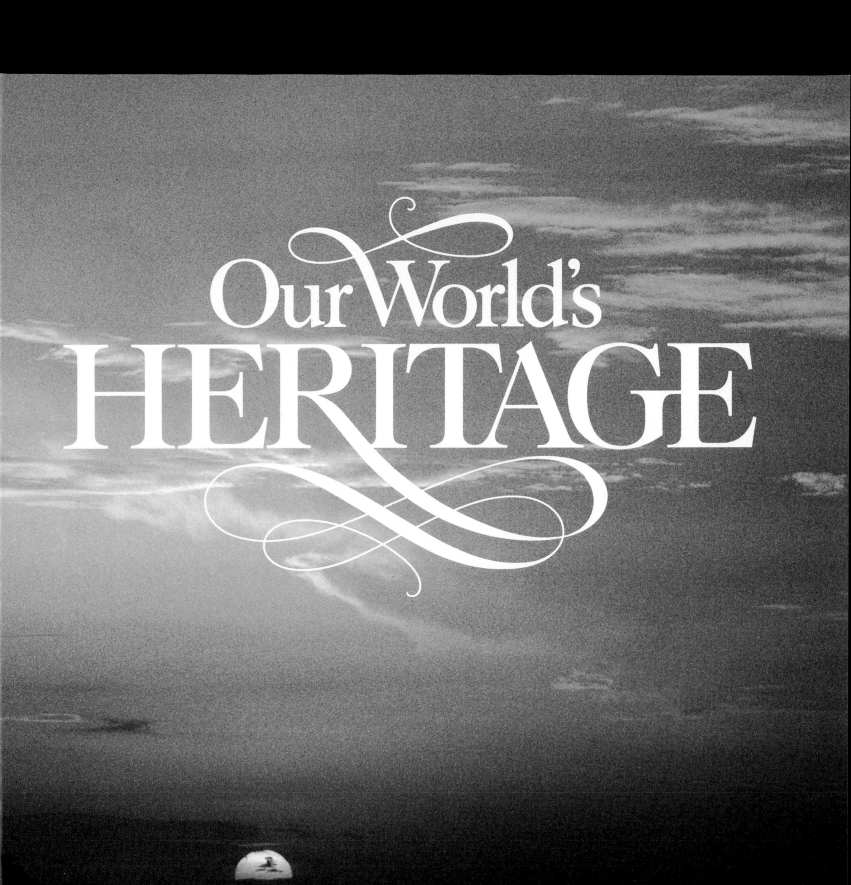

Our World's
HERITAGE

Our World's HERITAGE

Published by
The National Geographic Society

Gilbert M. Grosvenor
President and Chairman of the Board

Owen R. Anderson
Executive Vice President

Robert L. Breeden
Senior Vice President, Publications and Educational Media

Prepared by
National Geographic Book Service

Charles O. Hyman
Director

Ross S. Bennett
Associate Director

Margaret Sedeen
Managing Editor

Susan C. Eckert
Director of Research

Staff for this book

Carol Bittig Lutyk
Editor

Jennifer Gorham Ackerman
Assistant Editor

Carole Douglis
Catherine Herbert Howell
Edward Lanouette
Anne Meadows
Elizabeth L. Newhouse
Robert M. Poole
Margaret Sedeen
Lynn A. Yorke
Writers

Ratri Banerjee
Gretchen C. Bordelon
Cathryn P. Buchanan
Susan C. Eckert
Anne Elizabeth Ely
Catherine Herbert Howell
Mary P. Luders
Melanie Patt-Corner
Suzanne Kane Poole
Jean Kaplan Teichroew
Editorial Researchers

Gretchen C. Bordelon
Map Researcher

Joyce B. Marshall
Geography Intern

Linda B. Meyerriecks
Illustrations Editor

Greta Arnold
Illustrations Researcher

Michael Frost
D. Samantha Johnston
Illustrations Assistants

Karen F. Edwards
Traffic Manager

R. Gary Colbert
Administrative Assistant

Teresita Cóquia Sison
Editorial Assistant

Teresa P. Barry
Indexer

David M. Seager
Art Director

Charlotte Golin
Design Assistant

John T. Dunn
Technical Director

Richard S. Wain
Production Manager

Andrea Crosman
Production Coordinator

Leslie A. Adams
Production Assistant

David V. Evans
Engraving and Printing

Elisabeth B. Booz
Mary B. Dickinson
Marguerite Suarez Dunn
Julie V. Iovine
Werner L. Janney
Richard Lo Giudice
Tom Melham
Lise Olney
Patricia Penfield
Suzanne Kane Poole
David F. Robinson
Jonathan B. Tourtellot
L. Madison Washburn
Jayne Wise
Anne E. Withers
Contributors

Pages 2-3: The eighth-century A.D. Shore Temple at Mahabalipuram in southern India.

First edition: 200,000 copies 312 pages, 219 illustrations.

Contents

Javier Pérez de Cuéllar
Secretary-General of the United Nations

LEGACY FOR A SMALL PLANET

The idea that we are all part of earth and that earth is part of us goes back to the beginnings of human history—a notion enshrined, in one way or another, by most ancient cultures. But the belief in this intimate unity faded over the centuries. It took the advent of manned space flight in the 1960s and the visible deterioration of the environment to bring the concept back into focus and to make us realize that we are all inhabitants of a tiny blue-and-white oasis in the black desert of space.

The rapid growth of human populations and the spread of towns and cities and highways after World War II threatened important historic and cultural areas, as well as natural realms with unique plant and animal life. We humans were misusing earth's resources—its clean air and water, forests, minerals, and wildlife. Gradually, we became aware of the need to preserve our earthly heritage on a global scale.

A 1965 conference on international cooperation called for establishing "a trust for the world heritage that would be responsible to the world community for . . . efforts to identify, establish, develop and manage the world's important natural and scenic areas and historic sites for the present and future benefit of the international citizenry." The idea became reality in 1972 with the adoption of the World Heritage Convention under the auspices of the United Nations Educational, Scientific and Cultural Organization (UNESCO). Every nation was free to join the effort and, to date, almost a hundred countries have become participants. The convention seeks to compile a global Who's Who of unique natural and man-made sites. To qualify, each prospective entry must celebrate mankind's creative genius or demonstrate the natural diversity of our planet. Thus, as readers of this book will find, the list includes sites ranging from the Galápagos Islands to Chartres Cathedral, from the Grand Canyon to Islamic Cairo.

By 1986 the World Heritage Convention had recognized 247 sites as outstanding examples of their kind. Every year the sites proposed by participating nations are reviewed by two nongovernmental agencies—the International Union for Conservation of Nature and Natural Resources (IUCN) and the International Council on Monuments and Sites (ICOMOS)—for appropriateness, authenticity, and quality before they are designated World Heritage sites. Each may then display the World Heritage symbol: ⊗. The circle symbolizes the natural world; the square represents man-made structures. By linking nature and culture, the symbol encompasses the heritage we share as inhabitants of this planet, a heritage transcending both time and national boundaries.

For the most part, the cultural sites on the World Heritage list celebrate mankind's noblest achievements—the Taj Mahal, Versailles, Mont-Saint-Michel, Florence, St. Peter's and the Vatican, İstanbul, Machu Picchu, Stonehenge, ancient Thebes, the Statue of Liberty. But not all sites exemplify our finest moments. The World Heritage Convention also recognizes that we can learn from past mistakes, from places such as Auschwitz, the Nazi death camp in Poland that claimed nearly four million victims during World War II, and Gorée Island, a slave-trading depot off the coast of Senegal.

Natural wonders on the World Heritage list include such varied splendors as Iguazú Falls, the Giant's Causeway, Yellowstone, and Mammoth Cave. The Great Barrier Reef, the Serengeti Plain, and Ngorongoro Crater encompass unique ecological habitats, as do the Everglades and Royal Chitwan park.

Cataloging the world's special places is not a new idea. As early as the second century B.C., the ancient Greeks compiled a list of the Seven Wonders of the World: the marble lighthouse at Alexandria, the Colossus of Rhodes, the marble Temple of Artemis at Ephesus, the gold-and-ivory statue of Zeus at Olympia, the Hanging Gardens of Babylon, the colonnaded tomb of Mausolus, and the Great Pyramids at Gîza.

These colossal public works enshrined man's deepest beliefs and collective visions. Though they span just a few centuries of the millions of years we humans have lived on the earth, these monoliths of stone and metal represented mankind's striving for permanence. Even when they glorified gods and goddesses, kings and queens, they celebrated the genius of man as builder, defying mortality. But only the Great Pyramids still stand. The other wonders have vanished, swept away by natural disasters or the ravages of time and war. Today we have only tantalizing rubble to recall their grandeur.

Putting together a list of worthy sites, as the Greeks did, is one thing; protecting them against the ravages of man and nature is something else. In recent decades such efforts as UNESCO's International Campaigns have undertaken salvage and restoration work. A case in point was the multinational effort in the 1960s to raise the temples at Abu Simbel above the encroaching waters of the Nile River. The gigantic statues of Pharaoh Ramesses II and his queen, Nefertari, carved out of sandstone 3,200 years earlier, were cut into carefully marked pieces and reassembled on a bluff above the new lake forming behind the Aswân High Dam. Dozens of nations took part in the project—a four-and-a-half-year effort that cost 42 million dollars. Similarly, in the 1970s an international team of archaeologists, geologists, engineers, and artisans relocated some of the ancient buildings from the sacred island of Philae, also threatened by dams on the Nile.

On the island of Java, 27 nations helped the Indonesian government rebuild Borobodur, the ancient Buddhist temple built in the eighth century, then abandoned for hundreds of years until its discovery in the 1800s. The decade-long task, on a scale not seen since the rescue of the Nile temples, required the removal, chemical treatment, and replacement of 1,300,000 deteriorating stones from the midsection of the stepped pyramid. Thousands of stones and carvings that had tumbled from their niches had to be cataloged and restored to their proper positions—a job *(Continued on page 13)*

8

Workmen move heaven and earth at Abu Simbel (opposite) to save an ancient cosmos from the rising waters of the Nile River in Egypt. The construction of the Aswân High Dam 175 miles downstream created a lake that threatened to drown two dozen tombs, temples, and monuments—some of them dating back more than 3,000 years. Here a 3,200-year-old sandstone statue of Pharaoh Ramesses II undergoes a monumental facelift as it is hoisted piecemeal to higher ground. The seated figure, 67 feet high and weighing 1,200 tons, is one of a colossal quartet flanking the pharaoh's temple of the sun. Rescue teams had to saw the statues and two riverside temples into more than a thousand massive blocks. They then reassembled the pieces on a site built to resemble the original cliffside setting. The project, supported by 50 member nations of UNESCO, cost 42 million dollars and took four and a half years to complete —the most massive moving job ever undertaken.

Near the Aswân High Dam, launches (below) bring visitors to view Egyptian, Greek, and Roman monuments that for millennia stood on the now submerged island of Philae—the Pearl of Egypt, as it was called. Engineers in the 1970s built a cofferdam around Philae to hold back the water, then moved most of its buildings to a higher island shaped by dynamite and bulldozers to resemble Philae's contours. Such projects, in the words of the late Egyptian President Anwar Sadat, prove that "when people work together for a good cause they can achieve miracles."

Kluane & Wrangell-St. Elias

Wood Buffalo

Anthony Island

Burgess Shale

Olympic

Yellowstone

Québec City

Redwood

Bryce Canyon

Yosemite

Mesa Verde

Grand Canyon

Independence Hall   Statue of Liberty

Mammoth Cave

Great Smoky Mountains

Everglades

Hawaii Volcanoes

Teotihuacán

Tikal   Citadel

Copán

Cartagena

Gorée Island

Galápagos Islands

Jaú

Chan Chan

Machu Picchu   Cuzco

Salvador (Bahia)

Ouro Prêto

Iguazú/Iguaçu

Urne Bryggen

Giant's Causeway

Durham

The parks, wilderness areas, cities, buildings, monuments, and archaeological sites illustrated in *Our World's Heritage* include places on the World Heritage List of Recorded Sites as well as other places renowned for their natural or cultural qualities.

● World Heritage site
■ Site of World Heritage caliber

Easter Island

Los Glaciares
■ Torres del Paine

St. Michael's at Hildesheim
Warsaw
Stonehenge
Aachen • Falkenlust
Kraków
Amiens
Trier • Würzburg
Nancy
Auschwitz-
Birkenau
Wieliczka
Mont-Saint-Michel
Versailles
Chartres • Fontainebleau
Vézelay
Chambord
Bern
St. John's at Müstair
"The Last Supper"
Lascaux Cave
Plitvice Lakes
Orange
Pont du Gard
Florence
Arles
Dubrovnik
Gaudí's Works in Barcelona
Vatican City • Roman Forum
Ávila
Pompeii & Herculaneum
Ohrid
Batalha • Escorial
Córdoba • Alhambra
Coto Doñana
Valletta
Fez

St. Basil's at Moscow

Białowieża

Rila
Srebarna
İstanbul
Göreme & Cappadocia
Forbidden City
Acropolis
Great Wall
Saihō-ji & Fushimi-Inari • Fuji-san
Paphos
Meidān-e-Shāh
Royal Chitwan
Qin Shi Huangdi's Tomb
Jerusalem • Petra
Persepolis
Sagarmatha
Islamic Cairo
Keoladeo
Rās Muḥammad
Mohenjo Daro
Kathmandu Valley • Wolong
Memphis &
Thebes
Taj Mahal
the Pyramids
Abu Simbel & Philae
Kanha
Tassili-n-Ajjer
Ajanta & Ellora Caves
Ṣan'ā' • Shibām
Hampi
Fasil Ghebbi
Mahabalipuram
Angkor
Lalībela
Āwash Valley
Anuradhapura &
Polonnaruwa
Mount Apo
Garamba
Virunga
Tanjung Puting
Serengeti
Ngorongoro • Tsavo
Vallée de Mai
Bali
Lake Malawi
Kakadu
Etosha
Okavango Swamps
Namib-Naukluft
Great Barrier Reef
Uluru
Lord Howe Island
Australian East Coast Rain Forests
Willandra Lakes

Westland & Mount Cook

COLOSSVS SOLIS.

The Colossus of Rhodes—as imagined by a 16th-century artist—stood as a beacon to ancient mariners. Completed in 280 B.C., it fell during an earthquake 56 years later.

made possible by a computer. The temple's foundations had to be rebuilt and a hidden drainage system installed to prevent monsoon rains from undermining the structure.

In 1966 world attention focused on Venice as winter storms and high tides inundated the city of canals, threatening the very foundations of its architectural splendor. For decades Venice had been sinking as deep wells siphoned away an aquifer beneath its underpinnings. Air and water pollution from nearby industries corroded stone facades and statuary. Dredging and land filling altered the volume and natural tidal flow of Venice's lagoon. Decay and depopulation threatened the city long hailed as the Queen of the Adriatic. Since then dozens of governmental and private organizations from around the world have contributed millions of dollars toward restoring the city and its art—and to dealing with its underlying problems, both natural and man-made.

Since 1977 the World Heritage Convention has supported the sharing of technical expertise among nations and provided equipment, money, and training to help restore or preserve endangered sites. When floods threatened the Shalimar Gardens in Pakistan, World Heritage funds paid for workers and equipment to carry out emergency restoration projects. After an earthquake devastated the Montenegro region of southern Yugoslavia, the world responded to aid the victims—and to help rebuild the ancient city of Kotor, continuously inhabited for more than 2,000 years. World Heritage funds sponsored workshops and training programs for local artisans faced with the monumental task of rebuilding the city and restoring its priceless art treasures. At Sagarmatha National Park, site of Mount Everest, the world's highest peak, Sherpa villagers are planting trees to curb the deforestation brought about by the growth of tourism and its attendant demands for scarce firewood. World Heritage funds have helped build a small hydroelectric power plant and promote efficient energy sources, such as solar water heaters and airtight stoves.

In Pakistan continuing efforts are under way to save the ruins of one of the world's oldest cities—Mohenjo Daro. Once home to 40,000 people, the city flourished near the Indus River more than 4,000 years ago. In the words of one of its excavators, Mohenjo Daro provides the world with "the oldest example yet known of systematic town planning." Its streets, laid out in orderly grids, were lined with mud-brick apartments served by courtyard wells and an elaborate sewer system. But rising groundwater—the result of modern irrigation—now threatens the city's walls and foundations. Salts leached from the soil crystallize on the ruins and crumble the brick; the river itself poses a threat during periodic floods. To forestall further damage, Pakistani officials are planning to divert Indus floodwaters with a series of deflective rock spurs. Working closely with an international team of experts, they have also devised a system of wells, pumps, and drainage canals to help lower the water table. Venerable brick walls are being shored up and protected from groundwater with a layer of new, waterproof bricks.

In Vatican City specialists are removing layers of grime that obscured Michelangelo's masterpiece, painted in fresco on the ceiling and altar wall of the Sistine Chapel.

Meticulous cleaning has wiped away the dullness of centuries, revealing the artist's mastery of bright, vibrant colors, sometimes used in unusual combinations. Restoration has also revealed that Michelangelo painted standing, not lying, as popularly believed, and that he completed some areas without preliminary drawings.

Work is under way, too, to protect some of earth's unique natural sites. In Tasmania conservationists are stemming unbridled development by loggers, miners, and real estate interests in the Western Tasmania Wilderness National Parks. At the Río Plátano Biosphere Reserve in Honduras, education programs have won local support for conservation measures, and a resident Miskito Indian is in charge of the area. In Costa Rica a program funded in part by the World Heritage Convention is helping train villagers to preserve and manage the Talamanca Range-La Amistad Reserves, biospheres ranging from sea level to more than 11,000 feet and containing eight distinct life zones. Within them live nearly 30 bird and mammal species found only in this region.

And on the Galápagos Islands scientists are trying to control or eradicate plants, animals, and insects introduced by visitors and settlers. The introduced species threaten to displace native species found nowhere else, such as Darwin's finches and marine iguanas. Captive-breeding programs have produced more than 200 land iguanas and 800 giant tortoises. When a brush fire blazed across the largest island in 1985, Canadian planes bombed the flames with 800-gallon plumes of seawater, and Ecuadorian scientists and soldiers moved 500 giant tortoises to safety.

International recognition of a World Heritage site conveys responsibilities and moral obligations to the host country, which agrees to protect the site. Such has been the case with India and Bhutan. Both governments have agreed to cancel a hydroelectric dam project that would have flooded part of the Manas Wildlife Sanctuary in the Himalayan foothills. Manas is home to the Bengal tiger and 20 other vulnerable creatures, including the pygmy hog, the hispid hare, and the crocodile-like gavial.

The task of protecting such sites is enormous. It is also imperative and urgent. Three considerations should motivate the accomplishment of this task.

First, we have to save the past for the future. Civilization will be greatly impoverished if we lose our cultural heritage.

Second, we must learn to balance the need to innovate, to build, and to progress with the need to preserve our natural heritage, the source of our biological well-being.

Third, side by side with the instinctive attachment we feel to our country and our culture, we must develop a sense of belonging to this earth as a whole. What nature and human hands have wrought should enrich all of us. Not only Americans are awed by the Grand Canyon. People the world over, not just the citizens of India, are enchanted by the Taj Mahal. One does not need to be of a specific religious denomination to marvel at St. Peter's. We are all citizens of this planet. An earth-patriotism can release us from the confines of our racial, ethnic, cultural, or national prejudices and sustain a global civilization shared by all peoples. Our future depends on it.

Workers replace crumbling foundations at Mohenjo Daro in Pakistan, a city that flourished along the Indus River more than 4,000 years ago.

Inch by inch, a skilled restorer lifts a veil of dirt and paint from Leonardo da Vinci's "Last Supper" in the monastery of Santa Maria delle Grazie in Milan. Five centuries of neglect and abuse (Napoléon's men stabled horses here, monks cut a door through the painting) have obscured the mural's original brilliance. But eight years of cleaning have done much to recapture the luminous drama of Leonardo's work. Searching for the artist's original pigments, Dr. Pinin Brambilla Barcilon examines the deteriorated surface through a microscope (below) before cleaning with solvent and scalpel. Here she works toward the center, where Christ sits among his disciples. At far left, Judas may appear more darkly sinister than Leonardo intended; past restorers repainted many figures, adding their own interpretations.

With nary a rhino in sight, Dr. Kes Hillman-Smith turns to data cards to tally the last northern white rhinoceroses in Garamba National Park. Information from the survey, partly underwritten by the World Wildlife Fund and the World Heritage Fund, may help save the animals. Poachers have killed all but 18 of the hundreds of rhinos that, just a few decades ago, grazed this 1,900-square-mile park in northeastern Zaire.

Since 1938 the park has tried to protect rhinos, giraffes, and other endangered animals from illegal hunting, but political unrest and the proliferation of automatic weapons in central Africa have made it increasingly difficult to safeguard the animals. Black market prices provide hunters with a strong incentive: Rhino horn sells for as much as $5,000 a pound for use in medicines throughout Asia and as ornamental dagger handles in Yemen. Elephant ivory goes for about $50 a pound.

Tame elephants (opposite, top) from Garamba's unique elephant training school may unwittingly benefit other endangered animals by bringing tourists—and much needed funds—to the region. Docile when domesticated, elephants can be taught to carry sightseers on safari, plowing through the six-foot-tall grass that grows throughout the park (opposite, bottom).

ortress in the clouds, King Henri Christophe's Citadel looms like a battleship on a mountaintop in northern Haiti. Laborers carrying sand and cement for repairs climb the only approach to this bastion. Built in the early 1800s, it now symbolizes a nation's hard-won victory over colonial slavery. After the fall of Christophe in 1820, neglect and nature—including an earthquake—brought ruin to 15-foot-thick walls impervious to cannonballs.

Since 1977 the Haitian government, working with the United Nations, has sought to halt the decay attacking the Citadel—and to restore nearby Sans Souci Palace and its grounds. Today a hundred masons, carpenters, and laborers work to repair the fortress's walls and roofs (below), hoping to repel the tropical downpours that are its most implacable foe.

owing that they may reap the rewards of a restored land, Sherpas of Namche Bazar in northeastern Nepal plant fir seedlings to replace forests harvested for firewood. Village elders once regulated tree cutting, but the nationalization of forestlands and the influx of refugees from Tibet in the 1950s—plus tourists since—has undermined many such traditions. Today visitors sometimes outnumber the 3,500 Sherpas who live in these mountains; erosion threatens pastures and muddies streams; Buddhist monasteries and trailside prayer wheels languish, neglected by villagers who pursue paying jobs as guides, porters, and suppliers.

Sagarmatha National Park was established in 1976 to help restore the cultural and ecological balance upset by Nepal's tourist boom. Sherpa children now learn the benefits of conservation; alternative energy sources, such as solar heating and more efficient wood stoves, are encouraged; and with a $75,000 grant from the World Heritage Fund, Buddhist temples inside the park are being repaired and tree nurseries have been established to reforest barren slopes.

WINDOWS ON THE PAST

It is impossible to imagine a million years. At least, I cannot. A *thousand* million years is certainly far beyond the stretch of my imagination. Yet if we are to understand the history of our planet, we have to grapple with such vast periods of time. And one way of doing so is to descend one of the trails that zigzags down from the lip of the Grand Canyon to the banks of the Colorado River a whole vertical mile below. The rocks you pass are sandstone and limestone, red, yellow, and brown. They lie in roughly horizontal layers. For every vertical foot you descend, you travel back in time about half a million years. In one hour you can walk past deposits that took a hundred million years to accumulate. At the end of the day, when you slump gratefully onto a boulder beside the swift green waters of the Colorado, you may look back to the distant rim of the canyon far above. Then, as your eye skims up the tiers of strata, you will get some intimation of what is involved in the passage of more than a thousand million years.

Without such a time scale in mind, the facts of geological history seem almost impossible to believe. When I travel through the Alps or Himalayas and gaze at the buckled, folded layers of rocks exposed in the mountain faces, I have to remind myself of the passing of millions of years in order to understand how rocks could be crumpled and bent in such a fashion. On the other hand, the stupendous forces that created those folds are readily visible in another form. Climb the volcano of Mauna Loa on the Big Island of Hawaii. Mauna Loa is a rounded dome with a base so huge—50 miles or so across—that even though its slopes are gentle, its summit is more than 13,000 feet high. Its sides are strewn with black rocks, cripplingly difficult to walk over, their jagged edges ripping your boots to tatters. These are the solidified flows of lava. If you are lucky, the mountain may treat you to a display of pyrotechnics. From a vent in its flanks, plumes of scarlet lava may shoot several hundred feet into the air, and a river of molten basalt pour down steep stretches of mountainside at 50 miles an hour. Such terrifying, humbling displays are vivid indications of the forces at work deep below the earth's surface.

Forty years ago, when I was a university student at Cambridge, I joined with others in my class in drafting a petition to our professor of geology, demanding that the decades-old theory of continental drift be debated if not taught. The theory proposed that continents moved, that South America had once been joined to the west coast of Africa, as the two coastlines so vividly suggest, and that elsewhere continents had collided with one another and built mountain ranges by rucking up the sediments that lay on the seafloor between them. Our professor replied sharply that until someone could demonstrate to him the existence of forces that could move continents, such theories were nothing more than profitless speculation. Today we know that continents do indeed move over the surface of the globe. From satellite surveys of astounding accuracy, we know that the Atlantic Ocean does each year widen by a few inches, that Mount Everest is still rising, that deep in the earth's interior the semimolten rocks churn as though driven by vast convection currents swirling above the immensely hot metallic core, and that in places where the outer skin of the earth has cracked, molten rock wells up through the rifts, driven by exactly the same forces that shift the continents.

The processes that destroy mountains, even though they operate on a similarly long-drawn-out time scale, are not so mysterious. You can see them at work when you travel among mountains. Daily the sun warms rock faces, melting the snow and ice so that water trickles deeper into cracks and crevices. Nightly the cold returns, turning those films of water back into ice, so levering off the flakes, breaking them away from the parent rock, and driving irresistible wedges deeper into the joints of the cliff. Every year, in due season, the snow falling on the peaks accumulates in such quantity that it is compressed under its own weight and turns into a blanket of ice. As it slips downward, it joins with others to form a glacier that grinds its way over the lower slopes and forces a passage down the valley, gouging out the valley floor, scraping away its sides. As the millennia pass, so the fabric of the mountains is reduced to sand and gravel and carried by the rivers down to the sea. Eventually even the mightiest ranges are laid low.

In drier parts of the world the sun itself, aided by the wind, is the primary eroding force. If the land is so hot and parched that no plants can grow, as it is over much of northern Africa or central Australia, then the rocks lie naked. The sun's rays roast them until they become too hot to touch. The grains and crystals of which they are composed crumble and fall apart. The wind picks up the fragments and hurls them against other rock faces, hastening the destruction of mountains and of the grains themselves. Eventually it dumps the particles in vast, shifting dunes of sand.

Just as changes in the landscape proceed at a slow, barely detectable speed, so do the processes that alter the structure of animals and plants. The important modifications are not those that happen to an individual organism during its life but the genetic changes that occur at the time of its conception, for they are transmitted—by those individuals that survive to breed—to the next generation. So we are able to watch the progress of evolution only in organisms whose life spans are but a tiny fraction of ours. A species of aphid or fruit fly may produce a hundred generations in a few years. But we cannot hope to observe genetic changes among animals with life spans comparable to our own, let alone those such as elephants or tortoises that may, indeed, outlive us.

Nonetheless, there are places where even such long-lived creatures as tortoises evolve at remarkable speed. Hundreds of thousands of years ago tortoises reached the Galápagos, a group of volcanic islands that rise from the floor of the Pacific Ocean 600 miles west of South America. Their successful colonization of all the harsh volcanic landscape depended on producing a few offspring that were particularly well suited to these new conditions. Over generations the tortoises became bigger and bigger. Eventually they reached their present adult size of roughly four feet in length and 600 pounds in weight. With massive shells they are now able, during good seasons when rains cause the vegetation to sprout, to accumulate enough reserves of fat and water to last them through months of drought and starvation. On those dry islands with little edible vegetation at ground level, the tortoises changed in an additional way. They developed extremely long necks that enabled them to reach up and crop leaves from the trees. When Charles Darwin visited the islands in 1835, he observed these differences between the Galápagos tortoises and the ancestral form on the mainland and pondered an explanation for many years. Eventually he published *The Origin of Species,* in which he suggested that the driving force was a mechanism he called natural selection.

As a result we have some understanding today of the workings of evolution. But we still know little about the most mysterious of all transformations that, for the first time, gave life to inanimate molecules. It seems that the first living organisms appeared in the primeval seas between three and four billion years ago. These microscopic specks of matter, wrapped in membranes, were capable of absorbing chemical substances such as carbon and hydrogen, iron and phosphorus, and building from them their own particular kind of molecule—and so reproducing themselves.

It may be that the ocean floor not far from the Galápagos can show us how even that crucial event took place. In 1977 scientists in a deep-sea submersible, the *Alvin,* investigated vents in the seafloor from which gushed clouds of hot water, black with compounds of iron and sulfur. And in it, feeding on these chemicals, were multitudes of bacteria. These very simple organisms, with their unique life-chemistry, may well have developed here in the inky depths of the ocean. If that is so, then they may have replicated the process that first started when the seas on the young planet were still hot and mineral rich and—until that moment—lifeless.

For the most part primordial organisms were so fragile that when they died, they simply dissolved and left little sign of their passing. But slowly they evolved into bigger and more complex creatures, and about 570 million years ago some began to secrete hard shells. Once this happened, a new kind of evidence appeared in the rocks, for when these organisms died, they left behind their empty shells.

Mud and sand carried into the sea by rivers slowly drifted down and entombed the shells. As the weight of the sediments increased, so they hardened and turned to rock, the shells remaining within them. In those places where the continents collided and the sediments were elevated into mountains, the vast majority of these relics were destroyed. Of the tiny proportion that survived relatively undamaged, a great number lie beyond our reach, deep in the hearts of hills and mountains. Only where the layers containing them crop out at the surface can we see these extraordinary objects we call fossils.

The miracle is, that in spite of all the hazards, fossils are not rare. I spent my boyhood in the middle of England, and one of my greatest pleasures was to hunt for fossils in the golden yellow limestones of the countryside near my home. It seemed to me then, as it still does today, marvelously thrilling to split open a rock with a blow of a hammer and reveal the shining beauty of a coiled shell that 150 million years ago held a live and swimming animal and that no human eyes had gazed upon before mine did. Such joys can be gained from rocks all over the world, but in one or two places there are sites that produce specimens of quite extraordinary interest.

One such outcrop lies high in the Canadian Rockies in Yoho National Park. The rocks there, known as the Burgess Shale, were laid down half a billion years ago, soon after the time the first shelled organisms appeared. This deposit originally lay at the bottom of an underwater cliff. At regular intervals the mud that accumulated on the cliff slope slumped downward in a submarine avalanche, carrying away all the animals that lived in it and burying them on the seafloor. The mud was so fine that it took the impression of even the soft parts of these animals and so produced some of the most completely preserved fossils of this period ever found. Even more exciting, this mud contains impressions of animals that had no shells at all and have never been found elsewhere. They are tantalizing reminders of just how incomplete the fossil record normally is.

The fossils that fascinate us more than any others, of course, are those of our own ancestors. Nearly two million years ago, long after the last dinosaur had died, a freshwater lake lay on what is now the Serengeti Plain in East Africa. Apelike animals that walked upright were occasionally washed into the waters and became embedded in the mud. Volcanic eruptions and earthquakes caused the lake to drain. A river flowed across the flats, cutting its way through the sediments and forming the great ravine that is known today as Olduvai Gorge. And from its sides, in the solidified sediments, scientists are now retrieving the bones of the creatures whose direct descendants were to become the most powerful and influential creatures on earth.

Only 300 years ago an Irish bishop believed that a reasonable way to calculate the age of the earth was to count the generations listed in the Bible between Adam and Moses. He eventually concluded that the world had come into existence in the year 4004 B.C.—on October 22nd at 8 p.m. The realization that such an estimate bore no relation whatsoever to reality, and that the world was incomparably older, was the essential first step in a true understanding of the past. It is only 150 years since the bones of extinct giant reptiles were recognized for what they are and the word "dinosaur" was coined for the creatures to which they had once belonged; less than 70 years since the first remains of ape-men were painstakingly picked out of the rocks of Africa; and a mere 40 years since Cambridge professors felt unable to acknowledge the most fundamental of all the processes to shape the face of the earth.

Today physicists can give absolute dates to rocks and the fossils they contain by measuring their radioactivity; paleontologists, almost unbelievably, are isolating organic molecules from the remains of animals that died several million years ago and deciphering their structure in such detail that it may someday be possible to determine their genetic relationships. Much more information about the way in which the shape of our planet has changed and life upon it has evolved still lies in the land around us and within the bodies of animals and plants. Slowly we are adding more and more details to the longest, the greatest, and surely the most astonishing story that man can ever tell.

Grand Canyon
National Park, *U.S.A.*

"There is a certain malady, commonly termed 'big head,' with which a large number of otherwise healthy people are afflicted," wrote physician Mary E. Hart in 1895. "Prescription: Stand upon the brink of the Grand Canyon, gaze down, and still further down, into its awful depths, and realize for the first time your own utter insignificance."

Where better to gain perspective and humility than on the rim of this great chasm in northwestern Arizona, facing both an overwhelming vastness of space—a gorge one mile deep and up to eighteen miles wide—and an incomprehensible vastness of time: nearly two billion years of earth's history. The delicately tinted layers of sediment exposed in the canyon walls—cream, brown, yellow, green, raw umber, sometimes magenta in morning light, sometimes lavender in the haze of distance—record much of the region's geological history. Though the canyon was carved during the last six to ten million years, these stratified rocks go back to Precambrian times. They tell the story of seas advancing and retreating, of lagoons and Sahara-like deserts, of creatures now extinct.

But evidence of the recent geological past, including the history of dinosaurs and vanished mammals, is missing. Either sediments were not laid down during this period, or the topmost layers have eroded away. Still, the view here of earth's more distant past is remarkably continuous.

The cream-and-buff strata of the canyon's uppermost cliffs preserve fossils of sponges, corals, snails, and shellfish that lived some 250 million years ago in a warm inland sea, and just below—in beige sandstone that records an earlier desert—the frozen tracks of a small reptile that once scurried across the ground. Halfway down the canyon, purple layers of limestone 350 million years old entomb fish skeletons as well as remains of sea lilies and brachiopods, or primitive shellfish, that flourished in an ancient shallow sea. Absent are all signs of reptiles.

Autumn colors tinge the Grand Canyon's North Rim. Visible in the distance are multihued sedimentary strata through which the Colorado River carved a mile-deep chasm.

Three-quarters of the way to the bottom, all traces of backboned animals have disappeared. In the 500-million-year-old greenish siltstone and shale appears evidence of spineless creatures only: clams, worms, and trilobites—small armored invertebrates that thrived on shallow seafloors for several hundred million years. A vertical mile below the rim there is no sign of life, only dark, fine-grained schist almost two billion years old—tilted, buckled, and streaked with seams of pink granite.

"There goes God with an army of banners," wrote poet Carl Sandburg of the canyon's strata. The dramatic appearance of the Grand Canyon—with its multihued layers, its towering buttes and spires, its labyrinth of gorges, ravines, and tributary canyons—may suggest to some a cataclysmic origin. In fact, the canyon was created by two gradual, ongoing forces: mountain building and erosion.

About 65 million years ago a huge area of land was uplifted a mile and a half above sea level, creating an enormous earth blister—the Colorado Plateau. The waters of the Colorado River, loaded with rock, sand, and silt, began to carve through the layers, cutting down into ancient bedrock. Other erosive forces—wind, rain, snow, and extremes of heat and cold—attacked the canyon walls, widening the gorge.

Even today the Colorado River carves deeper and deeper into the canyon floor: It may eventually gouge down to sea level, another half a mile. And, over millennia, the canyon will widen as its two great architects, time and the river, continue their work.

Above: Havasu Creek, a tributary of the Colorado, spills into mineral-tinted pools just outside the park's boundaries.
Opposite: The downward-cutting Colorado winds through Lower Granite Gorge near Travertine Canyon in the western section of the park.

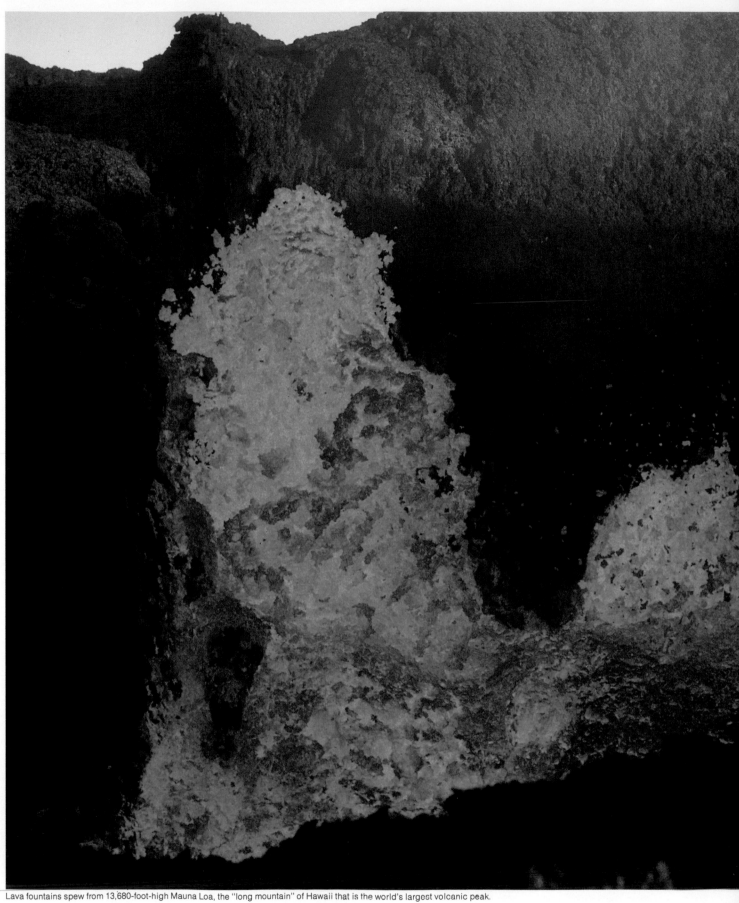

Lava fountains spew from 13,680-foot-high Mauna Loa, the "long mountain" of Hawaii that is the world's largest volcanic peak.

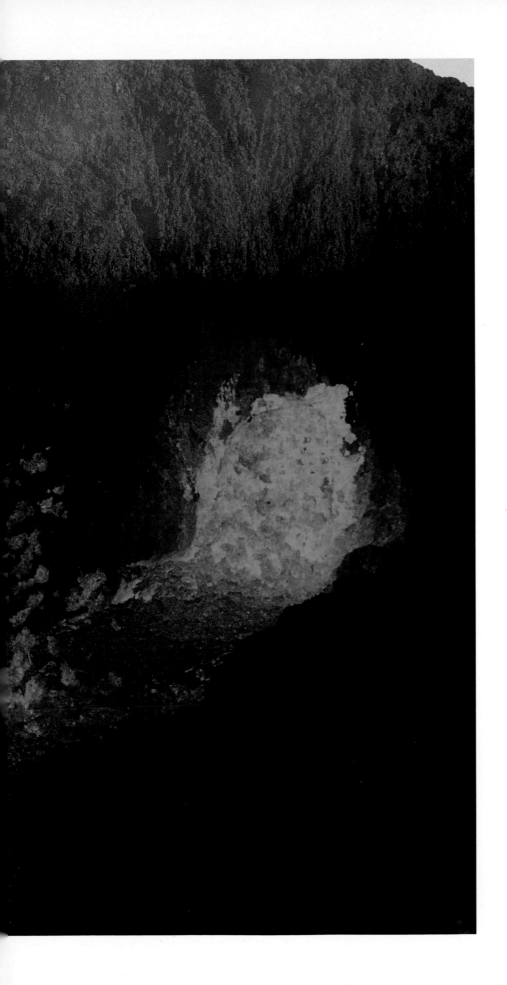

Hawaii Volcanoes
National Park, *U.S.A.*

When the wind shifts and the sky darkens over the Big Island of Hawaii, the salt air may suddenly turn acrid. Then visitors gaze inland, where the active volcanoes of Mauna Loa and Kilauea tower over the lush green landscape.

"The smell of sulphur is strong, but not unpleasant to a sinner," wrote a famous traveler who visited the island in 1866. What Mark Twain took as a foretaste of hell was in fact the smell of creation, for the island of Hawaii is continually being renewed by the forces of nature.

Scientists theorize that each of the eight major islands in the Hawaiian archipelago formed over a hotspot where magma, emanating from a chamber 30 to 40 miles beneath the ocean floor, pushed up against the slowly moving lithosphere, earth's outer shell. Where the molten rock punched through the crust, a volcano was born; successive eruptions over millions of years built up the chain of volcanoes, one by one, until they emerged as islands from the sea.

Two of Hawaii's active volcanoes—Mauna Loa and Kilauea —lie within Hawaii Volcanoes National Park. Hardened rivers of black lava fan out from their craters and ripple down to the sea, silent reminders of the red-hot lava flows that periodically destroy houses and forests and block the island's highways.

Despite the threat to property, Hawaii's gently sloped volcanoes usually give ample warning before they blow, allowing residents to evacuate. And eruptions sometimes bring the gift of land: Kilauea has added more than 850 million cubic yards of lava to the island since 1983—enough material to pave a four-lane highway, 31 feet thick, from New York to San Francisco.

Scientific understanding has modified traditional beliefs that eruptions are controlled by Pele, the legendary volcano goddess. But even today residents present offerings to placate the goddess. When trouble threatens, they carefully wrap up a bottle of good gin, place it near a hardened lava flow, and hope for the best.

Yellowstone
National Park, *U.S.A.*

Six hundred thousand years ago, what is now the northwestern corner of Wyoming blew sky-high in a volcanic eruption of such magnitude that it catapulted tons of hot pumice, ash, rock, and debris more than 30 miles into the air. Upwelling lava cooled to form a 2,600-square-mile plateau at an elevation of 8,200 feet in the Rocky Mountains. Airborne ash settled in layers that can still be found throughout the central and western United States.

And this, an eruption some 200 times greater than any other in human history, was a repeat performance—of eruptions that occurred here 2 million years ago and again 1.2 million years ago.

A history of the volcanic forces that shape our planet: That is the legacy of Yellowstone, designated a national park in 1872, the world's first. Though the 3,500-square-mile park is home to the grizzly, mountain lion, bison, bald eagle, and trumpeter swan, and though Gen. William Tecumseh Sherman pronounced the Yellowstone River "the best trout-fishing stream on earth," Yellowstone is first and foremost a geological park—a perfect laboratory for the study of heat flow within the earth.

Yellowstone lies over a hotspot—a place where molten rock, or magma, rises in a column called a thermal plume from deep within the earth's mantle. Yellowstone's thermal plume feeds a large magma chamber only 11,000 feet below the earth's surface. A similar chamber contained the stuff of Yellowstone's three giant explosions.

Once the magma chamber burst during the last eruption, its roof collapsed to form a crater, or caldera, in which most of the central

Visitors have watched Old Faithful erupt regularly since its discovery more than a century ago.

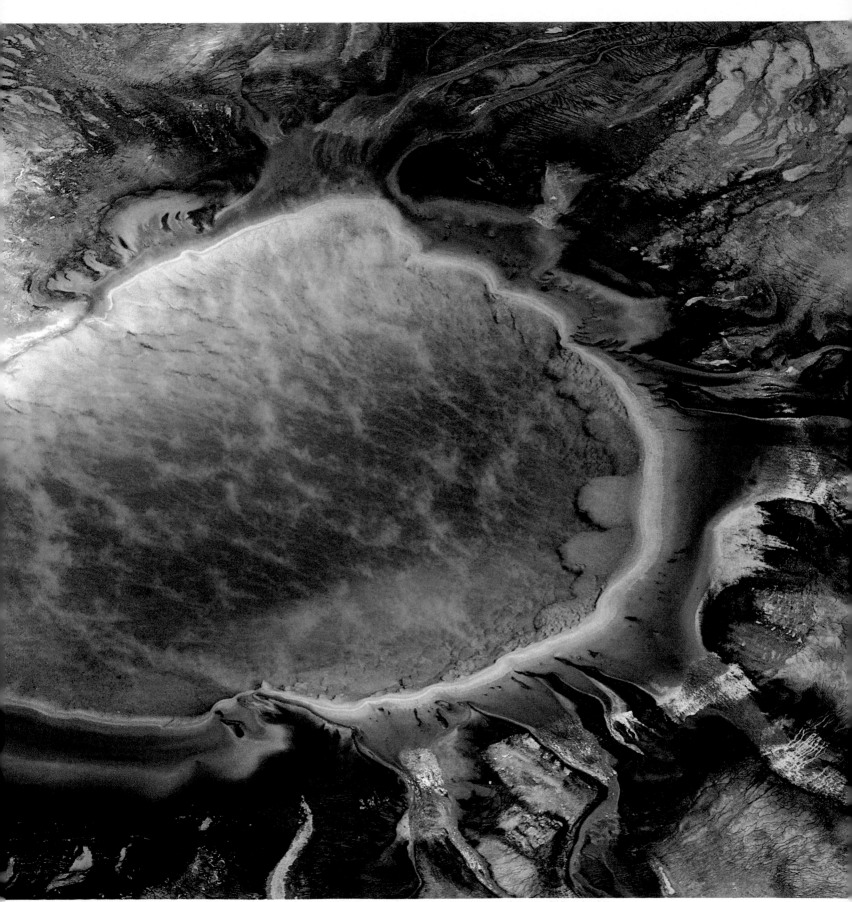

Grand Prismatic Spring is Yellowstone's largest hot spring—370 feet in diameter. Algae and bacteria that thrive in hot water tint its outer rings.

part of the park lies. The caldera is so large—some 1,300 square miles—that it was not clearly recognized until the 1960s, when scientists mapped it from the air. In and around the caldera—and fueled by the magma chamber now refilled with molten rock heated to more than 1000°F—are Yellowstone's 10,000 geysers, mud pots, hot springs, and fumaroles. Walking among them, wrote a 19th-century trapper, "one feels that in a moment he may break through and be lost in a species of hell."

Yellowstone's spectacular thermal displays take place because water from snow and rain seeps through the porous lava to be heated by the magma below. The resulting steam must rise. If unobstructed, it escapes through holes in the ground called fumaroles. If it reaches the surface as a trickle of acid-laden water instead, the clayish soil bubbles like a muddy stew.

Hot springs and geysers occur where hot water finds a route to the surface by moving slowly through a maze of water-filled cracks and fissures. The water becomes superheated, sometimes reaching triple its above-ground boiling point. Finally the expanding steam bubbles push the water through any available vent to the surface. A wide opening allows water and steam to well up in a hot spring; a constricted opening forces them to shoot up intermittently in one of the park's hundreds of geysers.

All the thermal activity adds up to a big question: When will Yellowstone erupt again? The first three explosions occurred 600,000 to 800,000 years apart, and it has been 600,000 years since the last one. The magma chamber, which now contains enough magma and hot rock to bury Wyoming some 13 stories deep, appears to be filling with more. But the question cannot be answered yet. For the time being, Yellowstone remains what it has been since the dawn of history—a wondrous sideshow put on by the mighty forces that sculpture the earth.

The Yellowstone River cascades twice into Yellowstone Canyon; Lower Falls drops 309 feet.

The Giant's Causeway,
United Kingdom

Irish giant Finn MacCool once challenged a rival Scottish giant to a duel of strength. How to reach his foe across the North Channel? "Och," said Finn Mac-Cool, "I'll build a causie." And so he did. Huge stones he carved, then heaved them into the sea to build himself a bridge.

Thus begins one Irish tale of the Giant's Causeway, a promontory of rock columns that cluster at the water's edge and line the cliffs for three and a half miles along the north coast of Northern Ireland. So perfectly shaped and precisely jointed are these polygonal fingers of stone that for centuries the Irish believed them the work of a giant master mason. In fact, the pillars were formed from molten rock deep within the earth.

Some 60 million years ago intense volcanic activity rocked the North Atlantic. In many places white-hot magma shot through the earth's crust in cataclysmic eruptions. But in this region it rose to the surface in a quiet, almost stately, manner. From reservoirs miles below the earth's crust, molten basalt welled up through fissures and vents, flowed over the undulating land, and hardened into rock. Flow followed flow. Then a prolonged pause, perhaps a million years or so. And suddenly another wave, hundreds of feet thick with a fine-textured, uniform consistency.

In one deep hollow, probably a river valley, the lava ponded. Slowly, evenly, the lava pool began to cool, shrink, and solidify. As the basalt at the bottom cooled and contracted, it fractured into near-perfect, multilateral columns. Erosion eventually wore away the upper mass, leaving the columns exposed—40,000 of them, rising to heights of 50 feet and ranging in diameter from 15 to 20 inches. Though weathered by ice, sun, wind, rain, and hammering waves, each pillar retains its prismatic form, and the Giant's Causeway the semblance of a flagstone path. As Irish poet W. H. Drummond wrote, "reason pauses, doubtful if it stand the work of mortal, or immortal hand."

Stepping-stones to pillars: Fracturing patterns and erosion cause height variations in causeway columns.

Uluru (Ayers Rock-Mount Olga) National Park,
Australia

"There they have stood . . . huge memorials from the ancient times of earth," wrote British explorer Ernest Giles of the 36 rock domes of Mount Olga. Called Katatjuta, or "many heads," by the Aboriginals, the Olgas and nearby Ayers Rock rise like leviathans from the Australian desert, isolated remnants of an ancient mountain range.

Six hundred million years ago in the heart of central Australia, sediments from eroding mountains hardened into layers of sandstone and conglomerate rock.

About two hundred million years later, forces within the earth uplifted the stratified ridges. Wind, water, and extremes of heat and cold then reduced most of them to fine sand, leaving only islands of resistant rock among the sandy plains.

Ayers Rock, the red sandstone monolith known by the Aboriginals as Uluru, rises more than a thousand feet. Weathering continues to erode its steep, ridged sides as air and moisture combine with surface minerals, forming iron oxides and clay that flake away. Eroded caves scallop the rock's

base. Many of these are decorated with ancient Aboriginal paintings depicting sacred objects, places, myths, and rituals.

At the Olgas, 20 miles west, erosion takes a more dramatic form. Large slabs of conglomerate rock split away at horizontal cracks, break down to boulder size, and fall or slide into the valleys below. Gradually, the domes' sides have become steeper, the tops more rounded. "Mount Olga is the more wonderful and grotesque," wrote Giles, "Mount Ayers the more ancient and sublime."

Runoff from the Olgas (foreground) and Ayers Rock (in the distance) creates oases at the base of each rock that support vegetation.

Kluane and Wrangell-St. Elias National Parks,
Canada/U.S.A.

Eleven thousand years ago, when Ice Age hunters gathered around dung-fueled fires in the bitter cold, rivers of glacial ice more than a mile thick were descending from the far northern mountains of North America. Slowly, inexorably, these giant sheets of ice ground their way south over fields and forests, driving all life before them and radically transforming the land.

A legacy of this last ice age lies amid the St. Elias Mountains in a remote wilderness area straddling the border of the Yukon Territory and Alaska. Within the national parks of Kluane and Wrangell-St. Elias, glaciers continue to shape the land, just as they did thousands of years ago. Here the continent's highest coastal range traps moisture-laden air from the Pacific, reaping as much as 20 feet of snow a year. These snowfalls nurture massive ice fields—including the world's largest outside the poles and Greenland—as well as some 2,000 glaciers, which radiate from the frigid fields.

Many of these glaciers advance slowly under the burden of their own weight, oozing forward a few inches or feet a year. As they advance, they grind, chisel, polish, and gouge the rock pavement over which they move. Glaciers that reach the Pacific calve mammoth icebergs, launched amid clouds of spray and ice.

In cycles that are little understood, some of the parks' large glaciers suddenly surge forward at different times, traveling as much as two miles a year at ten to a hundred times their normal rate. In 1986 a tributary of the Hubbard Glacier moved 112 feet a day, earning the Hubbard its nickname, Alaska's Galloping Glacier.

Over the centuries, several of the parks' glaciers have gradually retreated, leaving behind deep U-shaped valleys, angular peaks, river channels, and small, round lakes. These landforms stand as giant monuments to the sculpturing power of the glacier, the natural phenomenon that 19th-century naturalist Louis Agassiz called "God's great plough."

Ridges of debris, called moraines, stripe 45-mile-long Kaskawulsh Glacier in Canada's Kluane National Park.

Namib-Naukluft Park,
Namibia

Soo-oop-wa the Nama Khoi-khoi call the winds that blow through the dunes of the Namib Desert in southwestern Africa. In the language of the Nama, Namib itself suggests "area of nothingness." But this coastal desert defies its name. The heart of the Namib, which lies within 19,200-square-mile Namib-Naukluft Park, is home to an array of wildlife adapted to survival in a sea of shifting dunes. Animals and landscape alike owe their existence to the desert's ubiquitous winds.

Over millennia, wind has gradually built the Namib's massive mountains of sand. Some dunes are among the world's largest, 10 to 20 miles long and up to 1,000 feet high. The sands originated as inland sediments that rivers deposited in the South Atlantic. An offshore current swept the deposits northward and washed them onto the Namib's shores. Wind blew the sand inland and, grain by grain, shaped and reshaped the dunes into undulating ridges and crescents. Because the dunes vary in slope, compactness, and orientation to the sun, they provide a range of habitats for insects and reptiles.

Years may pass in the Namib without rain. But about one day in five, a cold current flowing northward along the coast from Antarctica generates heavy sea fog. Night breezes carry the fog inland 30 or 40 miles, bringing moisture to specialized dune dwellers. The headstander beetle tilts forward on its front legs to let droplets of water collect on its back and roll down to its mouth. Chameleons and other predators obtain moisture from the body fluids of their prey.

Breezes blowing through the dunes carry small insects and fragments of plants, providing a feast for scavenging beetles and other creatures at the low end of the food chain. More than mere sculptors, the Namib's ceaseless winds help ensure the survival of the richest variety of wildlife found in any dune desert, including some 200 species of beetles.

Pages 42-43: On the shores of the Namib, where desert meets sea, a lagoon nurtures flocks of migratory flamingos and marine birds.

In a reenactment of a 19th-century lighting technique, a guide hurls kerosene-soaked torches through the air, launching beacons into the inky recesses of Mammoth Cave.

Far below a stony valance, lights glow in Crystal Lake.

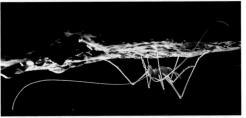

A cave cricket occasionally feeds outside at night.

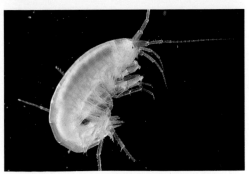

In this midnight world a shrimp needs no eyes or color.

Mammoth Cave National Park, *U.S.A.*

For millions of years water has seeped, trickled, and flowed through fossil-rich limestone deposits in central Kentucky, dissolving the rock and carving subterranean passages to the nearby Green River. Over time the water table dropped and the upper passages drained, creating the world's longest known cave system. This maze of tunnels, called Mammoth Cave, winds at least 300 miles on five connecting levels. Where underground streams once gurgled, narrow pathways with hundred-foot-high ceilings twist silently through the rock, opening into broad caverns, shafts as big as silos, and wide tubes with low, arched ceilings.

Most of Mammoth Cave lies beneath a cap of water-resistant sandstone that prevents the limestone from decaying. Where the cap has eroded, rivulets of water percolate through the soil and limestone, picking up minerals along the way. As the water seeps through the cave roof, the minerals form stalactites that hang from the ceiling like rusty icicles. Stalagmites sometimes build up from the cave floor to join them, forming dainty pillars or massive columns. In the cave's drier passages, moisture seeping through the walls leaves crystals of gypsum that grow into threadlike tendrils up to ten inches long or snowballs that burst into clusters of white "blossoms."

This vast underground honeycomb of passages and ornamented galleries first attracted tourists nearly two centuries ago, after a hunter stumbled into it in 1799 while tracking a wounded bear. Yet many insects and fish spend their entire lives in the cave without ever seeing the spectacle. Evolving through the millennia in utter blackness, their eyes have grown weak and, in some species, have disappeared. Isolated for untold generations, 50 species of cave creatures now risk annihilation from pollutants that seep through surface sinkholes to follow the water's ancient journey through Mammoth's measureless caverns.

45

Westland and Mount Cook National Parks,
New Zealand

The sawtooth spine of the Southern Alps marks New Zealand's main physical divide—and defines the border shared by Westland and Mount Cook National Parks. The two parks straddle a major fault system where tectonic plates slide against each other, fracturing, folding, and warping the land. The Southern Alps are young, made of rocks two hundred million years old but uplifted only within the past five million years by this plate movement. The peaks continue to rise. For some, uprising just offsets erosion's continuous whittling.

Within Mount Cook's 270 square miles, about 20 summits top 10,000 feet, while permanent snow and ice blanket more than a third of the park. Rugged steeps and extensive glaciation make this a realm of stark contrasts: stone against snow, shadow versus light. The crystalline air dissolves distances and evaporates depth, leaving only silhouettes. Sun and wind sculpture the frozen surfaces into dune-like waves and pattern them with swirls reminiscent of watered silk.

Westland plunges abruptly from the nation's highest mountaintops to the sea's edge, encompassing within a mere 18 miles rain forests and grasslands, glaciered spires and marine lagoons. A wide variety of birds—the alpine parrot, flightless kiwi, yellow-crowned parakeet, rare white heron—find refuge in its forests and marshes.

Highly varied in landscape and ecosystems, the two parks reflect the compact richness of New Zealand itself—a Colorado-size nation blessed with the diversity of an entire continent.

New Zealand's craggy main divide caps the glaciated reaches of the Southern Alps.

Great Smoky Mountains
National Park, *U.S.A.*

It is hard to picture now, but the Great Smoky Mountains once loomed perhaps as high as the Himalayas and as jagged as the Rockies. That was 300 million years ago, when the supercontinents of Gondwana and Laurussia collided, buckling the earth's crust toward the sky.

The hand of time softened the Smokies, smoothing the peaks and valleys by erosion. Ever so slowly, new trees and herbs and flowers crept in, following the same path across the Bering land bridge that much later brought the first humans to North America. To this day, that floral link with Asia can be seen in the Smokies' rhododendrons, ginseng, and other plants closely related to flora growing on the far side of the Pacific.

The Great Smoky Mountains National Park, covering just 800 square miles, includes some 50 mammal species, 1,520 flower species, and possibly the most diverse population of salamanders in the world—27 species. All thrive in the abundant moisture that sweeps in from the Gulf of Mexico and Atlantic Ocean, producing up to a hundred inches of rain yearly. Almost as wet as the Pacific Northwest, these southern highlands sustain 130 tree species, equal the number in all of Europe.

The trees lie thick upon the land, like a glimpse back to pre-Columbian America. Now as then, the forest exudes water vapor and oily residues, forming a haze that skirts the peaks and dances down the valleys. Long ago, native Cherokee Indians looked upon these shrouded mountains and gave them the name that stuck: Place of Blue Smoke.

Among the oldest mountains on earth, the Smokies form part of the border between North Carolina and Tennessee.

Fossils: Chronicles of Life

"Above the plains of Italy where flocks of birds are flying today fishes were once moving in large shoals." Five centuries ago Leonardo da Vinci grasped the meaning of fossil seashells embedded in the rock of mountains.

The earth yields such secrets slowly. Stones do speak: The fossils found in sedimentary rock recount the history of life on earth. But the record they provide is incomplete, a puzzle with many pieces missing. Most animals leave no reminder of their existence. Their flesh decomposes; their shells, bones, and teeth disintegrate. Only under certain physical conditions are the remains of animals preserved—usually in sandstone, limestone, or shale. And in many cases these fossil-bearing rocks are destroyed by the fracturing, buckling, and erosion of the earth's crust.

Given the odds against their formation and survival, a remarkable number of fossils have been found throughout the world—from the stone impressions of 3.4-billion-year-old, single-celled marine plants at the Fig Tree rock formation in South Africa to the petrified bones of flying reptiles at Canada's Dinosaur Provincial Park; from the hominid skeletons at Ethiopia's Āwash Valley to the 40,000-year-old remains of a *Homo sapiens sapiens* settlement on the shores of the now dry Willandra Lakes in Australia, among the oldest known sites of modern humans.

High in the Rocky Mountains of British Columbia lies a most unusual fossil record of a diverse marine community that lived some 500 million years ago. Here in the Burgess Shale, underwater mud slides preserved the hard parts, and in some cases the flesh, of 140 species of animals—sponges, jellyfish, worms, mollusks, and hitherto unknown forms of life, such as *Hallucigenia,* which moved about on 14 sharp spines, and five-eyed *Opabinia.* These fossils provide a window on the first great radiation of multicellular life. From such fragmentary but telling clues emerges the history of life on earth.

Mounds near Australia's Willandra Lakes hold evidence of early human settlers.

Canada's Burgess Shale preserved this wafer-thin imprint of a trilobite.

The tusks of a prehistoric elephant lie in Ethiopia's Āwash Valley, near where paleontologists found the three-million-year-old skeleton of the hominid they called Lucy.

The volcanic ramparts of Mounts Lidgbird and Gower rise thousands of feet above Lord Howe Island — home to many native species and the world's most southerly coral reef.

Lord Howe Island,
Australia

A feisty little flightless bird with a long bill and large feet struts across the forest floor, searching for worms and crustaceans. One of the world's rarest birds, the Lord Howe Island woodhen gave up the use of its wings generations ago to better suit its habitat, a land free of terrestrial predators and stocked with food—Lord Howe Island.

Located 490 miles northeast of Sydney, Australia, this isolated South Pacific island is a living museum of the evolutionary process. Though only 5.6 square miles in area, it supports a profusion of native species: 57 kinds of flowering plants, 17 ferns, 50 spiders, and 4 earthbound birds live among its palm groves and scrubby grasslands, its swamps and lush mountain rain forests.

Nearly seven million years ago the geologic upheaval of an underwater plateau called the Lord Howe Rise gave birth to a large shield volcano. Over time the sea eroded 90 percent of the original volcano, leaving a slim crescent of land devoid of life, Lord Howe Island. As millennia passed, plants and animals began to arrive, mainly from nearby Australia, New Zealand, and New Caledonia. Strong winds brought birds and winged insects. Snails and spiders ferried to the island on driftwood and clumps of vegetation. Plant seeds drifted there or hitchhiked on the beaks, feet, and feathers of birds. Only one type of mammal, a small bat, made the voyage.

Once established, the creatures began to adapt to their new home. Evolution proceeded rapidly within the isolated and inbreeding island community, creating new species to fill almost every niche. But after Europeans discovered Lord Howe in 1788, many of these unique plants and animals—including more than half of the species of terrestrial birds—disappeared, victims of seamen, settlers, and their escort of predatory mammals. Recent captive-breeding programs and other conservation efforts by scientists and islanders have increased the numbers of woodhens and other threatened wildlife.

About the size of a sandpiper, the Lord Howe Island woodhen is both flightless and tasty—a risky mix.

The Galápagos Islands,
Ecuador

"Nothing could be less inviting," wrote Charles Darwin on his arrival at the Galápagos island of San Cristóbal in 1835. Here was a world of elemental harshness, barren and desertlike. Fields of twisted black lava streaked the island's shores like petrified rivers. Coal black lizards crawled about on the jagged rocks. Though Darwin did not realize it at the time, this austere and seemingly unimpressive world would revolutionize the study of biology.

The scattered group of 19 volcanic islands that make up the Galápagos archipelago straddle the Equator 600 miles west of Ecuador. Some three to five million years ago the first islands burst through the surface of the Pacific Ocean. Over millennia, chance migrants from the South American mainland colonized the young and remote shores. The isolation of the islands and the different conditions on each—from the bone-dry shores of Marchena to the moist highlands of Santa Cruz, from flat Genovesa to mountainous Isabela—made the Galápagos a natural laboratory of evolution. Species that found footing there evolved independently of their mainland ancestors, adapting to the islands they occupied.

Consider the giant tortoise *galápago*, for which the archipelago is named. From a single mainland ancestor evolved 14 subspecies, some weighing up to 600 pounds. Tortoises that lived on arid islands had to feed on cactus pads or tree leaves, and their shells evolved with high peaks in front that allowed them to stretch their extra-long necks upward almost vertically. Those on islands with abundant ground vegetation retained domed carapaces, curved upward only slightly along the front edge.

The variability of species from island to island captivated Darwin and laid the foundation for his theory of evolution by natural selection. In this "little world within itself," he wrote, "we seem to be brought near to that great fact—that mystery of mysteries—the first appearance of new beings on this earth."

A giant tortoise on Isabela Island rears its scaly head. Tortoises on the Galápagos may live as long as 150 years.

Known as "imps of darkness," the black iguanas of the Galápagos are the only lizards in the world that have come to depend on the sea for their sustenance.

TESTAMENTS OF VANISHED CULTURES

The spiring canopy of red pine filtered the sunshine down into a soft green shade in which the whorls of fern-tree fronds stood motionless, seeming to breathe out a palpable silence. Underfoot, the slopes of the long-dormant volcano were deeply felted with mosses and the slow accumulation of vegetable decay. Mounting soundless, one emerged into dazzling light beside the small lake that had formed in the crater. Great archaic trees grew down to the water's edge, and blackened trunks lay half submerged like reptiles, giving a sense of the primeval world. The bellbirds and a *tui* called and sang unseen. It might have been an age before man.

This memory comes back to me from New Zealand, from islands that lay so long in utter isolation they remained frozen in time. These islands allow us to experience a prehuman landscape. More important, they bring home to us the realities of the diffusion of living creatures and then of mankind in time as well as in space. It was a quarter of a million years ago and more, long before the full evolution of *Homo sapiens*, that humans in southern India were already flaking the oldest shapely and standardized type of tool, the hand ax. Tens of thousands of years went by before the skilled seamanship of the Maori brought them from central Polynesia to New Zealand. Victoria was on the throne by the time the British came from halfway round the globe to force overwhelming change on the ancient life and landscape of New Zealand.

This sweep through time in one region helps us to imagine the slow yet spasmodic advance of ever inquiring and adventurous human beings fitting themselves into the world map. Sometimes they would be led on by river valleys, open hills, or navigable coasts, sometimes checked or diverted by mountains, forests, and deserts—or barred by the oceans until their mounting intelligence provided them with rafts and boats.

One of the greatest marvels of this ever changing human scene is the flowering of rich cultures or high civilizations at different times and places. It would appear that a special creative gift had been granted to these societies, enabling men and women in exceptional numbers to become poets and painters, builders and craftsmen, thinkers and inventors, eager to beautify their surroundings and lift existence to a higher plane.

While undoubtedly these high points of human achievement often owe much to natural advantages, I have never believed that economic explanations, so appealing to our own materialism, reach the heart of the matter. Though technology has been a cumulative business, its inventions seldom lost, civilizations have had the organic quality of life and death. Sometimes they have risen fast to their heights of creativity, then entered a slow decline, at last losing all vitality. For me there remains something still mysterious, certainly not crudely economic, in the seed of these flowerings—as there is in individual genius or, indeed, in life itself.

For signs of the infinitely slow beginnings of the great cultural achievements of our species, we can look again at the hand ax, the first known manifestation of man's ability to hold in his mind a standard tool form—and moreover one with proportions that still seem right to us. Leaping to the time of the still archaic Neandertals, there is another development pregnant for the future: Neandertal hunters began the ritual burial of their dead, giving them food and red ocher to simulate the blood of life. Here in these rough graves were the emotional promptings that would later build the Taj Mahal.

About 30,000 years ago humans of modern type had inherited the earth and the Neandertals and their like had vanished, taking their faint dreams of immortality with them. It was then, during the minor fluctuations of the last great ice age, that our ancestors began to render their visions of the inner and outer worlds in realistic carvings of animals and human beings. This dawn of the visual arts led to one of the most improbable happenings in ancient history. Between 17,000 and 12,000 years ago, there arose among Old Stone Age hunters the first exceptional outburst of creativity. Its setting—southwestern France and the north of Spain—was a tiny space when it is remembered that by then our species had peopled vast areas of the Old World, had reached Australia, and was even thrusting southward through the Americas.

In their little terrain between Mediterranean and Atlantic, artists refined the tentative carving skills of their predecessors and learned to grind paints to satisfy an indwelling love of color. Before their way of life ended together with the ice age, they left us the masterpieces of the painted caves of Lascaux and Altamira.

As the ice age melted away, the centers of creativity shifted toward the rising sun, to southwestern Asia. Here New Stone Age societies advanced from dependence on nature for their food to true farming—the foundation of high civilization. At Jericho in the Jordan Valley, recognized as the oldest known town, farmers grew wheat and barley. By the eighth millennium B.C. about 2,000 inhabitants crowded inside Jericho's massive, stone-faced walls and turrets—as though some farsighted spirit of history knew for what this place was to be famed. Thus protected, the citizens of Jericho created shrines, a cult of human heads, and the image of the mother goddess.

At the second most ancient town the mother goddess was served with an extravagant devotion. Çatal Hüyük, on the Konya Plain in Anatolia, spread its confusion of mud-brick houses over 30 acres and sheltered perhaps 6,000 souls. Among these houses were many shrine rooms distinguished by strangely powerful wall paintings and figurines—the oldest religious buildings completely furnished with works of art.

Jericho and Çatal Hüyük, the height of achievement in the early New Stone Age, point the way to the high, fully urbanized civilizations that followed. Around 5000 B.C. the Sumerians settled the torrid and featureless alluvial plain of the mighty valley of the

Tigris and Euphrates. The social authority needed to establish and maintain irrigation systems may have stimulated the Sumerians to build the first literate urban civilization. With water the soil was prodigiously fertile. Populations grew. With more hands to carry out the prompting of the human psyche, the Sumerians built tiered, pyramidlike temples—the first truly monumental architecture—and developed writing for keeping temple accounts. In one small patch of the earth's surface, prehistory was at an end.

In the Nile Valley the Egyptians were late starters on the way to high civilization and at first owed much to the Asian pathfinders. Within a few hundred years, however, the Egyptians had in some ways surpassed the Sumerians. The Old Kingdom (2700 to 2200 B.C.) created some of the finest art and architecture the world has ever known. Here all at once were not only the kings' pyramid-tombs, raised to a superhuman scale, but also monumental architecture in finely masoned stone, fluted columns, elegant motifs on capitals and friezes, and portrait sculpture. The "form" of Egyptian civilization was to endure for 3,000 years without fundamental change.

During these millennia both banks of the Nile were arrayed with massive temples, statues, and tombs, all raised for eternity from Egypt's copious supplies of stone. With the New Kingdom (1600 to 1100 B.C.) the pharaohs again built on a colossal scale. Of them all, Ramesses II was the mightiest builder. His passion for colossal statues of himself—in the Ramesseum of West Thebes and at his rock-cut temple of Abu Simbel—are only the best known among a host of them. Megalomaniacs can be great benefactors of posterity.

These high points of Old World civilization now shifted northwestward in the Mediterranean. By 2000 B.C. the Minoans of Crete had given birth to the earliest high civilization of Europe. They have left us exquisite art and the ruins of palaces. These greatly gifted, nature-loving islanders did much to civilize the Achaean Greeks, or Mycenaeans, that martial people who came down from the north and whom we know best from their royal strongholds at Pylos, Tiryns, and Mycenae itself.

Of all the outbursts of creativity that light up our history, surely none was brighter than that of the Hellenic peoples of the seventh to fifth centuries B.C. It can be symbolized for us by the Acropolis of Periclean Athens, a city that had more men of truly great genius walking its streets than can be expected from a millennium in the ordinary world.

Of further supreme significance for our Western heritage was the Hellenic dominance over the founders of Rome. These early Romans respected the Greeks and took to themselves all that they could of Hellenic culture. So by the second century B.C., when the Romans had conquered their teachers, there was a fully fused Greco-Roman civilization to be spread to the far reaches of the empire. The Romans took over the Greek orders of architecture and carried off or copied the finest sculptures. Their temples, like their divinities, were variants of the Greek. But the Roman genius, with its masculinity and love of power, found expression in the roads and fortresses that bound their conquests, in triumphal arches, and in huge public baths for manly sports and physical well-being. Most revealing of this dual inheritance: While the Romans still built theaters for literary drama and ritual, their passion was for the amphitheaters they had designed to stage mighty martial spectacles and combats of men and of beasts.

A few of the buildings left to us by the Greeks and Romans have returned to use: theaters and amphitheaters, temples, and even adapted baths. Far more profoundly, their thoughts and feelings mingle with ours. Even if we have now all but thrown away their languages, we read their books, act their plays, draw on their philosophies.

During the long evolution of our kind on the other continents, there was no sign of humans or their handiwork among the teeming plant and animal life of the Americas. Then, about 30,000 years ago, soon after *Homo sapiens sapiens* had taken possession of the Old World, a few hunting parties from the eastern extremities of Asia moved into Alaska. Most headed southward, always advancing and spreading, adjusting their way of life to highlands and plains, lakes and rivers, extremes of heat and cold.

By 1000 B.C. nations, states, and empires began to rise. Maya civilization flowered first, around A.D. 250, in the tropical rain forests of Guatemala and neighboring parts of Honduras, Belize, and Mexico. Tikal in northern Guatemala is perhaps the finest gift to us of the Maya heritage, with its genius in mathematics, astronomy, and calendrical calculations. At Tikal the ornate architecture and monumental planning can still awe us: spacious plazas, elaborate palaces, temple-pyramids crowned with decorative roof crests.

Few of the cultures that formed, mingled, and dissolved along the coast and in the highlands of Peru have left us an architectural inheritance comparable with those of Mesoamerica. Yet the Inca Empire destroyed by Pizarro was on a par with the Aztec Empire that fell to Cortés. Bound by a network of roads, the Inca realm extended 2,500 miles from Ecuador to northern Chile and from the coast to the high Andes. The Sapa Inca, treated as a god in both life and death, administered a kind of nightmare welfare state of perfectly ordered subjection with taxation through agriculture, labor, and craft products. From its earliest mythological beginnings, the Inca state centered on Cuzco, meaning "navel." From Cuzco the four principal roads radiated to the Four Quarters of the empire. Cuzco was a modest town until the eighth Sapa Inca, Viracocha, and his son Pachacuti raised palaces and public buildings and Pachacuti crowned an adjacent hill with the fortress that still dominates the city. Cuzco would have been an extraordinary heritage had not the Spaniards and the resistance to them so largely destroyed it.

By great good fortune another Inca town has been left to us almost intact. Machu Picchu is only a few miles from Cuzco yet utterly remote, 8,000 feet up in what is surely the most dramatic natural setting of any ancient monument. Built in the 15th and 16th centuries, Machu Picchu is ingeniously clamped onto a rocky saddle between two summits and encircled by strangely glistening peaks with the Urubamba River winding far below. A palace, temples, houses of priests and nobles, baths, and fountains reveal the skill of master masons and the perfection of Inca architecture.

It is right to end with the Incas and, at a distance, with the Aztecs, for despite the sharp superficial differences, these New World civilizations had much in common with those of the Old. They were readily comprehensible to Pizarro and Cortés, and we can recognize their similarities to Bronze Age Egypt and Sumeria. Humans, it seems, carry in their mental world similar urges and imaginative forms that find common expression—those universals of the inner life, religious intuition, the urge to create fineness and beauty far in excess of earthly necessity.

Lascaux Cave, *France*

On a September day in 1940, four teenagers hunting rabbits in the countryside of southern France discovered a hole exposed by a fallen tree. When the boys slithered down the tunnel, they found treasure: Lascaux Cave, decorated in the last ice age, then sealed off by landslides.

Lascaux's paintings and engravings depict close to a hundred animals. Huge bulls—one of which measures 18 feet from head to tail—stride across the walls; a horse tumbles down a cliff; a speared bison confronts its human hunter.

The artists of Lascaux, working 17,000 years ago, outlined the animals in manganese or charcoal and filled in with yellow ochers and reds made from iron oxides. By the light of fat-fueled lamps, the painters blew pigments through a pipe or dabbed them on with brushes, fingers, or pads. The artists exploited the limestone walls' bulges and indentations to give shape to their subjects' shoulders and hips.

The painted creatures may have served a faith centered on the animal. Perhaps, as flickering lamps made the animals appear to move and music from bone flutes echoed through the chambers, shamans incanted lore to youthful initiates.

The Lascaux artists and other Ice Age hunters lived in dwellings of skin or turf, under rock overhangs, or sometimes in cave entrances—reserving the inner depths for rituals. In a creative flowering that began 30,000 years ago, they produced new technology as well as art. They invented spear-throwers that enabled them to kill game at a distance of 30 to 50 feet; they may have shot the first arrows. A twine fragment from Lascaux hints that Ice Age artisans twisted fibers into nets and baskets. They probably created fashion too, devising the first sewing needles and wearing ornaments of shells, teeth, ivory, and bone.

Though Ice Age artists left treasure on grotto walls as far east as the Ural Mountains, 90 percent of the sites are in France and Spain. Of the 29 decorated caves clustered in the Vézère River Valley, none is more elaborate than Lascaux.

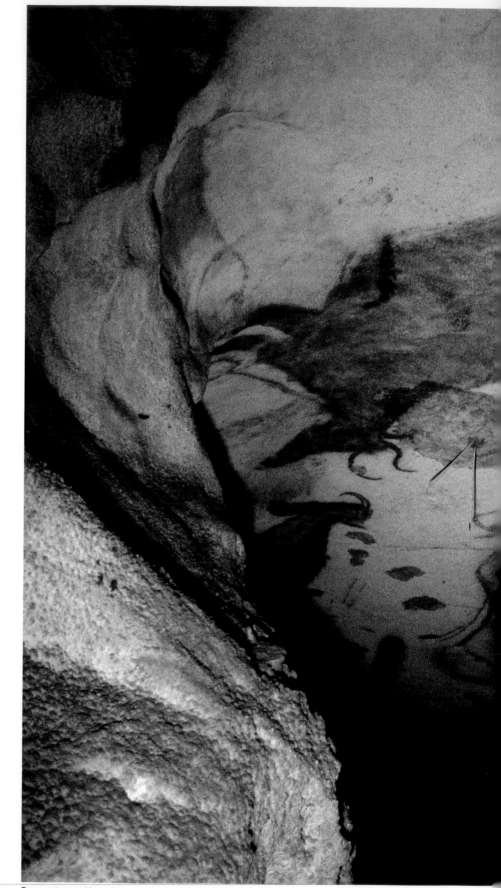

Temperature and humidity controls protect Lascaux Cave, closed since 1963; a copy nearby is open to visitors.

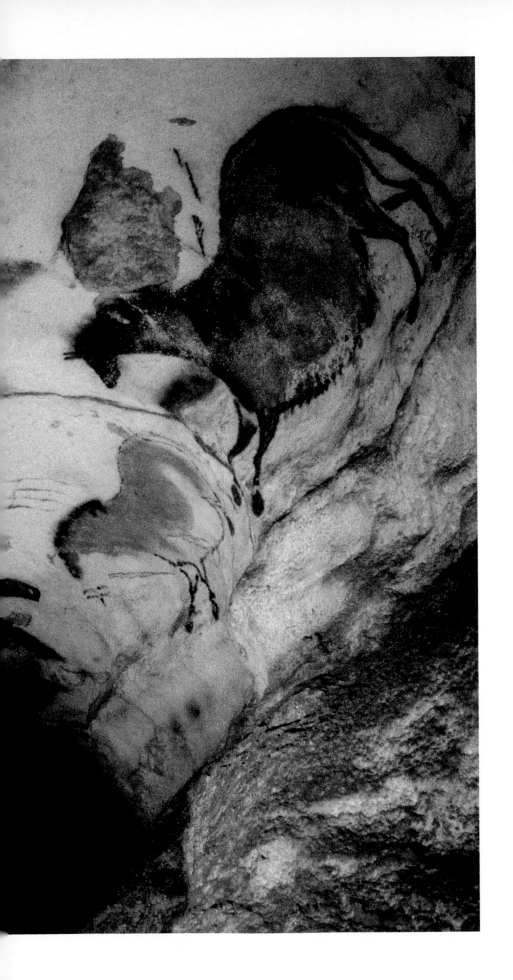

Stonehenge, *United Kingdom*

From the smooth chalk downs of Salisbury Plain in southern England rises a gap-toothed circle of gray sandstone megaliths: Stonehenge, unquestionably the greatest prehistoric monument in all of Europe.

This sanctuary of earth and stone had its beginnings in the New Stone Age, more than 4,000 years ago. A circular embanked ditch, or henge, defined a sacred area. Inside the ditch lay a ring of pits; outside stood the heel stone, a monolith of unhewn sandstone sited so that the sun rose directly over it on midsummer's morning.

Around 1700 B.C. early Bronze Age people erected a double ring of 80 stone blocks within the circular ditch. These slender bluestones, transported 250 miles from western Wales (probably by water), were imbued with holiness from their use at another sacred site. A hundred years later the temple of Stonehenge was raised to the magnificence known today from its noble ruins.

A structure of this scale, demanding immense labor and organization, can only have been the creation of a wealthy Bronze Age ruler, who amassed his riches through cattle and foreign trade. At the bidding of this supreme chieftain, the architects of Stonehenge had huge sandstone blocks dragged to the site from the chalk downs 20 miles away, where they lay exposed on the surface. Then, with stone mauls, workers shaped the blocks. Thirty of these stones, weighing about 26 tons apiece, formed an outer ring supporting curved, contiguous lintels. An inner horseshoe—made of five pairs of upright stones, each pair spanned by a lintel—completed the sanctuary's familiar form.

Aligned with the midsummer sunrise, Stonehenge probably marked the movements of the sun and, perhaps, the moon and planets. Above all, it was a grand stage for rites and ceremonies now only to be imagined—or aped by modern Druids who travel to Stonehenge for the summer solstice.

Pages 60-61: Sixteen feet of time-ravaged sandstone, the heel stone leans toward Stonehenge.

Ancient Thebes
with Its Necropolis,
Egypt

Ramesses II, the king of kings of Shelley's "Ozymandias," ruled ancient Egypt for 66 years; he left more than a hundred children—and scores of temples, monuments, and statues glorifying himself. Many of these he built at Thebes, a religious and political capital on the Nile.

Thebes reached its height during the New Kingdom (1600 to 1100 B.C.). In this immensely prosperous period, Egypt's empire stretched from the Euphrates River to northern Sudan. Ramesses and some 30 other New Kingdom pharaohs lavished their riches on shrine building, eventually arraying both sides of the Nile with temples bearing brightly painted figures of humans and gods.

On the east bank, at the site of the modern town of Luxor, a two-mile-long avenue of sphinxes once linked Luxor and Karnak, Thebes'

great temple complexes. At Karnak, the larger of the two, the main temple honored the sun god Amun-Re; temples to other deities surrounded it. In each, a progressively narrowing succession of gateways, courtyards, and halls led to the god's inner sanctuary.

Across the Nile the New Kingdom pharaohs favored richly decorated tombs hidden in the hillsides rather than highly visible pyramid-tombs accessible to robbers. In this desert necropolis, hundreds of painted galleries and chambers held mummies and their belongings. One such tomb, built by Ramesses II for his favorite wife, Nefertari, holds magnificent wall paintings now threatened by salt and moisture. In 1986 specialists began studying the tomb's physical setting to determine how to save these 3,250-year-old tributes to a pharaoh's great love.

Karnak's sacred lake reflects the remains of pylons that lead to the Temple of Amun-Re.

The head of Pharaoh Ramesses II tops a colossal body enthroned before the temple colonnade at Luxor.

Dignitaries in bas-relief—identified as Medes by their high, rounded headdresses—ascend stairs at the ancient Persian capital of Persepolis.

Persepolis, *Iran*

Designed to exalt the ruler of the largest empire the world had yet seen, ancient Persepolis brought together the treasures and artistic genius of 23 subject nations. Ionian stone carvers, Babylonian brick makers, Egyptian and Median goldsmiths labored two centuries to create the city that would symbolize the riches of ancient Persia.

Darius I began building his ceremonial capital around 515 B.C., soon after seizing control of Persia to become its third emperor. During Darius's 36-year reign the Persian Empire reached its greatest extent, stretching from the Danube to the Indus, and from the steppes of central Asia to the Nile. "King of kings . . . king of the great earth, far and wide," proclaims an inscription at Persepolis.

Darius regularly moved his court from Susa, his administrative capital, to Persepolis in the Marv Dasht Plain of southwestern Iran—perhaps in the spring, at the Persian New Year. Bas-reliefs flanking the city's ceremonial stairways mirror the procession of tribute-laden emissaries, their origins identified by hats or veils, capes or coats, breeches or long skirts. Babylonians hold fine fabrics and lead a prize bull; Armenians present horses; an Elamite carries a lion cub; Indians shoulder jugs possibly filled with pure gold dust.

The entire capital rises from an elevated terrace of limestone, dark gray like the hills behind it and covering 1.4 million square feet. Statues of winged, human-headed bulls guard the city gates. Palaces, harems, barracks, stables, a treasury, and an audience hall large enough to hold 10,000 people once stood on the platform. Darius himself appears on a palace doorjamb, stabbing a lion-headed, scorpion-tailed beast that personified evil.

In 330 B.C. Alexander the Great —ruler of Persia's enemies, the Greeks—conquered the Persian Empire and set his victor's torch to Persepolis. Ironically, rubble from the blaze buried the city for centuries and helped preserve the parades of stone figures, frozen in endless fealty to their king.

65

Protected by natural and man-made walls, Bedouin still live in the ruins of Petra.

Rather than pile stone on stone, the builders of ancient Petra constructed temples, storehouses, and tombs from living rock. They carved Jordan's rose-red city out of sandstone cliffs, first chiseling facades replete with Corinthian columns, garlands of flowers, and statues of gods and lions, then hollowing out the rooms.

Two thousand years ago Petra was one of the greatest commercial centers of the Near East and the capital of the Nabataean civilization. Once nomads of the Arabian Desert, the Nabataeans settled down to exploit Petra's strategic location at the nexus of six caravan routes. Gradually they took control of the luxury trade: frankincense from Arabia, spices from India, Chinese silks, Egyptian gold, Nubian ivory and slaves. "The camel caravans crossing the country were like armies on the march," wrote the Greek geographer Strabo of the traffic to Damascus, the Red Sea, and the Mediterranean by way of Petra.

Like ancient caravan traders, today's visitors must enter Petra—"rock" in Greek—via a mile-long ravine. In places the chasm walls soar to 328 feet and nearly close overhead. Suddenly, through an opening barely wide enough for two horses, appears a peach-and-pink tomb—or possibly temple—ten stories high. Farther on stand a vast amphitheater and other rock-hewn buildings that blend Assyrian, Egyptian, Hellenistic, and Roman styles. Soon the cliff walls widen to expose a plateau three-quarters of a mile across and about a mile long, where the shops and homes of 30,000 Nabataeans once stood.

After Rome annexed Petra in A.D. 106, alternative trade routes developed along the Red Sea and the Nile, and the city lost wealth and power. On the night of May 19, 363, an earthquake tumbled Petra's free-standing walls. Its residents finally dispersed after another quake two centuries later. In the 1100s Crusaders built a fort overlooking the abandoned city. Then, for almost 600 years, only Bedouin and wayfarers knew of Petra's hidden rock-faces and facades.

Paphos, *Cyprus*

Aphrodite, it is said, chose a rock off the coast of southwestern Cyprus for her earthly birthplace. Greek myths recount how the goddess of beauty, sensual love, and fertility, whose name comes from *aphros,* or "foam" in Greek, sprang from the sea froth produced by the severed genitals of Uranus, the personification of heaven, as they fell into the Mediterranean.

At Paphos, a flat-topped hill a few miles northwest of her birthplace, Mycenaean settlers from the Greek mainland dedicated a three-chambered temple to the goddess in the 12th century B.C. Although Phoenicians, Egyptians, and Romans in turn occupied Cyprus, the cult of Aphrodite thrived and the sanctuary drew her followers from all over the ancient world.

At the end of the fourth century B.C., King Nicocles built a harbor town ten miles from Paphos. He called it New Paphos. On festival days, worshipers crowned with myrtle marched in solemn procession to Aphrodite's temple in what was thereafter called Old Paphos.

New Paphos became the cradle of Christianity on Cyprus. When St. Paul preached there around A.D. 48, he converted the first Roman official known to have accepted the new faith.

At New Paphos mosaics decorate Roman villas and palaces, now in ruins. Scenes in one house show Dionysus teaching a man how to make wine—and the first drunken humans falling to the ground.

Today local custom harks back to the fertility cult celebrated at Old Paphos: Young mothers offer candles to the milk-giving Virgin Mary at a stone in Aphrodite's temple.

Discovered at New Paphos in 1983, this mosaic shows Apollo ordering the flaying of a satyr who dared pit his flute against the god's heavenly lyre.

The Acropolis, *Greece*

The rising sun pierced the darkened temple and touched Athena's ivory cheeks, suffusing them with divine warmth; it struck her jeweled eyes, making them gleam; it caught the gold of her tunic, setting it aglow.

Today nothing remains of the 40-foot figure of Athena Parthenos, Athena the Virgin, who once reigned over Athens from the rocky hill called the Acropolis, the "high city." And only ruins survive of the Parthenon—the ethereal temple built to hold her image— and the other magnificent structures under her aegis.

For a thousand years before the Acropolis was given over to the gods, it served as a walled citadel. Gradually, sacrificial altars and small temples were raised atop the 260-foot limestone outcropping.

During Greece's Golden Age the great statesman Pericles ordered a temple erected to honor the city's patron goddess, Athena. By 432 B.C. a marble temple in the Doric style stood framed against the bright Athenian sky. The Parthenon's perfection rested in part on the slight "imperfections" in its design: subtle tiltings, curvings, and swellings of the sides and columns that offset any lifelessness in its symmetry.

In time Greece's fortunes fell, and Christian and Muslim conquerors adapted buildings on the Acropolis to their own use. The Parthenon survived—as church and mosque—until 1687, when occupying Turks used it as a powder magazine during a Venetian siege. A direct hit exploded its center.

In 1801 Lord Elgin, a British diplomat, received permission from the Turkish sultan to remove sculptures from the Parthenon. Pieces from both pediments and one-third of the frieze were carried off to England. Since Greece's independence in 1833, the restoration of the Acropolis—including recovery of the Elgin Marbles— has been a fervent quest. For the history-proud Greeks the quest goes on—to save the timeless symbol of their nation's spirit.

Floodlights illuminate the gateway leading to the 2,400-year-old Parthenon atop the Acropolis.

Pompeii and Herculaneum,
Italy

Around midday on August 24 in A.D. 79, workers set 81 loaves in the oven of a bakery in Pompeii. Ten miles northwest, in the wealthy seaside town of Herculaneum, a baby rocked in a wooden cradle. Near these two Roman provincial towns in southern Italy rose Mount Vesuvius, with olives and grapes ripening on its fertile volcanic slopes.

Suddenly, with the force of a nuclear explosion, Vesuvius blew a mushrooming column 12 miles high. A hail of ash and pumice, followed by asphyxiating ground surges—clouds of gas and ash— and fiery avalanches of gases and lava, buried Pompeii 20 feet deep and engulfed Herculaneum, closer by, in 60 feet of molten rock. In 18 hours it was all over.

At Pompeii hardened debris encased the 81 loaves and other everyday items, along with the shops, brothels, houses, and public baths of this prosperous river port that was home to about 20,000 people. Many died. Plaster casts, made from hollows in the ash where victims lay, preserve their agonized expressions and poses. Excavated wall paintings, floor mosaics, statuary, and ornamental gardens reveal a comfortable standard of living. Temples, theaters, and an amphitheater offered worship and entertainment.

Similar finds, from luxurious homes to a charred cradle with its pitiful heap of bones, have come to light in Herculaneum. But recent discoveries add a new twist. Archaeologists thought most of the population of 4,000 to 5,000 had fled. Then excavations in arched chambers on the ancient seafront uncovered the bones of more than 150 refugees, presumably trapped in a vain attempt to escape by water. More are likely to be found.

Romans cremated their dead, so these skeletons offer an unmatched opportunity for study. They also haunt the viewer. With teeth clenched in the throes of suffocation, they illustrate human horror and fragility. "A masterpiece of pathos," the director of excavations called one huddled group—a fit epitaph for all.

Above: A wall painting, probably of rituals connected with Dionysus, the god of wine, decorates the Villa of the Mysteries outside Pompeii. Opposite: Damp volcanic soil at Herculaneum preserved the skeleton of a female victim of the Mount Vesuvius eruption for 1,900 years.

The Roman Forum, *Italy*

"Here, where the Forum now is, was once dense swamp," wrote Ovid in the first century B.C. Where the Forum once was, a grassy expanse now lies strewn with marble fragments of temples, monuments, and halls —remnants of one of the great civilizations of the ancient world.

Here in the Curia the Senate deliberated affairs of state. Here Julius Caesar refused the crown, and here a mob set fire to his bier. Here Cicero addressed Roman citizens, and here his head and hands were nailed to the speaker's platform after his murder.

Begun around 600 B.C., the Forum grew into a congested assemblage of temples and civic buildings—the hub of Roman public life. Shops and markets crammed every available space along the surprisingly narrow Sacred Way running down its middle. Victorious generals led processions down the Sacred Way and up the Capitoline Hill to the Temple of Jupiter. Clowns were stationed along the route to jeer at the heroes lest the gods become jealous of their glory.

The Forum began to lose its status as the commercial center of Rome in the second century B.C. after the sale of meat and produce was relegated to separate marketplaces. During his reign Julius Caesar started to redesign the Forum to relieve congestion further and transform the motley conglomerate into a harmonious whole —a rectangular courtyard surrounded by religious and political buildings. By A.D. 14 Augustus had completed the transformation.

By this time, however, the Forum had come to play largely a symbolic role. Over the centuries, earthquakes, fires, wars, and looting eventually reduced it to ruins.

When excavations began in the late 1700s, the whole area was buried under 30 to 50 feet of rubble, including the stone that once proudly designated the *umbilicus urbis Romae,* the navel of the city. Today work continues at the Forum to save the public heart of ancient Rome from the effects of pollution and traffic.

73

The curved wall of the Colosseum hovers beyond the three pillars of the Temple of Castor and Pollux (right) and the Temple of Antonius and Faustina (left), now a church.

Qin Shi Huangdi's Tomb Complex, *China*

The man whose armies unified China built a garrison of clay to vanquish mortality. China's first emperor, Qin Shi Huangdi, ordered life-size soldiers buried near him 2,200 years ago to defend his subterranean tomb. So far, one of archaeology's most awesome discoveries has turned up 8,000 such battle-ready warriors plus hundreds of clay horses.

Stationed in three underground vaults covering close to six acres, the terra-cotta soldiers, each with a different face, may portray the ethnic groups Qin forged into a nation. Wood and bronze weapons reveal great skill in military technology and metallurgy. After 22 centuries some swords remain sharp enough to cut a hair.

China's future Caesar began building his mausoleum at age 13 after inheriting the throne of one of seven warring states. With his fast-moving army he conquered the rival kingdoms "like a silkworm devouring a mulberry leaf," as an ancient historian wrote. In 221 B.C. he proclaimed himself Qin Shi Huangdi (First Sovereign Emperor of Qin).

To protect his new empire, Qin built the Great Wall. Behind it he shattered the old feudal system, erecting a centralized bureaucracy and codifying China's laws.

Obsessed with death and the afterworld, Qin dragooned 700,000 men to labor 36 years on the cavernous mausoleum near his capital, in what is now Shaanxi Province. Still unexcavated, the tomb itself is guarded by the clay army garrisoned nearby. If ancient records prove correct, an enormous palace and a trove of artwork wait underground, protected by crossbows set to fire on intruders. A model of the universe is said to glisten with gold and silver, pearl and jade, its waterways flowing with mercury.

Qin's subterranean world sprawls across 20 square miles; archaeologists may need several generations to unearth all its treasures. But the discovery of the clay army in 1974 at last granted Qin Shi Huangdi the immortality for which he hungered.

Life-like legions of clay escorted China's first emperor through the afterworld for 22 centuries.

Ajanta and Ellora Caves,
India

The languid eyes of a celestial nymph typify the sensuality of Ajanta's paintings.

Legend says that the Hindu gods and nymphs once petitioned Indra, the king of heaven, for permission to spend a moonlit night on earth. Frolicking on the cliff of Ellora, the deities broke their promise to leave by sunrise—and turned to stone in the midst of dancing and lovemaking.

Images of Shiva, Vishnu, and their consorts inhabit some of the world's largest and liveliest sculptures—the temples carved into the basalt hillside of Ellora in western India. The Hindu pantheon shares the mile-long scarp with temples and deities of Buddhism and Jainism. Artists of the three faiths sculptured 34 monasteries and major chapels between the sixth and twelfth centuries A.D., carving every pillar, every goddess, elephant, and lotus blossom from bedrock.

The two-story, 164-foot-long Kailasa Temple is dedicated to Shiva, the god of creation and destruction. The walls erupt into a three-dimensional visual text of Hindu mythology. Shiva appears playing a stringed instrument whose music creates the universe.

Six centuries before chisel hit rock at Ellora, Buddhist monks had begun carving and painting cave sanctuaries at Ajanta, 45 miles to the northeast. Dating to the first century B.C., these temples and cells wind around a cliff overlooking the Waghora River and flank more elaborate sanctuaries created between A.D. 460 and 480.

As exquisite as Michelangelo's Sistine Ceiling, the well-preserved murals in Ajanta's caves influenced painting styles throughout Asia. The art illustrates Buddha's life and previous incarnations. One cave shows Buddha blanketing the sky with a thousand images of himself to impress and convert heretics. Palace scenes, ostensibly of Buddha's abodes in former lives, offer glimpses of the fifth-century royal courts that financed Ajanta's monks and artists.

Although Ellora continued to attract artists and pilgrims, Ajanta lost its inhabitants during the fifth century. It became the domain of bats and tigers until its rediscovery 1,400 years later.

Candles illuminate the columns and seated Buddha in Ellora's Vishvakarma Chaitya Hall; its carved ceiling imitates the wooden temples of the seventh century A.D.

Anuradhapura and Polonnaruwa, *Sri Lanka*

A joyful procession marched along a "road sprinkled with white sand, bestrewn with . . . flowers" to accompany a precious bough to Anuradhapura, the capital of ancient Sri Lanka, in 247 B.C. The branch, from the bo tree under which the Buddha had attained enlightenment in India, was planted with great ceremony. As the fig cutting flourished, so did Anuradhapura and ancient Sinhalese civilization.

Indo-Aryan invaders from northern India had settled the Indian Ocean island in the fifth century B.C. Around 380 B.C. King Pandukābhaya made Anuradhapura his capital. More than a hundred monarchs reigned here over the next 1,400 years. Hoping to win rewards in future lives, citizens ringed the walled city with Buddhist monasteries. Carved palaces surrounded brick-and-plaster dagobas—large spired domes, some as high as 40 stories, that held relics or symbols of the Buddha.

Over the centuries Sri Lanka grew wealthy on agriculture and trade. With the help of elephants, islanders dug elaborate irrigation systems, reaping triple harvests of rice yearly. From crowded ports, boats carried pearls and rubies to the empires of Rome, India, and China. Art and literature flourished in the kingdom the Chinese called Land Without Sorrow.

But invading armies from India sacked Anuradhapura again and again, finally destroying it in 993. The new capital—Polonnaruwa, 60 miles to the southeast—flowered in the 12th century under Parākramabāhu I, who sought to create a festive island of tiered palaces and great dagobas, artificial lakes and colossal sculptures. Repeated invasions and neglect of the irrigation system hastened Polonnaruwa's abandonment in the 13th century.

Since the 1890s, archaeologists have been restoring Anuradhapura and Polonnaruwa, brick by brick. Dagobas and the gnarled bo tree, still alive after millennia, draw thousands of pilgrims each year.

At Polonnaruwa a 44-foot-long granite statue of the Buddha entering nirvana reclines next to a Buddha contemplating the sorrows of mankind.

A sandstone bas-relief at the temple of Bayon depicts soldiers of 800 years ago in full panoply.

Sagas in sandstone, the bas-reliefs at the city of Angkor boast of the military prowess and artistic glories of the Khmer Empire that ruled in Indochina for six centuries. Khmer sculptors carved eight epic friezes—6 feet high and up to 220 feet long—into the greatest architectural achievement of Southeast Asia: the temple now called Angkor Wat.

Between the 9th and 13th centuries, more than a dozen Khmer kings built their palaces and temples—Hindu, then Buddhist—at Angkor in northwestern Kampuchea (Cambodia). Suryavarman II raised Angkor Wat in the early 12th century to be his observatory and shrine—and his mausoleum.

Most Khmer Hindu temples are dedicated to the god Shiva and face the rising sun. Angkor Wat honors Vishnu, ruler of the western quarter of the compass, and so faces west. In the middle of the temple stand five multitiered towers—the five peaks of Mount Meru, home of the Hindu gods and center of the universe. Scattered throughout Angkor Wat are 1,700 bas-reliefs of celestial maidens. Crowned with gems and flowers, they represent the pleasures of paradise.

The Khmer reserved brick and stone structures for the gods. Mortals lived in wooden houses and palaces—long ago deteriorated—crowded inside the 75-square-mile metropolis. To care for a population of up to 750,000, the Khmer made Angkor a hydraulic city, constructing a glistening network of canals, moats, and massive reservoirs for irrigation, transportation, and purification rituals.

In the mid-1400s the Khmer succumbed to long-time Siamese rivals who sacked the city. For centuries only saffron-robed Buddhist monks worshiped at Angkor.

During much of the 20th century, preservation teams fought the forest's grip on Angkor's soft stones, but the Cambodian civil war forced them to leave in the 1970s. Restorers resumed work in 1987 so that Angkor's splendor might live, as its last great ruler intended, "as long as the sun and the moon shall endure."

The Gate of the Dead leads to 12th-century Angkor Thom, the last royal capital built at Angkor. Inside stands the temple of Bayon, with its stone forest of 49 towers, each carved with colossal faces.

The Monuments at Hampi,
India

In the early 14th century, as the Muslim conquerors of northern India swept southward over the subcontinent, a great bastion of Hindu faith and culture arose on the Deccan Plateau: the city of Vijayanagar, near the modern village of Hampi. Founded by two ambitious brothers, the city soon became the centerpiece of the vast Vijayanagar Empire, which dominated the south and held off the Muslim armies for more than 200 years.

Natural defenses made the capital almost invulnerable: The torrential waters of the Tungabhadra River protected the northern flank; massive granite outcroppings obstructed all other approaches. But the kings of Vijayanagar did not take chances. They built seven fortified enclosures: The inner four contained palaces, temples, and residences; the outer three, farmland. Despite constant wars with neighboring states, no enemy took the city by siege until 1565.

In the heart of the capital, a royal complex housed the king and his immense retinue of wives, advisers, guards, and servants. Even the royal elephants resided here in a palatial stable topped with domes and covered with plaster decoration. Each year the court played host to the governors and chiefs of the empire during a nine-day festival. In the early 1500s Portuguese trader Domingo Paes attended at the king's invitation. Dumbfounded by the display of wealth and power, Paes watched elaborate religious ceremonies, parades, wrestling matches, fireworks, and performances by hundreds of dancers. At a review of the royal army, he "could see neither plain nor hill that was not entirely covered with troops. . . . Truly, it seemed as if the whole world were collected there."

The increasing power of the empire did not go unnoticed by the Muslim rulers to the north. By 1565 five sultans had formed a coalition to defeat their Hindu enemies. At the Battle of Talikota, Vijayanagar's armies were overrun and the city was sacked. The royal family fled south, abandoning their capital forever.

Amid boulders tossed by the whims of nature, the 15th-century gateway of Virūpākṣa Temple still welcomes Hindu pilgrims to Hampi, site of the ruined city of Vijayanagar.

Easter Island, *Chile*

When the legendary Polynesian chief Hotu Matu'a pointed his double-hulled canoe toward the rising sun around A.D. 500, he launched a voyage that would inaugurate one of history's most intriguing civilizations. Hotu Matu'a and his companions became the first settlers on the triangular, windswept isle of Rapa Nui, later named Easter Island by Dutch explorers who reached it Easter Day in 1722.

According to legend, Hotu Matu'a fled from warring chiefs on his home island, which was probably in the Marquesas Islands more than 2,200 miles to the northwest. Another party of seafaring Polynesians—known as the "heavy-set people"—later joined Hotu Matu'a and the "slender people."

On the crater of a volcano, islanders began to sculpture the art that would symbolize Easter Island forever: towering, tight-lipped figures they called "living faces." With stone picks they carved the fronts first, then hacked the monoliths out of solid rock and, without benefit of the wheel, hauled them to 120 stone platforms lining the coast. After erecting the figures, which commemorate clan ancestors, islanders inserted eyes of white coral with inlaid pupils of red or black rock. They sometimes capped the heads with ten-ton topknots of dark red stone. Over time, clans vied with each other to hew ever more massive sculptures—up to 33 feet high and 85 tons in weight.

By 1680 the island had plunged into civil war. Clansmen destroyed crops, cut down forests, and overturned living faces. Hundreds of unfinished figures littered the quarry. The conflict climaxed when the slender people trapped nearly all the heavy-set people in a ditch and burned them to death.

Peruvian slave raids and European diseases ensured that Easter Island never fully recovered. When Chile annexed the island in 1888, the brooding giants outnumbered the living population; the tradition of megalithic carving never revived.

Megaliths on Easter Island stare inland with newly restored eyes of coral and volcanic rock.

Mesa Verde National Park, U.S.A.

Where the long fingers of Mesa Verde reach deep into southwestern Colorado, the Anasazi built some 600 sandstone dwellings in the sheltering alcoves of steep canyon walls. Scarcely a hundred years later, at the end of the 13th century, the pueblos were abandoned. The empty buildings stood forgotten on high, silent shelves until 1874, when surveyors spied a crumbling ruin in what is now Mesa Verde National Park.

Mesa Verde—"green table" in Spanish—takes its name from the juniper and piñon forests that blanket much of the plateau. The Anasazi, or Ancient Ones, first settled here during the sixth century, living in caves as well as in low log-and-mud shelters built over pits on the mesa top. In the eighth century they moved above ground to adobe houses.

By the late 1100s, when the Anasazi had perfected their masonry skills, they began building the cliff towns. With Stone Age tools they constructed apartment complexes several stories high and painted red-and-white designs in many rooms. No one knows whether they moved to the cliffs for religious reasons, protection from marauding nomads, or shelter from rain and snow. But these cliff dwellings were cold, damp, and crowded, and some could be reached only by using ladders or by clinging to hand- and toe-holds in the sheer rock.

On the mesa top the Anasazi raised crops in irrigated fields. They also domesticated turkeys and hunted deer and small game.

When the Anasazi left Mesa Verde in the late 1200s, they may have been fleeing drought or war. Or they may have brought about their own demise by exhausting the soil, stripping the forests, and hunting the game to extinction.

Today remnants of the old Anasazi culture live on in Arizona and New Mexico, where Pueblo Indians still follow many of the traditions their ancestors brought with them when they climbed down from the green mesa for the last time.

Abandoned by the Anasazi 700 years ago, Cliff Palace held perhaps 250 people in 200 rooms.

87

Teotihuacán, *Mexico*

Twelve centuries ago the first great city of the Americas went up in smoke as unknown arsonists prowled Teotihuacán and burned and sacked its temples. Residents fled. Six centuries later, when Aztecs visited this ancient center of commerce and religion, they found a ruined metropolis dominated by a hulking pair of terraced pyramids, the largest one rising more than 200 feet and covering ten acres.

Concluding that mere humans could not build on such a grand scale, the Aztecs called the city Teotihuacán—Place of the Gods. They incorporated the city into their myths and declared the huge pyramids the birthplaces of the sun and moon. They named one temple ruin for the plumed serpent Quetzalcóatl, the wind god whose gusty breath swept a pathway for the rain god Tlaloc. Although their obsidian eyes have been plucked out, sculptures of these deities still glower from temple walls.

Founded 2,000 years ago in the Valley of Mexico, Teotihuacán spread across eight square miles and supported a population of perhaps 200,000. At its peak, around A.D. 600, the city controlled a powerful state that was probably larger than imperial Rome.

Built of lightweight but durable volcanic rock and stuccoed with mud or lime plaster, Teotihuacán's 4,000 buildings were laid out in a rectangular grid. A broad avenue bisected the city and linked markets, monuments, and plazas. Thinking the low palaces along the route were tombs, the Aztecs later misnamed it the Street of the Dead.

Most Teotihuacanos lived in windowless, one-story apartments wrapped around sunny patios, often in compounds containing artisans' workshops. Obsidian production—the city's largest industry—provided spearpoints and cutting tools to trade with coastal lowlanders for feathers, jade, shells, and skins.

By A.D. 750 political decay had weakened Teotihuacán. No evidence survives to tell whether the city eventually succumbed to invaders or to enemies within.

A serpent bares stony fangs on the Temple of Quetzalcóatl at Teotihuacán, America's first major city.

Chan Chan, *Peru*

Along the narrow strip of desert separating the Andes from the Pacific, a mighty kingdom built castles in the sand. The crumbling walls of nine royal compounds still outline Chan Chan, the capital of an empire that once stretched 600 miles along Peru's north coast. The Chimú Kingdom flourished for 250 years, falling to the Incas around 1470.

The largest city in South America before Columbus arrived, Chan Chan sprawled across nine square miles and sheltered 50,000 inhabitants. Each of its kings built a compound to serve as his palace—and, later, his tomb. Artists transformed the tawny adobe walls into intricate friezes of marine deities. The kings lived well—robed in cloth as fine as the best in medieval Europe, surrounded by musicians, dancers, and jesters. When a king died, he was buried with hundreds of sacrificial females and great stores of gold and silver. Conquering Incas melted and recast the gold into life-size statues.

Now riddled with tunnels and pits from centuries of looting, the ruins are melting back into the desert. Walls once strong enough to withstand earthquakes are crumbling in the moist sea breezes or dissolving in the torrential rains that occasionally fall.

Archaeologists must hurry to preserve Chan Chan and complete a detailed portrait of its regal personality. Despite the looting, clues survive: jewelry, textiles, pottery, ornaments of gold, copper, and inlaid shell. But even this abundance of artifacts, wrote archaeologist Victor W. von Hagen, gives only an idea "of the almost Arabian Nights splendour . . . of Chan Chan."

When rain falls on Chan Chan's adobe walls, each drop scars the stylized fish leaping over a row of pelicans.

Tikal National Park,
Guatemala

Sacred man-made mountains soar clear of the Guatemalan jungle at Tikal, one of the grandest capitals of the ancient Maya. At 20 stories, the loftiest of Tikal's temple-pyramids survives as the tallest pre-Columbian building in the Americas.

Atop these limestone skyscrapers, the god-king and his elite may have contacted the gods and ancestor spirits through hallucinations induced by bloodletting, tobacco, and intoxicating enemas. The priestly elite also predicted conjunctions of the planets that might prove auspicious for declaring war or planting crops. Using an elaborate calendar system, they measured time to the day over millions of years. And they developed the most sophisticated writing system in the New World.

Recently deciphered hieroglyphs from Tikal and other Maya sites belie scholars' early view of these Native Americans as peace-loving mathematicians and stargazers. The inscriptions tell of wars, power plays, torture, and even self-mutilation by piercing the penis, tongue, or lips with obsidian lancets and stingray spines to nourish the gods with human blood.

Settled in the seventh century B.C., Tikal flowered with the Classic Maya civilization from A.D. 250 to 900. At its zenith the city sprawled across 50 square miles and may have counted as many as 40,000 inhabitants. Supported by intensive agriculture and a far-flung trade network, Tikal boasted temple-pyramids and palaces, wide causeways and a covered marketplace. Archaeologists have so far excavated about 500 structures and mapped the remains of some 3,000—all constructed without the aid of wheels or metal tools.

After a millennium and a half of continuous building and rebuilding—at least 50 temples lie beneath the dozens visible today —construction at Tikal suddenly halted. By A.D. 900 the city's population had all but vanished. To this day, no one knows why.

The jungle surrounding Tikal shelters an array of forest creatures, including the endangered jaguar, once the symbol of Maya royalty.

REALMS
ROYAL & SACRED

When I served as a second lieutenant in Nigeria in the 1950s, I spent a fortnight on maneuvers in the Ibo territory near Enugu. This jungle country caught my imagination because it was full of religion and magic. Every few hundred yards along the roads, little chapels of wood or corrugated iron carried the name of a different sect or brotherhood. The magic was to be found farther into the jungle. As I sweated with my platoon through the undergrowth in pursuit of imaginary enemies, we kept coming across miniature shrines of stick or earth, amulets or pieces of cloth mysteriously tied to branches.

But I found the strangest place when wandering on my own. I saw a grove of enormous trees in the distance and made my way to them. The trees formed a canopy, supported by smooth, silvery trunks like columns. Under the canopy was a patch of beaten earth; in the middle of the patch was a little shrine; and in the shrine was a skull.

I then noticed something else very curious. The trees in the grove stood in two groups, with an opening between them for the shrine. I looked along the axis of the opening to a hill about half a mile away. The side of the hill had been cut away on the line of the axis. It was a man-made cut, overgrown now. Its only conceivable function was to open a processional approach to the grove. I shall never forget the still evening, the low sun, the huge trees, the little shrine, the cut in the hill. There wasn't a soul in sight in the wide, lush landscape. Something was here that I didn't understand. I was frightened.

Groves have often become sacred places, as have caves, hilltops, and springs. Something out of the ordinary, mysterious, or exciting about these places has led people to see them as the homes or resorts of gods. Some sacred places remain little altered, like the cave by the Gulf of Naples at Cumae, where Apollo inspired the Sibyl to speak her prophecies. Others acquire an open-air altar, where sacrifices are made to the gods, and a shrine or temple for the gods to live in. Such are the temples of Athens and Corinth, set in sacred enclosures on craggy hilltops, and the temples of Olympia amid their groves and springs, miraculously lush as one comes down to them from the parched mountains.

Shrines are usually secret places accessible only to their priests. Worshipers are confined to courtyards or halls outside, where they can watch sacrifices at the altar or the emergence of the god or sacred object for processions. A barrier marks off the whole complex from the everyday world, and often some kind of processional way leads to the complex. In an Egyptian temple the courtyard for worshipers and the inner shrine fuse with an inexorable sense of occasion. Avenues of giant columns lead through one courtyard and then another to the labyrinth of secret rooms round the inner shrine.

In the great Christian churches of northern Europe, everything is put under cover. The naves of English and French cathedrals were often far too large for any local congregation; they can best be seen as processional ways leading to the culmination of columns and vaulting around the sanctuary. One instinctively compares the massive stonework of Romanesque churches like Vézelay and Durham to caves, and thinks of forests among the soaring piers and lacy vaults and tracery of Chartres and Amiens or the endlessly repeating columns of the Great Mosque of Córdoba or Bernini's colonnades outside St. Peter's in Rome. In spite of huge differences in context and belief, the vista down the nave of St. Peter's to Bernini's baldachin over the high altar and the tomb believed to be St. Peter's has something in common with my vista through the cut in the hill to the shrine and its canopy of trees in Nigeria.

Whatever the format, a principal object of builders of shrines and temples the world over was to please the god or gods. When the Sumerians came to live on the Mesopotamian plains, they built tall ziggurats as man-made mountains to link earth and heaven and provide a fitting home for the divine patrons of their cities.

But clearly no model could be better than the universe itself, the supreme divine creation. Some cultures thought of the universe as a flat sky supported on four pillars above a flat earth. Others saw the sky as a dome suspended over a square earth. At the Pantheon in Rome and Hagia Sophia in İstanbul, the mighty domes were envisaged as models of the sky. Domes are the most sensational examples of the way in which technology has been put to religious use. To enter the Pantheon or Hagia Sophia is to experience immediate and overpowering awe; in terms of the natural world, it is like standing on a hilltop on a still night, under a star-filled sky. All over the world, city after city acquired presiding domes, like slices of eternity come to rest on earth.

Church and temple enclosures were deliberately created earthly paradises, foretastes of bliss to come, full, often, of greenery and water and cut off by walls and gates from the everyday world outside. Light could be used too, to create the impression of another and better world. Such impressions are strong enough today for us, when we come in our well-made clothes and out of our comfortable buses or cars into the glow and mystery of Chartres. They must have been immeasurably stronger for medieval peasants, coming into their cathedrals from thatched hovels and a life of disease and poverty.

As sacred buildings become more complex, they acquire extra ceremonies, altars, shrines, and tombs of saints or holy men and women. They are given treasure or property and need treasuries for the former and offices from which to administer the latter. More and more decoration and ornament encrust their structure.

Inevitably, from time to time reaction sets in—a call to clear away clutter and get back to direct contact between man and God. Early Protestant meetinghouses had no elaborate decoration, no shrines, and often no priests; they were not sacred places but convenient buildings where people assembled to pray and be instructed. The first mosques were similar. To this day they are essentially prayer halls for the faithful. But even these types of buildings tend to grow more elaborate over the centuries. The Friday Mosque in Eşfahān, with its shimmering, multicolored courtyard and floating domes, has come a long way from the prayer hall of earlier centuries.

In many ways palaces have more in common with churches and temples than with houses. Kings tend to acquire divine attributes. Egypt's pharaohs and some of the kings of the ancient East were worshiped as gods. The emperor of Japan is still considered divine by many of his subjects; until 1946 they were forbidden to look down on him and had to shutter windows above the ground floor in Tōkyō when he went through the city.

A Christian king could not, of course, declare himself a god. But he had a special status: He was the Lord's anointed, God's representative and viceroy in secular matters, just as archbishops and bishops were in religious matters. His coronation poured divine force into the king, even if it did not turn him into a god. As Shakespeare put it, "There's such divinity doth hedge a king."

In the palaces of Gonder the Christian kings of Ethiopia presided over their councils from behind a screen. They were too sacred to be seen. Visitors having audience with the Byzantine emperors in Constantinople had to prostrate themselves and touch the ground three times with their foreheads—a ceremony much resented by embassies from Western monarchies, where no such ritual took place. When a delegation from the king of Siam came to Queen Victoria in 1858, its members insisted on crawling on their bellies across the audience chamber, much to the amusement of the English court. But the contrast was only one of degree. Queen Victoria, following the tradition of Western monarchs, only allowed her subjects to sit down in her presence as a great and occasional privilege. At Osborne, where she went for holidays, her big drawing room was built on an L-plan so courtiers could at least get round the corner and have a rest. She never ate at the same table with commoners.

As the seats of gods or their representatives, palaces were planned in a way similar to churches and temples. A processional approach led to the halls of state, where the monarch showed himself to his subjects; beyond lay sumptuous smaller rooms, inner sanctuaries accessible to only a favored few. And palaces, like religious centers, tended to grow in size, richness, and complexity. Those serving as the seat of government were inevitably very large; apart from accommodating the king and all the ceremonial surrounding him, they contained large numbers of government officials, each with his own retinue of servants. Hence the size of Versailles or Windsor Castle or the Escorial.

Other palaces were built for hunting. The more animals a king slaughtered, the better; a mighty hunter was the peacetime equivalent of a mighty warrior. The most sensational hunting palace is Chambord, built for François I in the 1520s and '30s.

Other palaces were for pleasure. Many, especially in Mogul and Moorish kingdoms, imitated Paradise—enclaves of greenery, pools, and fountains scattered with little pavilions. Capacious loggias looked out onto the gardens. Here sumptuous meals were eaten in the intervals of drinking, singing, watching dancers, or listening to poetry and music; ultimately, perhaps, the monarch would retire to a private room with a favorite.

The life lived in these magical realms set the king apart from his subjects and added to his mystique. So did the image of him slaying tigers by the hundred from the back of an elephant. In palaces as in churches, all the resources of art and invention increased the aura of majesty. State apartments were often up on the second or even third floors, approached by a superb staircase. The acme of grandeur and inventiveness came with the baroque and rococo staircases of the 18th century. Above tumbling flights of steps at Brühl and Würzburg, ceilings open into limitless worlds where gods and goddesses disport and allegorical figures pay homage to the ruler.

The elector of Cologne at Brühl, the prince-bishop of Würzburg, and countless other monarchs and minor potentates all emulated the architecture, ritual, and life of Versailles. Louis XIV set the pace for royal Europe. Let us spend a day with him in the 1680s.

The palace's rooms focus upon the king's bedroom. It lies behind the windows near the center of the second floor, adjoining the grand Hall of Mirrors to the west and looking out through gilded entrance gates along a great avenue to the east. Dominated by the state bed, the king's bedroom rises up through two floors. A carved balustrade, like an altar rail, separates the bed from the rest of the room.

The king awakens at 7:30. Only a few people may go behind the balustrade—among them the valet of the wig closet, who brings the king a selection of wigs. A hundred or so courtiers have the right to watch the king dress and have breakfast. Dressing is an elaborate ritual. Different people are privileged to help him on with different articles of clothing; the royal shirt is reserved for his son, the Dauphin.

In a room next door the king devotes his early hours to state business. Dinner is at one and supper, the main meal, at ten. The king normally eats dinner alone while everyone else in the room stands watching. His skill at cutting off the top of an egg with one blow of his knife never fails to appeal to his subjects. Other than the inner sanctum, almost the entire palace is as open to the public as the nave and aisles of a cathedral.

In the afternoon the king walks in the gardens or hunts. At night he enjoys regular court entertainments in the gilded reception rooms running along one side of the palace. He plays billiards in one, watched by his courtiers. In another there is music, in a third dancing; the king is a superb dancer. In a fourth, courtiers play at cards for high stakes.

Every now and then, evening entertainments take place in the gardens. After the masques, music, and dances, the king and court take to boats on the water while trumpets blow and the sky becomes a sheet of fireworks. Then the king retires.

The king's emblem is the sun. The king is the sun who warms his people; he personifies the Greek sun god Apollo. His bedroom faces due east, toward the rising sun. Suns and Apollos are everywhere, in the gardens and the decoration of the palace. Allegory and ornament raise him to godlike status. But he remains a Christian king.

King and court attend Mass every morning at ten in the palace chapel. The king worships up in a gallery, looking along the length of the chapel to the altar. The courtiers kneel below, facing the gallery, not the altar. When the king enters, the courtiers bow to the king and the king bows to the altar. The hierarchy is made clear; God and the king, the king and his subjects. Realms royal and sacred meet and fuse.

The Château of Chambord,
France

You first see Chambord as it was meant to be seen, from afar. Through a forest clearing a bold hodgepodge emerges—towers, pinnacles, turrets, chimneys, gables—a fairy-tale roof made all the more striking by the classicism and serenity of the stone walls beneath it.

Had you been there four centuries ago, you might have seen ladies of the court strolling the roof terrace of this Loire Valley château. From that vantage point they watched their lords set off to hunt wild boar, pheasant, and deer in the surrounding forests. The château was designed as a hunting lodge and pleasure palace for François I, the exuberant Renaissance king. To many it represents the French Renaissance in its most magnificent flowering.

"It was a building that would cost as much as a campaign," wrote one of the king's biographers. "To create it would cramp him. But he had the impulse to crown the earth with one of these vast, sumptuous, regal experiments." Sumptuous it is, and paradoxical too in its blending of medieval and Renaissance features.

Chambord's ground plan follows that of a medieval castle: an enormous square block, or keep, with massive round towers at each corner, enclosed by a rectangle also flanked by towers. Though partly fortified, the château was never intended for military purposes. Instead of the slits for windows typical of feudal castles, Chambord's windows are large and decorated with stonework. Its builders erected thick walls not for defense but to support the elaborate rooftop ornamentation.

Constructed mostly between 1519 and 1541, with as many as 1,800 workmen employed at one time, Chambord took inspiration from Italy, where François dallied for four months after defeating the duke of Milan in battle. The king brought home a passion for the Italian Renaissance, then at its height, and soon after embarked on building the château with its 400 or so rooms. Italian designers, sculptors, and painters flocked to

The French Renaissance château of Chambord sits in splendid isolation on the Cosson River, surrounded by a 13,000-acre park.

the court at François's invitation; from their collaboration with French master craftsmen and masons emerged the lively French Renaissance style.

Among the artists François lured from Italy was Leonardo da Vinci, who lived in nearby Amboise until his death the year that Chambord was begun. Leonardo may have had a hand in designing the château's grand double-spiral staircase in the center of the keep. The staircases wrap around each other so that a person ascending one catches only fleeting glimpses of a person descending the other, a feat of engineering that set the scene for centuries of peekaboo games. The staircases continue up through the roof, becoming an elaborately sculptured open tower which, though masterful in design, made the château nearly impossible to heat.

Since François had other châteaus, he spent a total of only 27 days at Chambord. With scores of horses, dogs, nobles, huntsmen, archers, and grooms, his hunt was an elaborate ritual accompanied by pomp and music. "When the hunt came home at dusk," a biographer wrote, "another concert of braying horn music took place ... before huntsmen drawn up in ranks like soldiers."

François and his court spent the evenings feasting and dancing. He loved beautiful women, but evidently they did not always love him back, for in March 1545, on perhaps the final visit before his death from syphilis in 1547, he is supposed to have scratched on a Chambord window the couplet:

Woman is often fickle;
He is a fool who trusts her.

Above: The keep's ingenious double-spiral staircase connected four apartments on each of three stories.
Opposite: Members of the court of François I found the nooks and crannies of the ornamental rooftop ideal for frolics.

The Fountain of Apollo: Water for Versailles's fountains was pumped from the Seine to the top of a 525-foot hill so it could flow down to the park.

The Palace and Park
of Versailles, *France*

"Versailles! It is wonderfully beautiful! You gaze, and stare, and try to understand that it is real . . . that it is not the Garden of Eden—but your brain grows giddy. . . . The scene thrills one like military music!" Even as cynical a commentator as Mark Twain called the palace and park of Versailles overwhelming. The magnificent château, more than a third of a mile long, holds 700 rooms adorned with art treasures and masterpieces by France's finest craftsmen: porcelain, tapestries, glass, furniture trimmed with silver or set with mother-of-pearl. Beyond the château, 247 acres of manicured gardens display a rigorous geometry. Wide, grassy avenues radiate to seemingly infinite distances, walled on both sides by rows of trees whose branches form perfect arches.

The palace began as a small hunting lodge near the obscure village of Versailles, 11 miles southwest of Paris. In 1661 Louis XIV decided to move his seat of government to this unlikely spot—away from the civil strife of Paris. To convert the small brick-and-stone building into an appropriate setting for a king's court, Louis called upon the great French artists of his time.

Architect Louis Le Vau retained the original hunting lodge, surrounding it on three sides with a massive, U-shaped classical structure of honey-colored stone. At the center of the palace was the king's splendid bedchamber. In 1678, at the peak of his power, Louis XIV decided to enlarge the château even further. Architect Jules Hardouin-Mansart added an elegant array of courtyards, new buildings, and the Hall of Mirrors, giving the palace its familiar form and making it a model of grandeur imitated by monarchs throughout Europe.

But it was landscape gardener André Lenôtre who created the crowning glory of Versailles: its gardens, with their radial avenues, extensive flower beds, water basins, colossal statues, and fountains—1,400 of them, ranging from delicate spouts to spectacular curving jets of water spewing from great bronze effigies.

To the end of his 72-year reign, Louis XIV continued to alter the château, redesigning the rooms and gardens, creating a physical embodiment of the famous expression, "*L'État, c'est moi.*"

Above: Shrubbery trimmed into precise cones adorns the South Parterre. Pages 102-103: In the 240-foot-long Hall of Mirrors, 17 windows face 17 panels made of 400 mirrors.

The Würzburg Residence,
West Germany

If the staircase ceiling in the Würzburg Residence should hold, a rival architect is supposed to have said, he would have himself hanged beneath it. Not only has this immense structure withstood the passage of two and a half centuries, it also survived the bombs that in 1945 destroyed much of the rest of the palace.

In 1720 Prince-Bishop Johann Philipp Franz von Schönborn of the principality of Würzburg began to build the 300-room palace as his dwelling and seat of government. The bishop's enthusiasm—he admitted to a disease he called the "building worm"—and the guiding spirit of architect Johann Balthasar Neumann combined to create an edifice about ten times the size of the White House. The bishop's successors lived there until the early 1800s, when Würzburg came under Bavarian rule.

Considered by many the 18th century's secular masterpiece, the restored palace represents the height of the German baroque. A harmonious synthesis of styles, the building has both a central courtyard and interior ones, fusing the French courtyard design with the multi-courtyard plan of Rhineland residences.

Architect Neumann invited Europe's best known painters, sculptors, and stucco artists to decorate the residence. Chief among them were the Venetian master Giovanni Battista Tiepolo and his two sons, who covered the 100-by-60-foot ceiling with a fresco mingling historical and allegorical themes. As Fame carries aloft a portrait of one of Bishop Schönborn's successors, Neumann, his work done, rests in the foreground with his dog.

A rococo cherub sculptured in the 1770s straddles the staircase balustrade.

Opposite: Tiepolo's exuberant allegory of the arts, including portraits of residence artists, unfolds above Würzburg's main staircase. Above: The sun god Apollo, one of the Venetian painter's flying figures, crowns the masterwork.

Palaces and Castles:
Regal Homes
for Reigning Monarchs

Palace: the official residence of a sovereign. The word comes from the Latin *palatium,* which in turn stems from the hill called Palatine, where emperors of Rome beginning with Augustus (27 B.C.-A.D. 14) erected their grandiose dwellings. From the Romans, too, came Europe's notion of a palace as a monumental seat of power located in the heart of a capital city—and of outlying estates devoted to lighter monarchal moments. In time, such edifices would come to rival temples and churches—the earthly abodes of the divinities.

The collapse of the Roman Empire in the fifth century brought strife and turmoil to much of the Western world. Palaces became battlemented castles—thick walled, slit windowed, and often moated or set on some strategically located and impregnable crag.

But castles—whether in England or Ethiopia—were gloomy and forbidding. In Europe the gradual return of peace and prosperity in the 16th century saw castles give way to manor houses and sprawling estates decked out with pavilions and gardens. Large, glass-paned windows replaced slotted embrasures once used for firing arrows; moats evolved into decorative ponds and ingenious waterworks displays; opulence and ornamentation prevailed. The palace again became truly palatial—culminating with regal extravaganzas such as Hampton Court Palace in England, the Alhambra in Spain, Schönbrunn in Austria, Falkenlust in Germany, and Versailles, Chambord, and Fontainebleau in France.

Half a world away, in China, the early 15th century saw the rise to power of the Ming Dynasty. In 1404 the Yong Le Emperor began to build his Forbidden City within the imperial precincts of Beijing. The palace compound covered 250 acres and was protected by walls and moats, including a stream shaped like a Tatar bow. Today the Forbidden City stands as a vast museum, a repository of treasures spanning a thousand years of China's heritage, and a monument to imperial splendor.

The Forbidden City presides over the bow-shaped Golden Water Stream in Beijing, China.

Top: Since the 18th century, Falkenlust Castle has graced Brühl, West Germany. Bottom: Built during an era of civil strife, the 17th-century fortress of Emperor Fasilides has outlasted time and turmoil at Fasil Ghebbi in Ethiopia.

The Alhambra in Granada, *Spain*

llāh cast the Moors out of the Alhambra, legend says, because they dared make it too much like Paradise.

But the Alhambra sprang from earthly beginnings: a modest fortress the Moors built to protect themselves from peasant revolts in the ninth century. Set on a spur of the Sierra Nevada overlooking Granada, the Alhambra gave no hint of the splendor to come.

By 711, four generations after the Prophet Muḥammad's death, North African converts to Islam had streamed across the Strait of Gibraltar to Spain. On their spirited Arabian horses, these Moors—Berbers and Arabs from the Atlas Mountains—galloped across most of the Iberian Peninsula, claiming the land for Allāh. The Moors would rule in Spain for nearly 800 years, bringing science, universities, and religious tolerance to a country mired in the Dark Ages. In 1085 Spanish Christians launched the Reconquest and slowly drove the Muslims south.

After Córdoba fell to the Christians in 1236, Granada replaced it as capital of the Moors. Muḥammad I founded the Naṣrid Dynasty there and reinforced the decaying fortress. Eventually thick ramparts punctuated by 24 watchtowers surrounded the stronghold's 35-acre plateau. Behind the massive walls Muḥammad I's successors created one of the finest examples of Islamic architecture in Europe. The fairyland palace was called the Alhambra—a corruption of "red castle" in Arabic—for the rubicund glow of its walls in torchlight.

A large, outstretched hand carved above the Alhambra's main entrance symbolizes Islam's five requirements: prayer, fasting, pilgrimage, almsgiving, and belief in the oneness of God. Inside, the decor generally respects Islam's taboos against depicting animals or humans. But everywhere there are patterns: Ceilings with plaster stalactites resemble enormous kaleidoscopic images exploding outward. Geometric and floral motifs of mesmerizing complexity,

Some 4,400 tiny plaster cells honeycomb the celestial ceiling of the Hall of the Two Sisters.

The Alhambra's somber walls and towers, never tested in battle, conceal all hint of the fairyland of arcades and courtyards, gardens and fountains within.

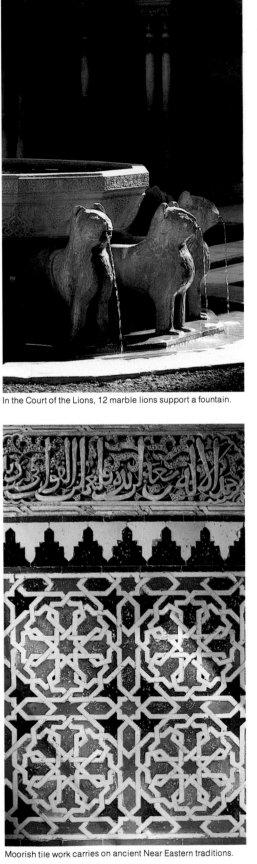

In the Court of the Lions, 12 marble lions support a fountain.

Moorish tile work carries on ancient Near Eastern traditions.

sculptured in stucco, wind across walls and over arches. Inscriptions carved in ornate Arabic calligraphy on walls and doorframes praise Allāh, Moorish rulers, and the Alhambra itself, while filigree windows mold even the light into designs on the floors.

The Naṣrid monarchs built for their own lifetimes, not for posterity. The arabesque flourishes molded, stamped, and carved into the wet plaster often conceal shoddy brickwork and carpentry.

Water, the ultimate luxury to a people who remembered the desert, was vital to Moorish architecture. With fountains and rivulets the Naṣrids displayed water like jewelry. Large pools reflected columns standing like palm trees at an oasis. Water fed lush greenery in the courts and in the Generalife— the architect's garden—where a fountain-studded canal ran through beds of fragrant flowers and herbs. The Alhambra became an earthly heaven in a culture whose holy book speaks of Paradise as "pavilions beneath which water flows."

Folk tradition insists that magic holds the palace together. But pragmatic diplomacy maintained the Naṣrid state. The sultan received official visitors in the throne room for formal audiences and receptions. In other halls the monarch heard his subjects' disputes twice a week, administering justice as had his desert forebears.

Some say the Moors transacted more business in the royal baths than in the royal halls. The monarch and his guests soaked in marble tanks of perfumed water, then proceeded to a steam room and a rest hall. On other occasions the sultan bathed with his wives. Afterward, it is said, he would send an apple to the one he desired to see alone.

Moorish rule quietly ended in 1492. After Christian sovereigns Ferdinand and Isabella signaled their plans to storm the Alhambra, Muḥammad XII, 22nd in the Naṣrid Dynasty, rode off without a fight. He burst into tears, tradition holds, as he last glimpsed his capital from a mountain pass still called the Sigh of the Moor.

111

The Meidān-e-Shāh
of Eṣfahān, *Iran*

"Eṣfahān is half the world," the city's poets once proclaimed. So it must have seemed in the 17th century after Shāh ʻAbbās I moved his capital to this oasis city in central Iran. Among tree-lined avenues and gardens, palaces and shimmering pools in a city of half a million people, a French chronicler counted 102 mosques, 273 public baths, and 1,802 caravansaries—courtyarded inns where travelers and traders fed their camels and stayed the night.

Shāh ʻAbbās I ascended the throne in 1588 at the age of 17. Not one to risk losing power, he later blinded two of his sons and had a third son executed. The shah united Iran's warring factions, drove back encroaching Uzbek and Turkish rivals, and forged alliances with Western powers against the Ottoman Empire.

ʻAbbās built the Meidān-e-Shāh, or Shāh Square, to be Eṣfahān's centerpiece and the Image of the World, as he called it. In the Meidān—a rectangular plaza nearly a third of a mile long—and the exquisite buildings framing it, sports and diplomacy, trade and prayer took place side by side.

From the palace balcony the shah watched polo matches or wild-beast fights on the Meidān. Other days, merchants covered the plaza with their tents. ʻAbbās could take ambassadors to the coffee shops on the Meidān's north side or to the bazaar, where stalls of fine fabrics, leatherwork, and jewelry lined miles of arcaded lanes. At night the shah delighted in illuminating the buildings bordering the Meidān with 50,000 oil lamps.

On the square's southern end ʻAbbās raised the Mosque of the Shāh, set at an angle to face Mecca. So eager was he to finish the great mosque, legend says, that he ordered its brick walls built before the foundation had settled. To gain time, the chief architect went into hiding—knowing that no work could proceed without him—and emerged, begging forgiveness, only after the foundation had stabilized.

The mosque's 177-foot-high dome recalled the shape of the Zoroastrian fire temples that flourished in Persia before the Muslim conquest. The dome, courtyards, and minarets glimmered with floral and geometric tile work reminiscent of a Persian carpet.

Although the shah's immediate successors continued to embellish Eṣfahān, the city later fell into decline; Afghan armies sacked it in 1722. For much of the 20th century, restorers have been reassembling the monuments around the Meidān, reviving in brick and tile a monarch's Image of the World.

Above: The Loṭfollāh Mosque, the shah's private sanctuary completed in 1618, gleams inside and out with mosaics of enameled tile.
Opposite: Shāh ʻAbbās I built his great plaza—the Meidān-e-Shāh—as a microcosm of his world, a center for trade, prayer, and princely pleasure.

The Mosque of Córdoba,
Spain

One of history's strangest marriages united not two people but two buildings. In the eighth century the armies of the Prophet Muḥammad spilled westward across North Africa and then seized Spain. At Córdoba, which became the capital of Muslim Spain, the Moors raised the Great Mosque in 785. The largest mosque outside Mecca, it eventually covered six acres. Its mélange of architectural styles echoed the alliance of East with West: an Eastern world transplanted to southern Spain, with a taste of Byzantium, a flicker of Rome, and the potent radiation of Islam.

Moorish builders tested and innovated, borrowed and synthesized to create an architecture for the new religion of Islam, a faith whose desert birthplace had no tradition of monumental buildings. The Great Mosque's open floor plan reflected the spiritual democracy of Islam, the belief that Allāh hears all prayers equally. The new faith needed neither priest nor sacrament. In the ghostly light of the prayer hall, worshipers stood row on row like the columns, facing the mihrab, a niche that directed the eyes and thoughts of the faithful toward Mecca. Byzantine craftsmen from Constantinople embellished the mihrab with stylized floral and geometric mosaics, heeding the Islamic prohibition against realistic portrayals of nature.

Had the prayer hall's expansive roof rested on a single tier of pillars, it would have seemed oppressively low. So Moorish architects, probably inspired by Roman aqueducts, added a second story of columns. Like the cooling palm canopy of a desert oasis, a seemingly endless web of arches entwined overhead.

Córdoba fell to the Christians in 1236. Three centuries later, clerics desiring sumptuous surroundings built a cathedral amid the Great Mosque's forest of columns. Without this bizarre addition, one of the glories of Islamic architecture would surely have been torn down during the Spanish Inquisition.

Atop hundreds of columns the Moors strung double arches to raise the prayer hall's roof.

Rila Monastery's irregular layout conforms to a rugged, mountainous terrain.

Rila Monastery, *Bulgaria*

On a steep mountain slope in the wilderness of western Bulgaria stands a secluded retreat that once held the heart of a nation. Fortress-like walls enclose an inviting arcade of colorful arches and a treasure house of paintings and wood carvings. For much of its history Rila Monastery has been stronghold and art repository, monastic refuge and cradle of national consciousness.

The Bulgarian Orthodox monastery was founded in the tenth century by followers of St. John of Rila, a critic of the Bulgarian court and clergy who sought a life of solitude and prayer in the Rila Mountains.

In 1396 Ottoman Turks invaded Bulgaria. During the long centuries of Turkish oppression, the monastery suffered frequent attacks by bandits and Muslim invaders. Even so, the monks of Rila continued their religious and literary activities—teaching, studying, copying scores of old manuscripts, and writing chronicles in the modern Bulgarian language.

When the nation began its struggle for independence in the early 1800s, the monastery found itself the symbolic center of an energetic cultural and political awakening. Three large wings were raised to house the growing numbers of monks, pilgrims, and students. Disaster struck in 1833 when a fire gutted the buildings. Almost immediately, stonemasons, bricklayers, painters, and wood carvers settled at the monastery. They worked with feverish haste and a year later completed the new Rila.

Today the red-roofed quadrangle juts from the thickly wooded mountains. Its massive outer walls, designed to discourage bandits, rise 154 feet in places. The courtyard facades and the five-domed monastery church are visually linked by exuberant red-and-white-striped masonry. Carved wooden ceilings and elaborate murals decorate the 250 or so guest rooms and monks' cells. Only a few of these cells are occupied now, but the monastery, with its extensive art collection and library, remains a monument to the persistence, hope, and pride of the Bulgarian people.

A gilded wooden screen embellishes the monastery church.

117

The Moss Garden
of Saihō-ji in Kyōto, *Japan*

The path winds through a dark forest, veering first toward a lichen-covered evergreen, then toward a gleaming sheet of water—a pond shaped like the Japanese symbol for "spirit." Radiant green moss of a single, luxuriant texture carpets every surface, softening edges and blending rock with soil. Draw near, and the verdant blanket separates into distinct patches, each its own shade of green with tiny flowerlike shoots of various hues. More than 120 kinds of moss thrive in the bosky garden of Saihō-ji, a Zen Buddhist temple in western Kyōto.

The temple was founded in the eighth century. In 1339 Musō Kokushi, a Zen priest, redesigned it to conform with medieval Zen aesthetics, which esteemed the small, simple, and natural over the grandiose and artificial. Musō built several modest villas, halls, and pavilions, all of which were destroyed during the civil wars of the 1400s. Only a more recent hall and two teahouses stand today. But the 4.5-acre garden remains.

In a daring departure from tradition, Musō created a stroll garden at Saihō-ji. Unlike aristocratic gardens, which were designed to be viewed from a single vantage point, Saihō-ji yields ever changing vistas. To aid contemplation and meditation, the path focuses attention on the immediate: a bamboo grove, a moss-covered stone, a group of rocks carefully positioned to capture the essence of a mountain waterfall —without the water. Rich in both illusion and allusion, Saihō-ji encourages the viewer to see large within small, a whole universe within the bounds of a garden.

Due to damage done by Saihō-ji's many visitors — up to 8,000 a day — access to the garden is now restricted to entry by appointment only.

Donors' names are inscribed on *torii* at Fushimi-Inari Shrine.

The Fushimi-Inari Shrine in Kyōto, *Japan*

Ten thousand *torii* gateways form a vermilion tunnel 2.5 miles long at the Fushimi-Inari Shrine in Kyōto. Donated by worshipers—successful businessmen in particular—the wooden torii mark the precinct as sacred.

Built in 711 on Mount Inari, this celebrated shrine was later moved to the foot of the mountain, where it stands today amid giant Japanese cedars. Fushimi is one of 40,000 Shinto shrines throughout Japan dedicated to Inari, a deity widely worshiped by the Japanese because of its association with rice cultivation and prosperity. Like all Inari shrines, it has a main sanctuary building painted deep red, long rows of torii, and numerous stone statues of Inari's messenger, the fox.

The Shinto religion centers on the worship of eight million *kami*—either legendary deities, such as Inari, or the spirits of natural phenomena, including caves, mountains, waterfalls, even individual trees or rocks. At Fushimi-Inari and other shrines, believers worship these deities through offerings, prayers, and festivals.

St. John's Convent in Müstair, Switzerland, is famous for frescoes inside depicting Bible scenes.

Cut from solid rock, one of the Lalībela churches in Ethiopia looks as if it were built with blocks.

When the emperor Constantine made Christianity the state religion of the Roman Empire in 313, he created the need for a new architecture. Greek and Roman temples had sheltered only the statues of gods; Christians needed churches large enough for the faithful to gather within as a priest celebrated Mass.

The earliest churches took two basic forms. Some were rectangular, modeled after the basilica, already an important architectural feature of the Roman forum. Others were circular or octagonal.

In 330 Constantine moved the imperial capital from Rome to Byzantium, which he renamed Constantinople. By 365 the Roman Empire had split in two, and the practice of Christianity, along with church architecture, took two distinct paths. The Eastern Orthodox Church, with its preference for mysticism, adhered to the circle—a symbol of perfection. To emphasize the circle, architects developed the dome; in Russia, on churches like St. Basil's Cathedral in Moscow, it took an onion shape that would shed snow better than the saucer-shaped Byzantine dome.

The Eastern churches retained their centralized, domed form for 14 centuries. But in the West the increasing size of Roman Catholic congregations stimulated an architectural inventiveness that resulted in variations on the basilican theme. One change was the Carolingian style, named after the emperor Charlemagne and exemplified in the multiple chapels and fortress-like design of the eighth-century Benedictine Convent of St. John in Müstair, Switzerland.

In Ethiopia, cut off from the rest of the Christian world by Muslim conquests, a king named Lalībela sought to create a new Jerusalem in the early 1200s—and in so doing created a wholly different church architecture. In the Welo Province he had 11 churches hewn from volcanic rock—masterpieces of architectural ingenuity carved as monoliths from the top down, then hollowed out and embellished.

Ivan the Terrible built ten-domed St. Basil's Cathedral in Moscow during the 16th century.

The Urnes Stave Church,
Norway

Where a North Sea fjord reaches deep into Norway's west coast sits the hamlet of Urnes. Here on a nobleman's estate in about 1150, master craftsmen built a tall wooden place of worship, called a stave church for the vertical posts that form its framework.

Between the 11th and 14th centuries, more than a thousand stave churches sprang up in isolated sections of Scandinavia. For centuries historians have been reluctant to credit the natives of the "heathen north" with the sophisti-

cated designs of these churches. Yet they remain without parallel in architecture, eluding classification.

Tall wooden posts, or staves, rise as high as 35 feet, joining the churches' floor and roof beams to form several box-shaped skeletons. Multiple roofs—steeply pitched and shingled—rest on top of these self-supporting units. Like the glass panels of modern skyscrapers, wall planks fill the sides, carrying little weight beyond their own. Inside, benches rim a 300-square-foot area.

Who designed these engineer-

ing oddities? Perhaps they simply grew out of northern Europe's long tradition of building in timber, from pagan temples to Viking ships. Dark and narrow, the interiors of stave churches resemble inverted ships' hulls. Or possibly the idea for stave construction came from Anglo-Saxon England.

In any case, the Urnes craftsmen imitated many of the design elements of Norman stone basilicas in their stave church. The 16 inside columns that rise to connect floor and roof resemble the rows of columns in Norman basilicas. Into

Urnes's wooden stave church has overlooked the Lusterfjord through time, termites, and the Reformation.

On the carved capital of a column, a figure displays a processional cross and a pastoral staff.

the wooden columns the craftsmen carved bases and capitals and decorated the rounded arches between the columns with fluting.

The craftsmen also incorporated carvings from an earlier structure built on the site. Swirling animals cut in high relief enliven the north wall and western gable. Bordering the keyhole-shaped door, broad and narrow bands of wood interlace to form a serpent battling a four-legged animal.

After the Reformation, Protestants tore down many of the stave churches, preferring to build their own airy structures. The church at Urnes is one of the oldest of Norway's 30 surviving staves. Some display carvings of St. Andrew's crosses mingling with dragons, as Christian and pagan beliefs must have mingled in the minds of the congregations.

Through centuries of long winters and short summers, these pagodas of the north stood tall and silent, architectural eulogies to a distant past. Stave churches remain a unique form of architecture, wooden arrows of faith pointing to the sky.

A four-legged beast struggles against a world of serpents on Urnes's carved entryway.

Flanked by allegorical and biblical characters, Eve hands Adam an apple plucked from the tree of knowledge in a scene from the painted ceiling in St. Michael's Church.

St. Michael's Church at Hildesheim,
West Germany

In March 1945 an 18-minute air raid by Allied bombers all but destroyed the German industrial city of Hildesheim. Fire gutted 944-year-old St. Michael's Church, one of the earliest and finest examples of Romanesque design. Fortunately, its ceiling's brilliantly colored allegorical painting escaped damage. In 1943 the "Tree of Jesse" had been dismantled carefully—it is made of 1,300 oak boards roughly three feet long and seven inches wide—by a prescient Hildesheim art lover, who hid the pieces during the war.

It took 13th-century monks about four years to paint these biblical scenes, which depict human salvation from the fall of Adam and Eve to Christ's redemption. To produce the rich hues, the monks used cinnabar for red and lapis lazuli for deep blue. Over the centuries other artists added several layers of new paint. These were removed as experts worked on the panels for five years, restoring each one under magnifying glasses. Long considered the most significant medieval painted ceiling, the "Tree of Jesse" was put back in place in 1960, the last step in St. Michael's restoration.

The church itself is no less important than the ceiling. Several features—three aisles, semicircular apses at each end of the church, and twin transepts bisecting the front and back of the nave—influenced later Romanesque design.

Bishop Bernward commissioned St. Michael's around 1001, while the German Ottonian kings were busy expanding the Holy Roman Empire. The building and adorning of churches glorified imperial power and won the loyalty of the peasants. Although Bernward may have had some help from an architect, the unusually symmetrical, six-towered design is believed his. The bishop's biographer described him as "eminent in scholarship, experienced in painting, excellent in the art and science of casting bronze, as well as in all kinds of architectural enterprises."

It was human vision that built St. Michael's . . . and saved its precious ceiling almost a millennium later.

125

The Basilica and Hill at Vézelay, *France*

Bathed in golden light, a procession of columns and striped arches moves so rhythmically down the basilica's nave it has been called the "dance of Vézelay." Balance, clarity, and serenity also suffuse this treasury of Romanesque art and architecture that rises on a hill over the Burgundian countryside.

A place of worship since the ninth century, the hill at Vézelay grew famous when news spread that relics of Mary Magdalene, the repentant sinner, rested in an abbey there. An influx of pilgrims called for a large church. By 1140 the 200-foot-long nave was built and the Basilica of St. Mary Magdalene consecrated; 60 monks lived in its monastery. So important a mecca did Vézelay become that, in 1146, St. Bernard convoked the Second Crusade on its hillside. And, 44 years later, the armies of England's King Richard the Lion-Hearted and France's Philippe-Auguste met here before setting out for Palestine on the Third Crusade.

But then Vézelay fell on hard times. Authenticity of the relics was cast into doubt, and pilgrims stopped coming. Eventually the monks abandoned the abbey; during the 16th-century Wars of Religion, the Huguenots used the basilica as a military barracks and barn. It was not until the mid-1800s that a young restorer named Viollet-le-Duc returned the basilica to its original splendor.

With rounded arches, heavy pillars, and other motifs borrowed from ancient Rome, Vézelay's Romanesque style expresses the fervent spirituality of the early Middle Ages. Its order and harmony bespeak divine reason; its massive vaulted ceiling induces the worshiper inward, away from the sensual world; its colored masonry creates a dusky, mystical atmosphere; its sculptured decorations use stories about God, ordinary people, saints, and monsters to inspire and cajole, awe and terrify. With secular as well as sacred portrayals, Vézelay's sculptures—crowning achievements of the Romanesque —embody both the humanism and holiness of the age.

At summer solstice, light streams through Vézelay's upper windows, creating a row of sun prints down the aisle.

Durham Cathedral,
United Kingdom

"Half church of God, half castle 'gainst the Scot," wrote Sir Walter Scott of Durham Cathedral and Castle, massive redoubts on a bluff over the River Wear. Though successive bishops altered the castle, leaving little that is original, the cathedral still exudes the strength, audacity, and faith of its Norman builders.

In 995 monks from the holy island of Lindisfarne, fearing Viking raiders, buried the remains of St. Cuthbert on this river bend in northern England for safekeeping. Almost a century later William the Conqueror appointed a bishop to organize a Benedictine monastery and military center here as a frontier bulwark. The bishop's successor, William of St. Calais, admired the abbey-churches of Normandy and came home inspired to build Durham's immense cathedral.

It is England's finest Romanesque creation. Designed as a whole and constructed between 1093 and 1133, the church typifies the Norman Romanesque yet displays daring innovations. The unknown architect experimented with vaulting that would render Romanesque methods obsolete and presage the Gothic style.

A desire for more space and light in the nave—thus higher walls—led him to eschew heavy vault constructions in favor of a ribbed skeleton that could hold a much lighter shell of stone. To meet the need for a support where ribs converged on the upper walls, he designed a half arch, or flying buttress, which he hid under the aisle roofs. This buttress and the pointed arch, a feature born of the rib vault, would become standard elements of Gothic churches.

For all its departures, Durham looks unmistakably Romanesque: Its walls, piers, and columns are massive, more so than the building's structure demands. Deep incisions in four bold patterns focus attention on the columns, away from the engineering feats above. Thought to have once been lavishly decorated, its columns painted, the cathedral emits a mood of majestic solemnity that overwhelms today's visitor.

Durham's rib-vaulted nave, held by alternating piers and columns, allows a third level of windows.

The Gothic:
An Age's Spirit Soars in Stone

Deep in the heart of France —in a church on royal land called the Île-de-France— there rose in 1140 or so an architectural style that would sweep the Christian world. Over the next two centuries the French alone built some 80 cathedrals in the style a Renaissance historian later scorned as "gothic."

A new aesthetic purpose, born of religious idealism, combined with new building techniques to create the style. Whereas the massive, groin-vaulted ceilings of Romanesque churches forced the believer down into his conscience, the new spirit lifted him upward to another world. Now one strove to throw off worldly concerns and mystically unite with God.

The rib vault and pointed arch suited this new concept perfectly; they enabled architects to build much taller, airier churches that reached toward heaven. At the High Gothic cathedral of Amiens, below, the nave soars to a breath-taking 139 feet, three times its width. Outside, flying buttresses bolster the towering structure. They and a 180-foot-high spire reinforce the skyward thrust.

Sculpture also expressed this new idealism. Unlike the crowded jumble of forms that sprang from Romanesque churches to spread doomsday admonishments, Gothic sculptures sought to educate clearly and calmly about the divine, to serve as Bible for the illiterate. Early figures, like the one below at Chartres Cathedral, are stylized and severe. Later sculptures, including those opposite from the 15th century on Portugal's Batalha Monastery, display the realism of the High Gothic.

Above: An Old Testament prophet from about 1145 ennobles Chartres Cathedral's west portal. Left: Amiens Cathedral, France's largest, forms a cross in the Gothic tradition. Opposite: The portico of Portugal's Batalha Monastery drew inspiration from the High French Gothic style.

Chartres Cathedral, *France*

"The architect . . . undertook, once for all, to show how a great cathedral should be lighted," wrote Henry Adams in his masterful study of Chartres. Stained-glass windows, 176 of them covering 22,000 square feet, turn the cathedral's interior into an ethereal cosmos.

In these 12th- and 13th-century windows, the most complete set of originals in any Gothic cathedral, biblical events unfold as though from an illuminated book. As the sun moves across the sky, light brings each wall to life in turn, transforming the deep reds, blues, and violets from muted to blazing. Overall a brilliantly intense blue —the legendary Chartres blue— predominates. Flying buttresses made the jewel-like glass mosaics possible by relieving the walls of their weight-bearing function.

The windows offer proof that medieval cathedral-building was a community effort. Pictorial signatures of donors include everyone from craftsmen to the royal family.

Finished in 1220, Chartres Cathedral honors the Virgin Mary. A tunic given by Charlemagne's grandson and said to be hers lies in the treasury. At least five earlier churches had burned on this site, not far from Paris; the final one was all but destroyed in 1194. Miraculously the tunic survived, a sign to townspeople that Mary desired a more majestic shrine. With donations from all over France, they built her one in just 26 years.

To make the stained glass, glaziers added color to molten glass, then blew it to the desired thinness and baked it. When the glass had cooled, they cut it into shapes specified by an artist, who etched in details, added enamel to them, and baked it on. Then the artists assembled the pieces in panels and bound them with lead. Finally came the unenviable task of wiring the panels to a window grid without breaking them.

So sublime is the result that, in the words of Henry Adams, "one becomes, sometimes, a little incoherent in talking about it."

Pages 130-31: The Virgin's death in stained glass blazons the south aisle of Chartres Cathedral.

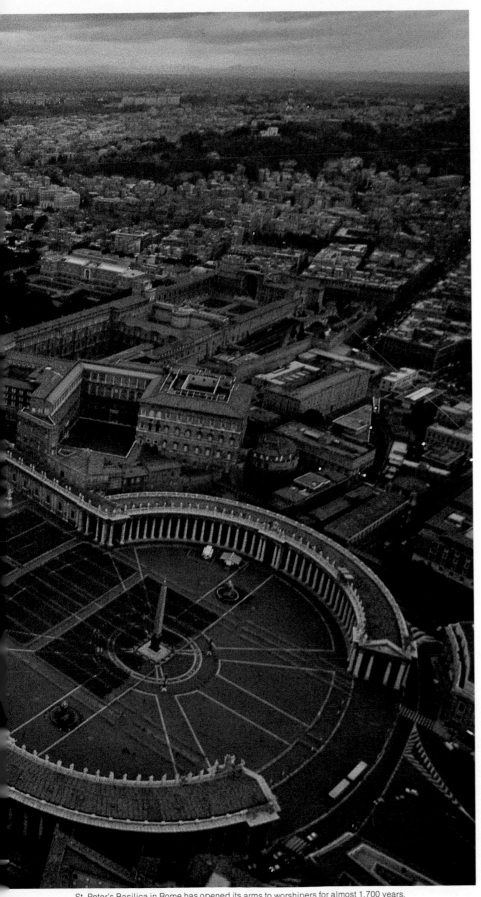

St. Peter's Basilica in Rome has opened its arms to worshipers for almost 1,700 years.

The smallest country in the world is a city: Vatican City. Even though it is small—a scant sixth-of-a-square-mile enclave near the Tiber River in Rome—it looms large in realms of the spirit.

Seat of the papacy, the city is the spiritual, political, and administrative center of the world's largest Christian denomination, the nearly 700-million-member Roman Catholic Church. As an independent state since the 1929 Lateran Treaty with Italy, the Vatican issues its own coins and stamps and maintains a standing army of a hundred or so Swiss Guards. It has its own bank, an influential daily newspaper, a diplomatic corps of a hundred papal legates—even a seldom-occupied jail. A high stone wall built during the Renaissance surrounds most of the city, enclosing parks and gardens, museums and art galleries, libraries and archives, chapels, offices, and living quarters for its thousand permanent residents.

St. Peter's Basilica—its enormous dome designed by Michelangelo and sometimes referred to as Rome's eighth hill—dominates Vatican City and serves as a beacon of faith to millions of pilgrims each year. The church, nearly 700 feet long and 450 feet wide at the transept, stands as a triumph of Renaissance art and architecture, the work of a succession of architects that includes Bramante, Sangallo, and Michelangelo. The world's largest Christian church, it can hold as many as 50,000 worshipers.

Consecrated in 1626 after more than a century of planning and building, St. Peter's occupies the site of a basilica erected early in the fourth century by Rome's first Christian emperor, Constantine. Under the high altar lies the tomb believed to be that of the Apostle Peter, crucified in A.D. 67 during the reign of Emperor Nero. Archaeological excavations beneath the church in the 1940s uncovered the tomb, lending credence to the idea that St. Peter's rises from the bones of its namesake.

In front of the basilica spreads the colonnaded expanse of St.

Peter's Square, designed by Bernini in the mid-17th century. The piazza, partly encircled by 284 columns, holds more than a quarter million people who gather here on holy days for papal blessings.

Beyond the church, the museums of Vatican City house priceless sculptures, including the "Apollo Belvedere" and the "Laocoön" group, the statue of a Trojan priest and his sons set upon by snakes for angering the gods. The museums also display Egyptian and Etruscan masterpieces, pagan and early Christian inscriptions, and paintings by modern artists such as Renoir, Seurat, Matisse, Picasso, and van Gogh.

Rooms, chapels, and corridors glow with the works of Fra Angelico, Pinturicchio, Raphael, Titian, and Leonardo da Vinci. Some of Michelangelo's greatest paintings grace the ceiling and altar wall of the Sistine Chapel, where cardinals from around the world meet occasionally to elect a new pope.

"The place is wrong and no painter I," protested Michelangelo when Pope Julius II demanded that he decorate the chapel ceiling in 1508. But the pope insisted and Michelangelo, more accustomed to chiseling stone than working with paint and wet plaster, set about his task. He raised a scaffold 80 feet above the chapel floor and worked four years, head bent back, face and beard splattered with paint. A quarter century later, at the age of 61, Michelangelo at the behest of Pope Paul III once again returned to the chapel to paint "The Last Judgment." One prelate, who complained about the nudity displayed, found his face adorning Minos, judge of the underworld, complete with donkey ears and a serpent tail. An amused pope shrugged off the cleric's protest, saying he had no authority in hell.

Over the years, grime, soot, and shellac have darkened and obscured Michelangelo's Sistine masterpieces. Now restorers are working to clean and preserve the frescoes, once again revealing the dazzling array of colors used by the master painter, sculptor, and architect nearly five centuries ago.

Above: Laocoön and his sons battle serpents through eternity. Opposite: Bernini's bronze baldachin has canopied St. Peter's high altar since 1633. Here deacons become priests.

THE SILENT CATACLYSM

The passenger pigeon perches in its museum case, wings lifted slightly as if ready for flight. But no one will ever see the bird aloft again. In 1813 John James Audubon observed flocks so large that the "light of noon-day was obscured as by an eclipse," when for three days the pigeons darkened the skies near Louisville, Kentucky. He calculated that more than a billion birds passed overhead in just three hours. The last passenger pigeon, a bird named Martha, died on September 1, 1914, in the Cincinnati Zoo. Abundant and successful as a species, the pigeon was relentlessly destroyed because it so pleased the palate.

I like going to museums, those dead zoos, those reliquaries of dead beauty, because it is my only contact with the many animals that have recently passed. And I am always indignant and saddened by their loss. Having spent all my professional life in the wilderness stubbornly fighting for the survival of endangered species, I know that there is no logic in such extermination, only greed and thoughtlessness.

The list of vanished animals is long and tragic. Steller's sea cow, a 14,000-pound relative of the manatee, grazed peacefully on kelp in the Bering Sea until fur hunters noted its meat was like veal. It disappeared in 1768, only 27 years after its discovery. In 1638 Englishman Sir Thomas Herbert wrote that dodos, 50-pound flightless birds from Mauritius, are "better to the eye than stomack." Nevertheless, Dutch settlers clubbed the last dodo to death around 1680, and today it symbolizes both extinction and stupidity—though this is more a reflection on ourselves than on the bird. Include the Labrador duck, great auk, quagga, bluebuck, names that are almost gone from memory, yet these species were with us during the 19th century. And no matter how vibrant many others are now, they too will go out of our lives.

At least 150 vertebrate species have vanished since 1600, a small percent, it would seem, of the 50,000 or so species of birds, mammals, fish, and other vertebrates cataloged so far. Many of the vanished species lived on islands where their small populations were vulnerable to habitat destruction by introduced herbivores, such as goats and rabbits, and to predation by rats and cats. Now extinction rates are accelerating, everywhere.

Noah took "every thing that creepeth upon the earth" into his ark. But he forgot the plants. Of the 250,000 or so species known, thousands have vanished in recent centuries. On St. Helena, Napoleon's island of exile, fewer than half of more than 100 endemic plant species survive. As a rough measure, when a habitat is reduced by 90 percent of its original size, 50 percent of the plant species there will become extinct. The unique forests of Brazil's Atlantic coast now occupy 2 percent or less of their former range.

To most people the loss of a species means the loss of a spectacular animal—the Indian rhinoceros or the orangutan or the whooping crane. But most animals are small, more than 99 percent of them invertebrates such as insects. Some 40,000 beetle species alone have been described. As British biologist J.B.S. Haldane noted, the Creator appears to have had an inordinate fondness for beetles.

Actually more is known about the number of stars in the heavens than about the number of species on earth. Although 1.7 million species have been described, no one has any idea, even to the nearest order of magnitude, how many there are. Guesses range from 4 to 30 million. There may be many more than 30 million if the tiny forms in the soil—mites, roundworms, protozoa—were all known, and if the continental shelves of the sea, perhaps the richest habitat of all, were properly explored. But there is not enough time, enough money, enough trained staff to make the necessary inventory, for life's diversity is rapidly and quietly slipping away. Estimates about the rate at which species are disappearing vary from 10,000 to 40,000 per year.

We need to concern ourselves more with conserving ecosystems than with saving individual large vertebrates. A natural habitat will collapse if you take away the nutrient-producing plants and the decomposers—soil bacteria and fungi—that break down those nutrients. In addition to food and fuelwood, ecosystems provide humanity with other essential services, all free, among them cleaning water and air, manufacturing soil, and controlling floods. Large animals are generally less important to an ecosystem than obscure species. The loss of the California condor from the wild in 1987 is an ethical and aesthetic tragedy, not an ecological one. Often, however, by protecting a large species such as a jaguar in its natural habitat, giving it the great space it needs, we automatically assure the survival of thousands of other species in that same habitat.

The ever increasing destruction of resources has one major cause: the human population, which has grown to nearly five billion in the past decade and will almost double worldwide within 40 years.

One destructive force is the small-scale farmer and herdsman. Being poor, they have no option but to chop down the last trees and convert soil to desert in an attempt to raise a crop. The recent drought in Ethiopia and the Sahel occurred in areas first made barren by deforestation, overgrazing by livestock, and other misuse of the land.

Just as destructive are the industrialized nations, overdeveloped and wasteful, which deplete the resources of the Third World with their huge appetite for raw materials. It will take a readjustment of values and priorities to change current attitudes.

Why be so concerned about extinction? In the history of life on earth, extinction is the norm, survival the exception. A species survives, on an average, less than 10 million years. There have been five mass extinctions in the earth's history. The most widely known was at the end of the Cretaceous 65 million years ago, when the last dinosaurs vanished, as well as 60 to 80 percent of all marine species.

Mass extinctions proceeded slowly—the one at the end of the Cretaceous took about 8 million years—and most lineages had at least some survivors, which then showed high speciation rates. New species originate mainly when a small segment of an ancestral population becomes isolated and the animals change form and behavior through natural selection until the population is well established. This process may be so rapid that no intermediate forms—missing links—are found in the fossil record. Then, having settled in, the new species may remain unchanged for millions of years.

We are now in yet another extinction spasm but one very different from those of the past: Humankind is the sole agent of this silent cataclysm. The earth may well lose as many species now as during the mass extinction 65 million years ago. But there are differences. More lineages will be destroyed, as will a greater proportion of plants. We are not only causing extinction but also reducing future speciation rates. Evolution will lack a reservoir of species, except perhaps cockroaches, rats, garden weeds, and other organisms adapted to living with humans. Too much will be gone, not just shifted or modified, but gone forever. It will not be the dead who accuse, but the emptiness.

In 1987 Vermont placed the tiger beetle on its threatened species list. Do we really need the tiger beetle? Often asked, such questions imply that every species ought to have value, preferably economic value. There are those who assert that we should develop an altruism toward other organisms that celebrates them for their uniqueness and diversity. I agree. A tiger is more precious for its beauty than the Taj Mahal, for once destroyed, the tiger can never be re-created by human hands. The real battle, I think, is less to save the Komodo dragon or a rare orchid than it is to shape a new attitude.

In conservation, however, both idealism and realism must be served. Whether one lists nonconsumptive uses of wildlife, such as whale-watching, or the importance of fish as a food source, the actual and potential economic value of wild species is enormous: China and India make birth control pills from wild yams. The euphorbias, desert plants resembling cacti, store food not as carbohydrates but as hydrocarbons, the basis of petroleum. A wild perennial maize has been discovered in Mexico, giving hope that its genetic material will turn domestic maize from an annual to a perennial crop.

Each species may prove valuable to medicine, industry, or agriculture. If for no other reason than to help us survive, we must protect the unique genetic resources of each species. Many countries today depend mainly on just one crop, and 90 percent of the world's diet is based on but 20 species. If a problem arises, genetic engineers cannot create new genes, only rearrange existing ones, and for that they will need wild stock.

The basic issue, then, is to conserve biological diversity. At stake is not what will happen to us but what will happen after us. As Harvard biologist Edward O. Wilson wrote: "The one process ongoing in the 1980s that will take millions of years to correct is the loss of genetic and species diversity by the destruction of natural habitats. This is the folly our descendants are least likely to forgive us."

Yes, we need the tiger beetle.

What can be done to protect ecosystems, to preserve biological diversity? The needs of peoples must always be considered: Conservation is more a social than a scientific problem. The demand for fuelwood from native plants can be reduced by using solar cookers and planting fast-growing trees, such as the Philippine *ipilipil*. In Zimbabwe, South Africa, and elsewhere, ranching a combination of wild and domestic animals on the same land has proved more profitable than ranching either on its own.

Reserves established to protect scenic wonders, dramatic species, and various habitats cover about 2 percent of the earth's surface. Unfortunately most reserves consist of mere fragments of nature surrounded by agriculture and settlements. When a population is small, as it often is on islands or in isolated habitats, it becomes vulnerable to extinction from natural disasters, disease, and inbreeding. Species cannot be saved two by two. When related individuals mate, deleterious gene combinations are likely to affect reproduction—lowered fertility, smaller litters, poor viability of the young. Inbreeding also reduces the genetic variability of a species, lessening the animals' ability to adapt to environmental changes. And changes are inevitable. Over the next century the earth will probably become warmer and rainfall patterns may shift. Many reserves will be altered, and many species will have to adapt, disperse, or die. The conservation strategy for any species or ecosystem cannot depend only on a scattered network of reserves.

As a final resort a few species can be salvaged in captivity with the hope that some day they may again find a wild haven. Extinct in the wild, European bison, China's Père David deer, and Mongolian wild horses owe their existence to a few individuals taken into captivity. In 1986 the last known population of black-footed ferrets, North America's rarest mammal, crashed when ferrets died of distemper, and prairie dogs—the ferrets' main food—were decimated by plague. The ferrets' future now rests on 18 captive animals.

For some species money holds the key to survival. There are 1,200 Siberian tigers in captivity. To maintain an animal can cost up to five dollars a day, an annual bill of more than two million dollars for just this one tiger race. Can Siberian tigers ever be returned to the wild, or do we simply keep them as relics of a better past? How do we allocate space and money? To save the California condor, should 25 million dollars be spent over the next 30 years, or should the money go toward the protection of koalas or endangered mangrove forests? Zoos are not a solution, merely a palliative to buy more time for a few species.

Preservation in nature is the only sensible way to protect species and the only way to conserve ecosystems.

Conservation has as much to do with feelings and emotions as with arguments about human poverty, greed, and survival. I know that the priority is to protect ecosystems, the last square miles of American tall-grass prairie, the Serengeti savanna with its vast herds, not just a few spectacular animals and colorful plants. Yet my heart speaks to the snow leopard and mountain gorilla. In the future will only a few bones and skins in museums immortalize the giant panda? Today's concern for the panda is something new in human consciousness: For the first time there is a worldwide realization that a species matters.

We are at a turning point in our existence. We do not have two earths, one to squander and one to treasure. It is urgent that our mind comprehend what our hands are doing. When Peru's Inca ruler Atahuallpa was strangled by Francisco Pizarro's men, his last words were: "Why do you seek gold when our land has such lovely flowers?"

Will his cry of despair become our epitaph?

Coto Doñana
National Park, *Spain*

On the Atlantic coast of southern Spain, where the Guadalquivir River forms a marshy delta behind a 20-mile-wide band of shifting sand, lies one of Europe's greatest wildlife kingdoms. Gulls wheel through shimmering heat over the marsh, where flamingos glide on lagoons and where rails wade in seasonal pools. Wild boars root in the reeds, and azure-winged magpies dart through groves of pines.

Alongside the marsh sprawls the Coto Doñana, once the estate of Doña Ana and her husband, a duke whose family held the land nearly 500 years. This scrubby wilderness and former hunting reserve of kings and noblemen remained virtually unspoiled until the 1950s, when developers moved in. To thwart plans to drain the marsh for farmland, the World Wildlife Fund—with help from the Spanish government—bought chunks of the Coto and the wetlands for a nature reserve that became Coto Doñana National Park. The 310-square-mile park serves as home or way station for half the bird species breeding in Europe.

Herons and egrets nest in cork oaks near a 16th-century hunting lodge, formerly the home of Doña Ana. Nearby, a Spanish lynx pads through the scrub, listening to the hum of mosquitoes, the knocking chant of the red-necked nightjar, and the *hoop-hoop-hoop* of the hoopoe. Two-inch-long tufts spiking from the lynx's ears help focus sounds so the small, spotted cat can pinpoint the sources. Named for Lynceus, a mythological figure who could see through opaque objects, the lynx can discern a mouse 250 feet away. Spanish lynx once prowled the Iberian Peninsula. Only 400 or so survive in Spain and Portugal. About 50 live in the Coto Doñana area, hunting birds, rabbits, and fawns.

The park is also the last wild redoubt of another endangered predator, the Spanish imperial eagle. About a dozen pairs of the big brown birds nest in the cork oaks and pines of Coto Doñana, bestowing their regal presence on this former domain of kings.

Spent from battling for a doe, a red deer bellows among the rushes. Deer and other wildlife in Coto Doñana National Park support endangered predators.

Białowieża National Park,
Poland

When the acorns drop in Białowieża National Park, the bison begin to congregate. One by one the great beasts come plodding through the trees to root for food. They swing their ponderous heads back and forth, plowing the earth with an unhurried majesty that befits their long residence in the primeval forest.

The bison were there thousands of years ago when Ice Age people painted and carved images of the huge animals in Europe's caves. But with the spread of civilization, hunters reduced the herds and the ancient forest that once stretched from the shores of Brittany all the way to Moscow.

By the early 1900s the sheltering woods had been reduced to a mere scrap of land in the Białowieża region that lies between Poland and the Soviet Union. Only 700 or so bison still lived on the frontier as World War I began. All were gone when the war ended, shot for meat by soldiers and poachers.

Though vanished from the wild, a few bison remained in zoos—the one thing that saved them. In 1929 the Polish government brought two cows from Sweden and a bull from Germany to reestablish the wild stock at Białowieża.

War threatened again in 1939, but this time Hermann Göring, Hitler's second-in-command and a keen hunter, ordered special protection for the bison.

With that unlikely patronage, more than 40 animals survived, ancestors of the 250 bison that thrive today in and around the park. They wander through the oaks and spruces, reminders of a time when neither guns nor human voices disturbed the silent forest.

A European bison pauses in 20-square-mile Białowieża National Park.

Srebarna Nature Reserve,
Bulgaria

As the Danube River nears the sea, it is nothing like the famous blue that Johann Strauss ascribed to it. Between Romania and Bulgaria it flows milky brown, carrying a heavy load of silt that approaches a hundred million tons each year. It sweeps back and forth, carving new channels and leaving behind lakes and marshes—reminders of the river's wandering history.

One gift of the river, Srebarna Lake, covers a mere 2.3 square miles, but the water and marsh provide ample food and shelter for 179 bird species, including the endangered Dalmatian pelican.

Some 70 pairs of the graceful pelicans find refuge at Srebarna Nature Reserve, a nesting ground bristling with 13-foot-tall reeds and rimmed by hills. Each pelican fishes alone, bobbing on the water in search of prey. One spots a fish, plunges its head beneath the water to grab its dinner, and emerges with a splash. It swallows and paddles off, looking for more fish.

Such scenes were frequent throughout Europe just a century ago, when Dalmatian pelicans numbered in the hundreds of thousands and ranged from Eastern Europe to China. Their numbers declined as farmers drained the marshes for cropland and fishermen killed the birds, seeing them as a threat to their livelihood. Some 3,500 of the pelicans exist in the world today.

Those nesting at Srebarna benefit from regulations that limit human activity to research. Laws also protect the cormorants, glossy ibis, white-tailed eagles, and other rare birds that find shelter in one of Europe's most significant wetlands.

White spoonbills and pygmy cormorants, two of Europe's rare species, roost at Srebarna Nature Reserve.

143

Everglades National Park, U.S.A.

The sharp thwack of a scaly tail marks the end of the wet season in Everglades National Park; an alligator thrashes the drying marsh mud to break through to water trapped below. Later, as the winter sun turns scattered cypress trees to white skeletons, a bald eagle swoops down to catch a snake in the gator hole; black-and-white wood storks snatch catfish, and a Florida panther laps the water. As the years pass, a willow thicket may circle the pond and lilies blossom on its surface.

The American alligator, slaughtered by the millions for its hide, was threatened in the late 1960s. Now protected, its numbers are rising; its gator holes help some of the 35 other vulnerable species of Everglades animals survive when the rains stop between October and May. More than 300 types of birds find shelter in the park, including ibis, herons, and snowy egrets, species hunted almost to extinction for their fashionable plumes.

The 2,200-square-mile park occupies the tip of the Everglades, called River of Grass by Native Americans. The lifeblood of the region is rainfall and a vast sheet of water that spills from the banks of central Florida's Lake Okeechobee. For thousands of summers the lake created a river only inches deep but up to fifty miles wide. Its almost imperceptible flow took it a hundred miles south through the prickly, ten-foot-tall saw grass and around islands of mahogany trees and air plants before emptying into Florida Bay.

But as more people moved to south Florida at the turn of the century, engineers drained half the Everglades, controlling the water with 1,400 miles of canals, dikes, and levees. Supplying water to farms and cities took priority in the dry season. Droughts became so severe in the 1960s and '70s that the very ground blazed in the park. And when engineers dumped excess water in the rainy season, they flooded alligators from their nests. Today planners are using computers to reestablish a more natural flow of water into the domain of the gator and the eagle.

An Everglades alligator crunches a red-bellied turtle for lunch.

Above: An anhinga preens with its stiletto bill, also used to skewer prey.
Pages 144-45: Mangroves guard Florida Bay, haven for endangered crocodiles.

Tangled mangrove islands provide indispensable nurseries for wildlife, including the fish and shrimp harvested by commercial fishermen in south Florida.

Wood Buffalo
National Park, *Canada*

The shrill cry of the whooping crane can be heard three miles away, a voice from North America's wild past. It rings across the cattail marshes and sedge meadows of the vast wilderness that hid the big white birds for decades: 17,300-square-mile Wood Buffalo National Park, a refuge for whoopers and other vulnerable creatures—and for bison. One of the world's largest national parks, Wood Buffalo straddles the border between Alberta and the North-west Territories. It is a land of cold rivers, evergreen forests, and plains strewn with shallow lakes and meandering streams.

More than 50 million bison roamed this land and the central plains of North America until settlers and buffalo hunters annihilated the great herds. Following an unofficial United States policy of subduing the Native Americans by eliminating their main food source, hunters killed more than two and a half million bison yearly.

By the turn of the 20th century, fewer than a thousand plains bison remained. And only a small herd of darker wood bison survived, tucked away in the remote area that would become Wood Buffalo National Park. To preserve the plains bison, Canada bought 709 of the animals from a rancher and installed them in southern Alberta, where they multiplied and threatened to overgraze the range.

In 1925 authorities began shipping these plains bison north on trains and barges, releasing 6,673 into the recently established park. The wood bison interbred with the newcomers and were then considered extinct as a subspecies until 1957, when a purebred herd was

Some of the 4,200 hybrid descendants of wood bison and plains bison swim across Prairie River. Many drown when storms rise suddenly.

Spruce oases dot Wood Buffalo's salt plains, once a source of salt for natives and traders.

discovered in a corner of the park.

Three years earlier, a pilot investigating a forest fire in the park had spotted the only nesting site of the whooping crane, among the spruces and tamaracks in a bog. The birds, which stand almost five feet tall, usually hatch two chicks, but only one lives. Today scientists are stealing spare whooper eggs and flying them to Grays Lake, Idaho. There sandhill cranes act as foster parents and offer hope that the whoopers, whose numbers have slowly climbed to more than a hundred, will survive.

149

Torres del Paine
National Park, *Chile*

A haunting whinny resonates like a witch's cackle among the granite towers of the southern Andes: A guanaco alerts his family group to a puma skulking in the scrubby grass bordering the mountains. Only pumas can harm them here, for the guanacos, which come from a line of camel-like creatures hunted by man since the Stone Age, have found asylum in Torres del Paine National Park. In this remote corner of southern Chile, small herds of guanacos browse on dwarfed beech trees or graze in lush meadows. Condors circle slowly overhead. Black-necked swans also find a haven here, gliding across clear lakes in the 935-square-mile park.

The ancestors of the guanacos were jackrabbit-size animals that originated in North America 40 million years ago, then dispersed around the world and adapted to a variety of habitats. In Asia and North Africa their descendants developed their familiar humps. In South America guanacos, vicuñas, alpacas, and llamas evolved. Guanacos spread along the Andes and numbered more than 30 million. Their padded feet helped them negotiate the snowy slopes as well as the sands of coastal deserts. Decimated by overhunting, today's population stands at about 600,000.

Patagonian Indians, hurling lances or leather-thonged bolas, hunted the 250-pound guanacos for meat, clothing, and shelter. But the animals held their own until Europeans arrived with guns and horses. Even members of Charles Darwin's party lured the guanacos to slaughter. One man would lie on his back and wiggle his legs in the air. When the guanacos approached to investigate, the men would shoot.

Settlers later brought sheep and cattle, a threat to the guanacos' grazing lands. But if left alone in the wild, guanacos thrive. Preserves like Torres del Paine hold the key to their survival. Now protected in Chile, Argentina, and Peru, these aristocrats of the plains and mountains face an encouraging future.

Young male guanacos band together under the glacier-carved mountains of southern Patagonia.

Wolong Natural Reserve, *China*

In the twilight of a remote mountain forest, a soft wind sweeps down the ridge. It rustles the delicate leaves of a bamboo grove, breaking the evening stillness with a sound that brings the promise of spring to China and life itself to the giant panda.

The rare creature, which feeds almost exclusively on bamboo, once ranged throughout eastern China. But as the country's human population expanded, clearing bamboo from the land, the pandas began to disappear. Their decline continues today.

Today only a thousand survive in the wild, chiefly in the wet, rugged mountains of Sichuan Province, on the eastern edge of the Tibetan highlands. Perhaps half live in wilderness areas such as Wolong Natural Reserve, a haven for the animals the Chinese call *daxiongmao,* or large bear-cat.

The name indicates the difficulty of classifying an animal that has long bewildered scientists. Is it more closely related to bears or to raccoons? No one can say for certain. Originally carnivorous, the panda evolved into a vegetarian, with flat molars for crushing bamboo, and a sixth digit, or false thumb, for grasping bamboo stalks. Yet the panda retains the simple digestive system of its carnivorous ancestors and is ill-equipped to digest cellulose and other plant material. Pandas, which may reach 230 pounds in weight, compensate by devouring up to 40 pounds of bamboo a day.

With today's limited bamboo reserves, the pandas stay one step ahead of starvation. That threat came to world attention in the 1970s and '80s, when at least 138 pandas died during one of the dramatic bamboo die-offs that occur every hundred years or so.

To guard against such losses, China is planting other bamboo to supplement the species that will inevitably flower and die down in the future. And some pandas will be transferred to parts of the country where bamboo is plentiful—to ensure a future for the gentle animals that have come to symbolize all of earth's threatened wildlife.

Above: Bamboo, a prolific grass that includes a thousand species, provides a springtime delicacy for pandas. Opposite: A lone panda trudges through 800-square-mile Wolong Natural Reserve.

Rain Forests:
Life Vanishes
in Earth's Green Belt

Rain forests girdle the globe with a belt of green that is home to more than half the species on earth. With warmth and plentiful moisture, tropical life flourishes on a grand scale. Just 25 acres in Borneo support 700 tree species, equal to the number in all of North America. One river in Brazil's Amazon forest has more kinds of fish than all the rivers in the United States.

Thirty years ago rain forests covered 15 percent of the land; today they cover only 7 percent. Humans, using chain saws, axes, and fire to clear the land, are responsible. As the cover vanishes, so do countless species: Ten animal species die each time a plant species disappears.

In the Philippines, where clearing has reduced the rain forest by 70 percent, the Philippine eagle hovers close to extinction; fewer than 300 remain. Like other hunters, they need a large range to find the flying lemurs, palm civets, and monkeys that sustain them.

Logging also threatens orangutans, solitary primates of the rain forest. Perhaps as few as 5,000 survive today, living in remote areas of Borneo and Sumatra.

Thousands of butterfly species still find a haven in the rain forests of South America, which hold the world's greatest concentration of butterflies. But some, including members of the *Morpho* genus, are threatened by dwindling habitat.

The disappearance of the rain forest limits the birth of new species, raising the specter of a barren future for all who share the planet. "Death is one thing," wrote conservationist Michael Soulé. "An end to birth is something else."

A morpho butterfly, capable of flying 20 miles an hour, finds refuge in Brazil's Jaú National Park.

Above: An orangutan nests in Borneo's Tanjung Puting Reserve. Opposite: A Philippine eagle, formerly known as the monkey-eating eagle, feeds its young in Mount Apo National Park.

155

Mosses, ferns, and vines cloak a creek bed in New England National Park, where pockets of both temperate and subtropical rain forests flourish.

The East Coast Rain Forest Parks, *Australia*

Earth's driest continent seems an unlikely place for rain forests. Yet fragments of a once extensive forest lie scattered along Australia's eastern rim, where towering trees choke out the noonday sun, casting the mosses and ferns of the forest floor into dappled light.

Though at least half of this cover has been cleared for agriculture, about 785 square miles of temperate and subtropical rain forest survive in 16 protected areas of New South Wales. The plants and animals here reveal Australia's ancient links with equatorial regions as well as with Gondwana, the southern landmass that began to break apart some 140 million years ago, eventually forming Australia, Africa, South America, and Antarctica.

In Australia today the forest throbs with life, shielded from extremes of climate by a dense canopy. Thus protected, the leaf litter and humus of the forest floor have varied little through the millennia, and life here remains virtually unchanged. Many of the plants and reptiles of the rain forest arrived from the north, crossing the land bridge that once linked Australia and New Guinea.

Primitive insects called springtails, a source of food for other animals of the forest, are closely akin to the earliest fossil insects found in Scotland, half a world away. Fallen trees provide a habitat for fungus beetles, brightly colored creatures that feed on the luminescent fungi of the forest.

Snakes conceal themselves by day, emerging at night when the forest awakes. Then the warm air quivers with frog song. Some 25 species of frogs live here, including what may be Australia's most distinctive amphibian, the marsupial frog. Like kangaroos, these frogs protect their young by carrying them in pouches; but it is the father that has the pouch—and responsibility for rearing tadpoles.

Myriad other lives of these rich lands remain secret, unnamed and uncounted, for science is only just starting to catalog the diversity of Australia's rain forest.

A diamond python, one of the few reptiles endemic to Australia's rain forest, is common but rarely seen; its spots serve as camouflage.

Above: From the back of a trained elephant, visitors sight rhinos at Royal Chitwan. Opposite: The rhino munches 50 pounds of grass a day; birds eat insects off its back and warn of intruders.

Royal Chitwan National Park, *Nepal*

Like an armored tank, a two-ton Indian rhinoceros in Royal Chitwan National Park trudges through grass 20 feet tall, pausing often to sniff the air and the ground. Suddenly he snorts as he comes face-to-face with another rhino—a female. She raises her head and curls her lips, displaying her lower tusks. She honks. He stands his ground. She turns from the confrontation and trots away, effortlessly mowing a new path through the grass.

Such encounters might be a thing of the past were it not for Royal Chitwan, a 360-square-mile park in southern Nepal where rivers meander through a mosaic of grasslands and forests. Leopards and Bengal tigers roam the forested valleys of these outermost hills of the Himalayas. Langur monkeys swing from treetops. And here, about 400 endangered Indian, or greater one-horned, rhinos live under the watch of hundreds of military guards.

The rhino, a resident of earth for 40 million years, was not always as well protected as it is today. Since 1970, poaching and habitat destruction have reduced its numbers from 70,000 to 13,000 worldwide. Use of rhino horns for rituals and medicine has also played a part in the animals' decline. Even today the horns fetch a handsome price in Yemen, where daggers with rhino-horn handles are a status symbol for men. And in China, Japan, Burma, and Korea, the rhino horns are ground into powder for drugs to cure ailments ranging from fever and snakebites to nosebleeds.

Under protection at Royal Chitwan, one-horned rhinos are staging a comeback. By 1981 the rhino population had recovered enough to permit Nepal's monarch to fulfill a royal obligation—sacrificing a rhino once in his lifetime. Wearing a white robe, the king knelt in the abdominal cavity of the disemboweled beast and offered handfuls of blood to the Hindu gods. The royal ceremony, postponed during the years of the rhinos' decline, signifies new hope for a beleaguered species.

Keoladeo National Park,
India

Three Siberian cranes wheel and begin their descent, dazzling white and graceful as they drop from a blue November sky. They drift toward Keoladeo National Park, a patch of green almost lost in the immense brown of northern India's heavily populated plains.

The stately birds, which grow more than four feet tall, land on the marsh's edge. After resting, they probe for tubers and roots in the shallow water. They must replenish themselves after a 3,500-mile journey from their breeding grounds in western Siberia, one of the most desolate places on earth.

They find a haven at Keoladeo, though the park covers just 11 square miles. Only 1,700 of the birds exist in the world, and some fall to hunters' guns during the long journey south to China, Iran, and India, their major wintering grounds. Others starve as wetlands are converted to farms to feed Asia's exploding population.

At Keoladeo the cranes take their place among pintails and geese, teals and cormorants—an avian population that may swell to 200,000 between November and February during the winter migration. Egrets and spoonbills roost in the scraggly acacia trees, while openbill storks trudge in slow procession around the lake's fringes, plucking snails and mussels from the mud, extracting the meat with surgical precision.

The birds feed voraciously, but the marsh is a most generous provider. Even a small plot of this wetland—one square mile—provides the 8,000 to 12,000 pounds of food needed daily for a colony of 6,000 painted stork nestlings. People also come here to cut grass for their cattle, an illegal practice that began again when the sanctuary's protective wall fell into disrepair.

A maharaja created the wildlife area in the 1850s to attract waterfowl for hunting. But with shooting now banned at Keoladeo, what man built for killing serves as a strategic sanctuary, a place of tranquillity in a sea of humanity.

Openbill storks, one of more than 350 bird species that depend on the sanctuary at Keoladeo, nest in the trees during breeding season.

161

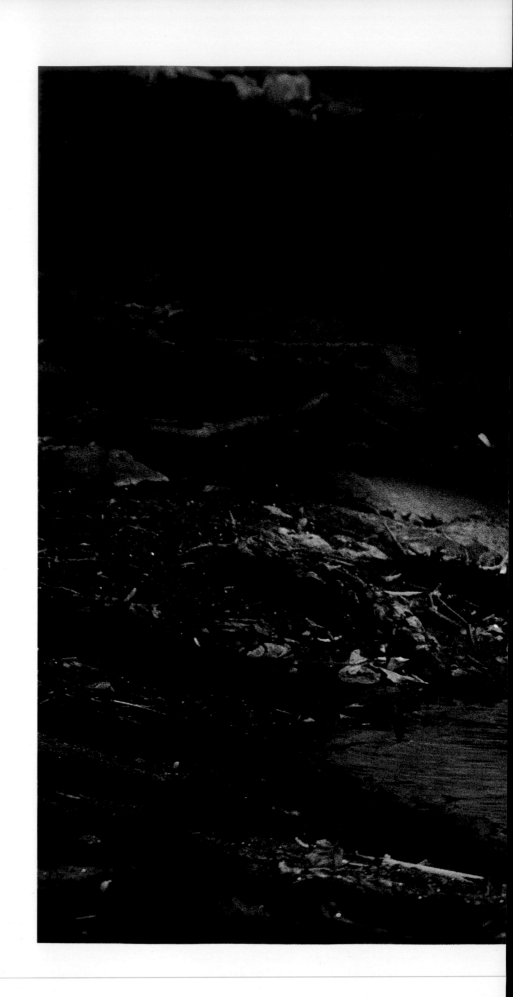

Kanha National Park,
India

Tigers: The Greeks revered them. A sultan viewed them as symbols of independence. The Chinese, ever practical, ground their bones for medicine. And the English poet Blake saw the good and evil of all creation in their "fearful symmetry."

Speak the name *tiger* and you conjure up the embodiment of stealth, ferocity, and energy. But long before tigers stalked the human imagination, they dominated a continent, from the Caspian Sea to the Pacific Ocean. For more than a million years they thrived in Asia, adapting to any realm—whether marsh, grassland, or forest—that offered water, prey, and protective vegetation.

By the turn of the 20th century, however, hunting had increased and the tiger's habitat had fallen to the plow. Local races of tigers vanished in Java, Bali, and Soviet Central Asia. And in India, which once boasted a huge population of tigers, the great cats numbered fewer than 2,000 by 1972, down from an estimated 40,000 in 1900.

With the tiger's extinction looming, conservationists from around the world inaugurated Project Tiger in 1973. The campaign called attention to the creature's plight, raised research funds, set up patrols to discourage poachers, worked to ban the international sale of tiger skins, and—most important—selected Kanha National Park and 14 other reserves to save the tiger's habitat in India.

Experts realized that saving the tiger meant saving a whole environment. Tigers needed deer for prey, deer needed grass for grazing, and grass needed water and good soil. All were considered when India established its tiger reserves, which also saved the endangered elephants, rhinos, and wild buffalo that shared the tiger's habitat. Gradually the great cats bounded back; by 1984 some 4,000 were thriving.

India helped lead the way for other Asian nations, which established their own tiger reserves. By making room for one spectacular species in trouble, they saved a world of others.

Symbol of conservation success, a tiger drinks at Kanha, India's 360-square-mile park.

The Okavango Swamps,
Botswana

Most rivers run to the sea, but not the Okavango. It begins as a trickle in the highlands of Angola, builds magnificently as it sweeps southeastward into Botswana, and forms an inland delta that sprawls across more than 6,000 square miles. Then, as gradually as it began, the river disappears, swallowed by the sands of the Kalahari, the "great thirst" desert of southern Africa.

The continent's largest and most fertile oasis, the Okavango Swamps each day take in some six billion gallons of water from the river. Innumerable channels run through the swamps, forming a maze that changes constantly. An island of ten-foot-tall papyrus that blocks the current today may break loose in the night and take root downstream, making a new island. Or one of the region's frequent earthquakes may shudder far beneath the water's surface, ripple up through a thousand feet of underlying sand, and reverse the flow of the currents.

Though changeable, the swamps provide a reliable refuge for crocodiles, hippos, buffalo, and other wildlife. Some 400 species of birds thrive here, including the African jacana, a lily-trotter that seems to walk on water as it sprints across lily pads. Rare birds such as the slaty egret also live in Moremi Wildlife Reserve, a part of the delta. When the dry season comes to Okavango, it brings elephants and even hippos from hundreds of miles away; they find water in the chain of depressions called pans that lead into the swamps.

Okavango's wildlife owes its splendid isolation—and perhaps its very existence—to the tsetse fly, the notorious swamp pest that can cause sleeping sickness in humans and an often fatal disease, nagana, in domestic cattle. For centuries the tsetse's threat kept humans away. But now Botswana, eager to expand its cattle industry, is spraying the delta to kill the tsetse. That could open the untamed swamps for grazing—and change Okavango forever.

The Okavango glimmers in Botswana, where a fifth of the land is set aside for conservation.

Tsavo National Park,
Kenya

Pools of cooling water, plentiful grass, and few human predators—this must be hippo heaven right here on earth.

Mzima Springs, home to more than 20 hippopotamuses, blooms like`a floral centerpiece of palms and fig trees in the parched expanse of Tsavo National Park in southern Kenya. The largest of Kenya's parks, 8,000-square-mile Tsavo supports diverse wildlife, including thousands of elephants. Forced off their ranges by farmers and poachers, the elephants have turned some of the park's acacia and baobab forests into bushland.

At Mzima Springs, an oasis in this scarred landscape, 50 million gallons of water fill the pools every day; the water flows not from nearby lakes or rivers but from a distant range of volcanic hills. There, ashy soil filters rainwater down to a layer of impermeable rock. The water courses underground until it spills into the two-mile-long chain of pools at Mzima —to benefit the hippos and the turtles, crocodiles, snakes, and fish that live there year-round.

The hippo, with its prodigious appetite, enriches life at the oasis. Eating more than a hundred pounds of grass nightly, the hippo produces equally impressive amounts of dung. The fertile droppings blanket the bottom of the pool and nourish crustaceans and plankton. These sustain insects, frogs, and fish, which in turn are food for birds, snakes, and other creatures in the food chain. Here in this domain of the hippo, the dust-caked elephants, lions, antelope, impalas, and zebras of Tsavo find food and water springing eternal in a dry land.

A two-ton hippopotamus, the "river horse" once common throughout Africa, lolls in Mzima Springs; *Labeo* fish clean the hippo's hide.

Lake Malawi
National Park, *Malawi*

"When I first put on a snorkel and mask and went down, I opened my mouth in amazement and almost drowned."

The diver was recalling his first plunge into the warm, clear waters of Lake Malawi, where clouds of gaudy tropical fish drift this way and that, flashing blue, yellow, purple, and orange in the gentle current. The lake, which forms part of the border between the countries of Malawi, Tanzania, and Mozambique, is home to possibly as many as a thousand fish species. Most of them are found nowhere else in the world.

Part of the Great Rift Valley, Lake Malawi is 360 miles long, with a maximum depth of 2,300 feet. Around the lake, hippos and crocodiles sun themselves, heedless of the fish eagles and cormorants that hunt nearby. To save a piece of this unique environment, Malawi set aside 36 square miles of land and water in 1980 for Lake Malawi National Park, the first national park in the world designated to protect freshwater fish.

The lake's residents have adapted countless ways to survive in this highly diverse setting. Several species of the colorful fish in the cichlid family provide maximum protection for their offspring: One parent shelters the fertilized eggs in its mouth, guarding them from predators until the young hatch and grow; other cichlids swim freely with their young by day, then gather them in their mouths and ferry them to a safe place for the night.

Scientists still have much to learn about the huge lake whose sun-splashed waters hold the greatest variety of freshwater fish in the world.

In tropical Lake Malawi a mouthbrooder fish hovers protectively near its fry.

Virunga National Park,
Zaire

In the heart of central Africa lies Virunga National Park, a last refuge for one of earth's rarest and most misunderstood creatures, the mountain gorilla.

Although a close relative to man, the gorilla has been falsely portrayed as a ferocious carnivore, miscast as a movie villain, and even maligned in our language, in which to call someone a gorilla is to call him a thug.

In truth, these shy apes are usually models of civility, rarely fighting over land, sex, or food. They travel in tight-knit families of 5 to 30, subsisting on nettles, fruit, bamboo shoots, thistles, wild celery, and other vegetation that grows on Virunga's moist, rugged mountain slopes. Gorillas often wrest food from the land, ripping out roots, splitting stems, and stripping bark in a display of strength. Females may reach 200 pounds in weight, males more than 400 pounds, making them the largest of the primates.

Despite their impressive size, these gentle giants are a poor match for humans. Trappers injure or kill many gorillas in snares intended for other animals. And some poachers have invaded gorilla sanctuaries, mutilated the animals, and sold their hands as ashtrays and their heads as coffee-table decorations. The pressure for farmland has also hurt the gorillas, which live in one of Africa's most fertile areas, surrounded by villages. The 3,000 square miles in Virunga National Park were once part of Africa's first national park, established in 1925 to protect the gorillas' habitat. Much of that original park has been turned into cropland.

As a result, fewer than 400 mountain gorillas exist today—about 115 in the Impenetrable Forest of Uganda and another 250 in the Virunga Mountains. This second population is now protected in Zaire, Rwanda, and Uganda, the three countries that share the volcanic range. All three countries have started patrols and education programs to reduce poaching and habitat destruction, giving hope that the beleaguered gorillas will not vanish from the earth.

A mountain gorilla finds protection in the Virunga Mountains.

THE URBAN LANDSCAPE

ometimes in autumn upon the hills of Fiesole, when a pale sun emerges from its clouds, perhaps, and casts a wistful gleam across the valley below, one can believe The City to be an aspect of the divine. Then the towers and domes of Florence look more than mere physical artifacts but seem to possess an insubstantial glory, and the whole jumbled construction down there, its narrow streets, its red-tiled roofs, its windows flashing in the sudden sunshine, suggests some fantastical image of Paradise.

It is no surprise that when St. Augustine of Hippo needed a metaphor for devotional correctness, he chose the City of God, for the city has always symbolized human aspirations at their loftiest. It was toward a celestial city that Bunyan's Pilgrim labored on his Progress. It was a Jerusalem that Blake wanted to build among the dark satanic mills. Earth had nothing to show more fair, Wordsworth thought in ecstasy, leaning over Westminster Bridge to survey the greatest metropolis of his time.

But of course the city pertains to the carnal as readily as it evokes the supernal, and in fact St. Augustine invented a twin city, the heretical Earthly City, to teach us how *not* to behave. The city is all things to all men, where the noble is balanced by the ignominious. When there is no soft sun to warm the scene, when the hills are less than Tuscan, when a drizzle falls upon gray slate roofs and all is stink, noise, and eyesore among the relentless traffic, even the best of cities can seem sufficiently profane.

The City Protective. The civic instinct is immemorial. Long before recorded history men and women were settling in communities, and we see the impulse toward urban life commemorated in some of the oldest human remains, the lake villages, the hill forts, the hut circles of remotest antiquity. In their time they served the same essential purposes as the conurbation of today. They provided security against danger or discomfort; they sheltered the amenities and institutions of society, cobbler's shop to chieftain's court; they offered the means of profit; above all, perhaps, they gave people a sense of membership.

The oldest city still extant is said to be Irbīl, which stands on a high circular mound above the flatlands of central Iraq and is supposed to have been continuously inhabited for 5,000 years. It is preeminently a place of mutual support. Jammed mazelike within the perimeter of its abrupt plateau, it is like a family secret in clay—an introspective enclave within which every resident knows every other, only citizens of standing can find their way around, and strangers in every century feel themselves baffled and excluded.

It is the archetype of the City Protective. Most of the ancient cities of the East, where the city proper was invented, share its sense of hugger-mugger privacy, and in a different way even great modern cities of Europe still sometimes appear familial or at least corporate; Naples for example, despite its splendors of topography and architecture, feels first of all a city of tight neighborhoods, while the burgher-cities of the Scandinavian north, Bergen, Oslo, or Stockholm, stand on their foreshores like so many comfortable clubs, allowing outsiders temporary membership only.

At another level of protection, any respectable citizen of the Middle Ages must have felt marvelously reassured when after a foray into the world at large he returned home to one of the great walled cities of antiquity, glowered all about by ramparts. Even now, when I pass into İstanbul through its indestructible fortress walls, I feel myself obscurely comforted by their presence behind my back, as though ghostly drawbridges have been raised back there, and imaginary portcullises lowered. There are some fortress-cities which are more like weapons of war than like living-places, but there are many others, such as the grand old city of Cartagena within its crumbling ramparts, or Dubrovnik castellated so precisely beside the sea, which feel like havens still, offering their citizens if not defense against cannon and cavalry, at least shelter against importunate suburbs.

Transported to the countryside, many city people even now feel themselves bereft: They miss those stout night-watchman walls, if only in the idea of them; they miss that womblike intricacy of lanes, even when translated into shopping malls; and they pine for the concentration of human activity that comforted our Neolithic ancestors.

The City Assertive. We look at those venerable cities and think of security; but if we look at one of the colossal cities of our own time, erupting in sheaths of concrete and mirror-glass, we think more probably of power. Down the generations the city has shifted its posture, from the defensive to the more generally aggressive, and all the human cravings for glory, wealth, and dominion have been channeled through its medium.

One by one cities have risen to supremacy, now in the East, now in the West, and even when their mighty powers are overtaken, they retain some numen of their apogee— the cloud of dust left behind, as the Spaniard Miguel de Unamuno put it, when a people goes galloping down the highroad of history. It is 15 centuries since the fall of Rome, yet still one senses some of the swagger of its imperial prime. Only a handful of colonies remains of that British Empire upon which the sun never set, but crossing St. James's Park on a summer night, say, seeing the signal lamp shining on the tower of Parliament, glimpsing the presence of the Queen's palace one way, the Arch of Admiralty the other —even now one can sometimes feel, shamefacedly perhaps, the excitement of dominion.

Far from the metropolitan centers, too, surrogate capitals of empire seem to fly spectral flags of conquest, however long ago they raised ensigns of their own. High in the Peruvian Andes the city of Cuzco, built with the cyclopean blocks of the Inca Empire, bears itself in the High Spanish style and feels to this day, when the jangled bells of its cathedral ring out across the dusty plaza, like a colonial settlement among the natives. In Goa and Macao polychromatic architecture of the Portuguese defies the tropic suns, and far from France the boulevards of Ho Chi Minh City remind the traveler that for a generation or two Saigon used to call itself the Paris of the East.

Money is power, too, and many a great city has been dedicated not to authority but to profit, coalescing around exchange or landing stage rather than palace or chancery. Incongruous among the barren deserts of the East, serene on Mediterranean headlands, one finds in their lovely ruins the scattered trading-cities of the Greeks, and along the merchant routes that link East and West stand some tremendous conurbations— Guangzhou seething beside the Pearl River, Bombay where the riches of India come down to the sea, or the irrepressible bazaar-city that is Damascus.

Temperamentally at least, the cities of money are more durable than the cities of authority—the haggle never changes, whether it be verbal or electronic, but brands of government come and go. One of the most salutary experiences of travel is to follow the ceremonial route of the former emperors of China through the city of Beijing, out of the Forbidden City to that high platform upon which, three times a year, the Sons of Heaven used to make their formal communion with the gods above. It is hard to conceive of such a mission now, in the city of concrete that is Beijing. As the royal procession clattered by, with tossing plumes and palanquins, every citizen was cleared from the streets, every window was shuttered; now the No. 116 bus follows more or less the same route.

The City as Civilization. Every day in the Polish city of Kraków a trumpeter blows a fanfare from a high gallery above the central square, but before he finishes his performance he suddenly breaks off, and the sound is left to echo silvery but uncompleted across the square. So it was one day in the 13th century, when the trumpeter was shot by a Tatar arrow, and the daily repetition of his interrupted call is a reminder that a city can also be the repository of all those traditions, talents, tastes, and accomplishments that constitute a culture.

The mere coining of cash, the mere acquisition of political power, are not among mankind's highest functions, and cities that seem to express the nature of a civilization stand farther along the pilgrim's progress to Paradise. They have mostly developed, it is true, out of power-cities, or money-cities, or cities of strategic meaning, but down the centuries they have come to embody profounder human fulfillments: kinds of art, schools of philosophy, achievements moral, aesthetic, or simply gastronomic.

Sometimes an entire national or even international culture has contracted down the centuries into a solitary conurbation, which then becomes a world in itself. In this kind Vienna, the old capital of the Austro-Hungarian Empire, is supreme. It is a ceremonious, conventional, sycophantic city, but its pompous boulevards and public buildings provide the framework for all the ramifications of a once brilliant culture. Here are the showy theaters and immense state museums, restaurants of celebrated cuisine, coffee shops where Brahms and Bruckner lingered, the royal stables of the Lippizans and the apartment where Freud first set up his couch—all that once seemed to represent the flowering of an inexpugnable order, embodied now in the idiom of a single high-and-dry metropolis.

The City Spiritual. But the highest purpose of a city must be to reach beyond the worldly, even at its most cultivated, and aspire to some spiritual summation. Many a famous city is dedicated to an idea—Hong Kong is one great powerhouse of capitalism, Moscow is Communism in concrete, Washington even at its most megalomaniac still speaks wanly of Jeffersonian democracy. Grander still, though, if more dangerous, are those cities that exemplify the energy of faith.

What could be more terrific than Lhasa, clustered around the palace-fortress of the god-king on his hill? Was there ever a more peculiar sensation than to wander through the brazen tumult of Kyōto from one hushed sanctuary to another? Is anywhere more frightening than Qum, the sacred city of the Iranian Shiites, or more formidable than Amritsar, where the masterly sages of the Sikhs sit in conclave in their Golden Temple?

My favorite city walk in the world is a walk through the original Cairo, the walled city which the Fāṭimids built in the tenth century, because it is dominated by all that is most impressive in Islam. One after another the minarets rise above the crooked, crowded back streets, here a dome, here a steeple, here a pair of sandstone pepper pots, and from their open doors, as one passes through the babel of donkey carts, trucks, blaring radios, goats, and bawling street-vendors outside, there seems to emanate an invincible calm. When the call to prayer sounds, violently amplified through a hundred loudspeakers, and even the market men and taxi drivers pause for their moment with God, the most cynical agnostic can only marvel at the sheer force of the civic conviction.

And so one arrives, as almost any piece about the meaning of cities must eventually fetch up, at the gates of Jerusalem. We are told there has been a city in this corner of Judaea since the 14th century B.C., but it is not the age of the place that makes it the last destination of topographical essayists, but its astonishing power of holiness. Held within those honeyed walls are memories found to be sacred by all three of the great monotheistic religions of mankind, embracing in one degree of conviction or another well over a third of all the people of the earth. The conjunction here of three of the most powerful of all creeds, in the hard, clean light of Palestine, surely makes Jerusalem the ultimate metropolis.

Of course there are holy places deep in the countryside, sacred stones solitary on moorlands, springs or lakes immemorially revered. The city, though, is above all else a microcosm of mankind, and it is proper and inevitable, as Augustine, Blake, and Bunyan saw, that to build our own Jerusalem wherever we are, our own City of God, our own Celestial City, must be the supreme allegory of the human purpose.

But only the human purpose; for when all is said, the city is not God's work after all, but man's, and must to my mind always be inferior to the mighty presence of nature on which it is imposed. There is in Wales a site worthy of any Florence—a wide, gentle bowl among rolling hills, with a sweet river running through it, only awaiting, one would think, its towers, domes, bridges, and palaces. In the 13th century a brand-new town was actually founded there and laid out to fulfill all the classic urban functions: a place of settlement, a market, a military outpost, a seat of power, a community. Somehow New Radnor never came to life, never acquired the city momentum, and to this day it stands uncompleted and unfulfilled, no more than a bypassed hamlet beneath the ruins of its sheltering castle. Some of its original building lots are still, after seven centuries, vacant of construction.

Around it the valley stands as it always did, sans domes, sans towers, sans kings, tycoons, or even saints, in all the matchless confidence of the land itself.

The Old City of Bern, *Switzerland*

Water carved a natural fortification in a crook of the Aare River, and threat of fire dictated a citadel of stone. But it took Swiss prudence to preserve Bern unspoiled for eight centuries.

Duke Berthold V fortified the peninsula tip in 1191 to guard its river crossing. He called the settlement Bern because, legend says, the name sounds like *Bären,* the German word for "bears." The bear became Bern's mascot, gracing its flag and coat of arms, decorating bronze bells and stone fountains. Alive, the animals have been fed and pampered by visitors for 500 years in the city's bear pits.

A free town when the duke died heirless, Bern burgeoned, extending broad streets along the river-girded spit in the only direction possible, pushing back its towered wall. Three cantons to the east united in 1291, declaring freedom from Austria. Bern, then an important canton, joined the new Swiss Confederation in 1353.

Fire devoured the wooden city half a century later, sparing little but its gutted towers. On the old foundations, citizens rebuilt Bern from sandstone, perching well-set houses above arcades where merchants and craftsmen could thrive, safe from the weather. Later, city fathers relieved the town's severe uniformity with ornate fountains. On one, blind Justice balances her scales over the heads of the proud and mighty medieval rulers: the pope, German emperor, Turkish sultan—and the mayor of Bern.

So well did the city, with its wide streets and plentiful water, work for its inhabitants that despite its growing power, passing centuries brought no urge to improve, only to refurbish. In 1779 Goethe called it the cleanest, most beautiful city he had seen. Napoléon, less sensitive to its charms, stayed a mere half hour before dragooning it into his empire.

Switzerland elected Bern its capital in 1848. Today fashionable suburbs lie beyond its bridges, but Bern's ancient heart continues to unite the folk of a polyglot nation in their common bonds of tradition, tenacity, and ordered beauty.

In spite of its spectacular setting and the pride of its citizens, Bern is one of Europe's least known capitals.

175

The Old Town of Ávila,
Spain

In Castile they know it as the "city of saints and stone." Sited on a promontory above the Adaja River, embraced by the Gredos Mountains of central Spain, Ávila today stands as the only completely walled city in Iberia. And, at nearly 4,000 feet above sea level, it also stands "nearest to heaven" as Spain's highest town.

In the words of novelist James Michener, Ávila is "a handsome sight" from any approach, with its massive, honey-colored battlements, red-tiled roofs, and gates that "look as if horsemen might clatter out through the portcullis." Many people judge Ávila the finest example of a medieval city in all of Spain—a city rife with twisting lanes, huddled shops and houses, and dozens of churches, convents, monasteries, and palatial residences, some now converted to public offices and museums.

Ávila's beginnings trace back to prehistoric times, when Celtic tribes settled the area. Some of their handiwork, hulking stone statues of pigs and bulls, survives in and around the city. Then came the Romans and, later, the Visigoths, who overran this outpost the Romans knew as Abula.

Christianity arrived in Ávila during the first century with St. Segundo, one of seven delegates appointed by the Apostles to convert the heathen world. He became Ávila's first bishop. Even today, it is said, he will grant a wish to anyone placing a fresh handkerchief on his tomb.

In 1090, soon after the expulsion of Muslim armies from the area, work began on the mile-and-a-half-long, 40-foot-high wall that surrounds the old city. Nine

176

Ávila's cathedral rises like a benediction above the city's serrated battlements.

years of construction produced 90 towers, 2,500 battlements, and 9 gates. A massive Romanesque cathedral became a built-in bastion along part of the eastern wall.

Almost as tangible as the city's fortifications is the aura of sanctity that pervades its streets and plazas. For here was the birthplace, in 1515, of St. Teresa, the great mystic and reformer of the Carmelite Order.

Born into a well-to-do family, she entered the convent as a young woman and, at age 40, chanced upon a statue of Christ standing along her path. In a moment of divine illumination, tradition holds, she beheld God. Thereafter Sister Teresa set out to imbue her order with a new, more ascetic sense of purpose. A young Carmelite priest joined her in her task. Today the two are revered as the city's towering saints —Teresa and John of the Cross.

Much of the city memorializes St. Teresa—the site of her birthplace, her school, her churches, the convents she founded, her rosary and confessional booth. At the Convent of St. Thomas, where she sometimes prayed, lie the tombs of Don Juan, the only son of King Ferdinand and Queen Isabella, and Tomás de Torquemada, the first Grand Inquisitor of Spain.

St. Teresa's memory also lives on in deeds recalled, such as the time she miraculously restored life to her little nephew after he was crushed by a falling wall.

Other tales linger, too, including the legend of the town beauty, St. Barbada, who beseeched God to make her ugly because she feared for her honor. God heard. She sprouted a bushy beard.

The Old City of Ṣanʻāʼ,
Yemen

"Ṣanʻāʼ be it must, however long the journey, Though the hardy camel droop, leg-worn on the way." Sounding like the slogan of an ancient chamber of commerce, the old Arab saying affirms the importance of this central highland city.

About 2,500 years ago Ṣanʻāʼ was a stronghold of the Yemeni kingdom of Saba and a crossroads for the caravan routes that etched the southern tip of the Arabian Peninsula. Saba, the biblical Sheba, gave the mountain-ringed town its name. In the Sabaean language Ṣanʻāʼ meant "well fortified." Early structures clung to the mountainside; gradually the town spilled onto the fertile plain.

By the fourth century A.D. brick walls with wooden gates augmented the protection of the mountains. But Ṣanʻāʼ was not impregnable. In the sixth century a brief Abyssinian domination ended with the arrival of Persian armies. During the Persian hegemony that followed, the town embraced Islam.

The new faith would change the face of Ṣanʻāʼ. Within its walls —rebuilt from time to time and capped by stone towers—the city filled with houses, gardens, mosques, public baths, and religious schools. The market flourished, famous for Arabian steel, fine textiles, polished gems, and aromatic spices.

Drawing on traditional materials and techniques, the builders of Ṣanʻāʼ achieved harmony with their environment. Square, tower-like houses of unfired brick on stone bases rose as high as ten stories. Myriad windows, skylights, portals, and niches outlined in whitewash provided light and relieved the imposing facades.

For more than a thousand years —spanning two occupations by Ottoman Turks—Ṣanʻāʼ remained unchanged. Then, in 1962, it became Yemen's capital, and rapid development threatened the old walled city. But preservation plans will ensure the survival of the urban masterpiece once known as the Pearl of Arabia.

Like icing on gingerbread, white trim outlines the fortress-like buildings of Islamic Ṣanʻāʼ.

Reaching 20 feet at its thickest and 50 feet at its highest, Dubrovnik's stone-and-lime wall encircles the old city.

The Old City of Dubrovnik, *Yugoslavia*

"This place owes its foundation to the ferocity of mankind towards its own kind," wrote novelist Rebecca West of Yugoslavia's medieval port city. If the painterly scene that Dubrovnik presents to the eye—the dramatic cliffs jutting into the turquoise Adriatic Sea, the sun-brightened white of its stone houses, the patchwork of red-tiled roofs—belies West's idea of ferocity, the impenetrable wall that frames the squarish peninsula does not.

It was to fend off mankind—first the Arabs, then the Normans, Byzantines, Venetians, Hungarians, Turks, and, finally Napoléon—that Dubrovnik girded and regirded itself over the centuries with a massive stone wall, ramparts, fortresses, towers, gates, and drawbridges, then protected itself still further with a deep moat.

Dubrovnik traces its origin to the seventh century A.D., when refugees from the nearby city of Epidaurum fled advancing tribes of Avars and Slavs and settled on a tiny island of steep rock. During the thirteenth century, residents joined this natural fortress to the mainland by filling in the shallow sea channel. Located between the Balkans and Western Europe, the city flourished as a medieval power. Independent and prosperous through trade and shipping, it was known as the Republic of Ragusa until the Napoleonic victories led to its downfall.

Episodes of natural ferocity—frequent fires and devastating earthquakes—prompted Rebecca West to see in Dubrovnik's history "the perpetual cancellation of human achievement." The earthquake and fire of 1667 killed thousands of residents and destroyed fine Romanesque, Gothic, and Renaissance buildings.

Fires threatened medieval Dubrovnik when its dwellings were made of timber, not the stone and lime of later times. As an incentive for homeowners to build with stone, Dubrovnik's magistrates, it is said, forbade those living in wooden houses to store more than two measures of wine. Owners of stone houses had no such limit.

The City of Valletta,
Malta

Malta—the Turks called the Mediterranean island "this cursed rock." For it was here in 1565, at what is now the city of Valletta, that Christian soldiers defeated Sultan Süleyman the Magnificent and checked the westward expansion of Islam.

Christianity's defenders were the crusading Knights of St. John of Jerusalem. Outnumbered almost five to one, they withstood the Turkish onslaught, swimming a narrow channel between two peninsulas to repair an underwater chain protecting their fleet. Led by their Grand Master, Jean de la Valette, 129 of the knights held Fort St. Elmo at the water's edge.

After 31 days under siege the fort finally fell. The Turks decapitated the surviving defenders, tied them to crosses, and floated them across the harbor to the knights' Fort St. Angelo. The knights killed Turkish prisoners and fired their heads back across the water with cannon. Some two months later help arrived from Sicily, and the Turks were ousted.

The knights built a fortified city here after the siege and named it Valletta for their Grand Master. The city, today the capital of independent Malta, remains largely unchanged. Fortifications surround a grid of houses and palaces rising in tiers that follow the natural contours of the terrain; all is mellowed by the golden glow of Malta's limestone. Suits of armor worn by the valiant knights stand in the Grand Master's Palace. The palace looks out on a building that once sheltered the Grand Master's bodyguards; today it houses a Libyan cultural center surrounded by flags of green—the color of Islam.

Strategically located in the central Mediterranean, Malta was dominated by ten different powers—from the Phoenicians to the British—until 1964.

Peg-legged, one-armed, half-blind Don Blas de Lezo defies an English fleet attacking Cartagena in 1741.

Outposts of Empire

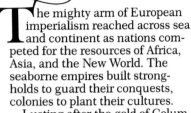

The mighty arm of European imperialism reached across sea and continent as nations competed for the resources of Africa, Asia, and the New World. The seaborne empires built strongholds to guard their conquests, colonies to plant their cultures.

Lusting after the gold of Columbus's Indies, Spain sent conquistadores and priests to loot and subdue. In 1533, two miles high in the Peruvian Andes, Francisco Pizarro conquered the Inca capital, Cuzco. Spanish culture reigned, but in the steely patina of Cuzco's perfect stonework, Inca sternness and sophistication endure.

For three centuries Spanish fleets carried treasure and trade goods between the New World and the Old. To repel the English, the French, and the Dutch, ships sailed in armed convoys and rode in fortified harbors. In the Caribbean, behind Cartagena's high walls and heavy cannon, Spanish bureaucrats piled up emeralds, pearls, gold, and silver, and built a city of gardens, fountains, and balconied white houses that reminded them of their Andalusian roots.

With a fleet of 20 ships Sir Francis Drake sacked the Colombian port in 1586. His brief occupation alarmed the Spaniards into building massive forts that protected Cartagena even 155 years later, when England threatened the Spanish Indies again.

As wars embroiled the European powers, colonial outposts in the Americas changed flags repeatedly. New Amsterdam found itself New York when the British took it in 1664, New Orange when the Dutch took it back, and, in 1674, again New York. In Canada a few moments of gunfire on a plateau over the strategic narrows of the St. Lawrence River won for England, in 1759, the walled, garrisoned, gray stone city of Québec and doomed French hopes for a Canadian domain. Soon after, to the south, the thirteen original British colonies formed a new nation in a war that grew partly from colonial resistance to taxes levied by the crown to pay for its expensive wars against France.

Château Frontenac crowns the rooftops of Québec.

Fine stonework makes Cuzco still an Inca city.

The Historic Center
of Salvador (Bahia),
Brazil

Charles Darwin called Bahia a "luxuriant hot-house made by nature for herself." Here in northeastern Brazil, amid a tangle of tropical vegetation, the Portuguese built their first New World capital in 1549. On a hill by the sea, the founders laid out narrow, cobbled streets and sprawling plazas in a grid that time has scarcely changed. Pirates soon harried the young capital. In 1624 the residents abandoned the city after spying Dutch warships, but a year later Bahians retook their city and ringed it with forts.

Most women in Bahia were Brazilian Indians or African slaves, and the races soon blended. The city became a cosmopolitan port of call and the major slave-trading center in South America. Tobacco and sugar booms financed opulent life-styles in the 17th and 18th centuries, when a landowner's wealth could be gauged by the jewelry his slaves wore. Baroque churches and palaces sprang up, embellished with rococo trim and imported tiles. This construction frenzy ended when the nation's capital moved south to Rio in 1763.

After the mid-20th century touched Bahia, the colonial buildings on the hilltop became too time-honored to tear down. Today the warm sea breeze carries the scent of palm oil from sidewalk kitchens, where turbaned mulattas in full skirts and lacy blouses sell coconut confections and sizzling fish stew. In the century since the slaves won freedom, a modern city of nearly two million has burgeoned below, yet colonial Bahia remains writer Jorge Amado's "splendid city, bride of the sea, lady of mystery and beauty."

Above: Bahia rises from the Bay of All Saints, discovered by Amerigo Vespucci on November 1, 1501. Opposite: Craftsmen carve a marble sink on a steep lane linking colonial Bahia with the modern city below; shops fill the arches of a retaining wall built in the 18th century.

The Old Walled City of Shibām,
Democratic Yemen

For 17 centuries the mud-brick city of Shibām has stood rooted on a rocky mound rising from the Wādī Ḥaḍramawt. This great valley that cuts across the Arabian Peninsula and brings seasonal water coursing to Shibām's palm groves was part of an ancient highway, the Incense Road.

Over the wadi's sandy bed wound camel caravans with goods from China, India, the Mediterranean world—dates, spices, grains, wine, textiles, indigo, gems, gold, slaves. And incense: Arabia's fertile southern coast furnished the best of the frankincense and myrrh vital to Egyptian religious ceremonies, processions, and offerings since before the second millennium B.C. Jews, Persians, Greeks, and Romans, too, coveted these precious gum resins as ointments and as incense that smoldered in their houses and temples, giving off the pungent balsamic perfume of the gods.

Frankincense made empires and unmade them. The Hadramis grew rich and built walled cities as entrepôts along the Incense Road. Around A.D. 300 Shibām became a center of power in the Ḥaḍramawt Kingdom. By the ninth century, when Islam had spread across Arabia, the trade and the kingdom had declined.

"Believer is to believer," said the Prophet Muḥammad, "as the mutually upholding sections of a building." Linked one to another, almost as cells in a honeycomb, the houses of Shibām uphold Muslim tenets: The family, the household, the city are microcosms of the nation of Islam. In Islam, the individual merges with the community; in Shibām, separate buildings fuse into the monolithic fortress that defied marauding nomads.

On the precious land inside the walls, houses rise as high as seven stories. Shibām has been rebuilt many times over the centuries. Always, houses go up under the hands of masons working with the methods of forebears who made a royal city from the desert earth.

The walls and towers of Shibām guarded the riches of an ancient caravan trade.

187

The Bryggen Area
in Bergen, *Norway*

Muted colors of earth and forest tint the wooden houses of Bryggen, Bergen's old port on the rugged coast of western Norway. Crowded between forested, rain-swept mountains and a sheltered harbor, Bryggen has welcomed ships from near and far for more than 900 years.

Norse sagas say King Olaf the Quiet founded Bergen in 1070. Olaf sought peace with his neighbors and prosperity at home; Bergen flourished by trading fish. Each January shoals of cod migrated toward the Lofoten Islands to spawn in the warm waters of the Norway Current. The catches of cod, dried by arctic winds into brick-hard stockfish, reached much of Europe from the warehouses of Bryggen—in Norwegian, "the wharf." The gabled warehouses, built by Norwegian trade lords from about the 12th century onward, held communal kitchens shared by vassals whose dwellings strung out behind.

Fire destroyed Bryggen nine times before the present houses were built after a fire in 1702. Reconstruction always followed the original pattern and the timbered style, even when German merchants occupied Bryggen.

In the 13th century merchants from independent trading cities in northern Germany formed the Hanseatic League to curb piracy and regulate commerce. Soon the league monopolized all the trade in northern Europe. By 1350, with Bergen in their stranglehold, German merchants ousted Norwegians from the stockfish trade. Bryggen's warehouses suited the harsh, extortive life of these officials, required by Hansa rules to live as bachelors. They disciplined their young apprentices with brutal lashes and used double-standard scales—one set for buying and another for selling.

Slowly the Hanseatic League crumbled; Germans and Norwegians pursued Bergen's trade. Then, in 1955, fire destroyed half of Bryggen, and archaeologists began to explore. They are revising the Norse sagas: The deeper they dig, the older Bryggen becomes.

Crowded along Bryggen's waterfront, these old warehouses are among the last remnants of the reign of the medieval Hanseatic League.

The Historic Center
of Florence, *Italy*

Florentines: Pope Boniface VIII called them the fifth element. Earth, Air, Fire, Water . . . and the Florentines.

Think of the Renaissance—the rebirth of classical culture and learning, the age of humanism—and Italy comes to mind. Think of Renaissance Italy, and Florence comes to mind. For more than 200 years, beginning in the early 14th century, no other city in Europe sustained such a continuous burst of intellectual and cultural achievement. In Florence the West saw its first opera performed, the first public library opened, the first nude sculptured since classical times. Here a trio of artists formulated the laws of perspective. And here the Florentine vernacular, Tuscan, became Europe's first modern language. The great figures of the Renaissance—the Medici, Brunelleschi, Donatello, Masaccio, Leonardo da Vinci, Machiavelli, Michelangelo, to name just a few—were all Florentines.

How did a city with fewer than 100,000 residents become the center of the Renaissance? How did the Florentines create their new Athens on the Arno?

Geography favored the city from the beginning. In the first century B.C. Romans founded Florentia ("flourishing town") on a flat piece of land beside the River Arno, a location that fostered the development of textile industries. The rapid-flowing Arno made the cleaning of wool easy and provided access to the port of Pisa in the west, and thence to the commercial world rimming the Mediterranean Sea. Mountain passes to the city's north, south, and east facilitated trade with other parts of Europe.

In this choice spot Florence prospered. By the early 14th century the city far surpassed most European towns in size and wealth. In 1328 it supported a population of 120,000. Just 20 years later the Black Death struck, eventually claiming one-half to two-thirds of the city's population. Despite the devastation of the plague, Europe's demand for luxury goods—

190   Brunelleschi's dome for Santa Maria del Fiore Cathedral dominates the heart of Florence.

especially fine cloth—rose. So did the fortunes of the Florentines. By the early 1400s their cloth reached markets from England to Egypt. Their coin, the gold florin, circulated everywhere, becoming Europe's preferred currency.

In the Florentine mind a new self-image began to form. Awareness of the city's international importance raised self-esteem. Poetry and chronicles, sometimes recited in streets and squares, gave voice to this *fiorentinismo,* praising prominent citizens and hailing the city as the daughter of classical Greece and Rome.

Florence was stable by the standards of the time, dominated by a group of wealthy families. The most powerful of these were the Medici. Under the patronage of this great family of businessmen, with their interest in classical ideals, Florence achieved renown

as the vanguard of the Renaissance. Florentine guilds and civic groups commissioned numerous works of art and architecture with Medici guidance, including the great bronze doors of the Baptistery cast by Ghiberti; statues by Donatello and Ghiberti for the niches in the grain market guildhall known as Or San Michele; and Brunelleschi's monumental dome for the Duomo, or Santa Maria del Fiore Cathedral.

In the early 1400s the Arte della Sela, Florence's powerful silk guild, commissioned Brunelleschi to design the Foundling Hospital. This refuge for the orphaned and homeless was the first building in the Renaissance style; its proportions and structural features—the Corinthian columns, rounded arches, and domed bays—derived from Roman models.

During their century of domi-

nance the Medici founded libraries and academies, including the Platonic Academy, a thriving center of humanist scholarship that helped foster the Renaissance's revolutionary new beliefs in the possibilities of human thought and creativity. The family encouraged artists Ghiberti, Donatello, Botticelli, Leonardo da Vinci, and Michelangelo—sculptors and painters who brought a masterful realism to Italian art using scientific perspective and chiaroscuro, or molding with light and shadow.

"Nothing is beyond the power of the Florentines," wrote one 15th-century Florentine goldsmith. Realistic, civic minded, educated in the classics, the leaders of Renaissance Florence gave direction to the genius of their time, making their city a cultural center second only to Athens and Rome in its impact on Western civilization.

Above: The 600-year-old Ponte Vecchio, which spans the Arno River, supports shops for goldsmiths, silversmiths, and jewelers. Opposite: A panel from Ghiberti's gilded bronze door of the Baptistery shows the Old Testament story of Joseph. Michelangelo named the door the Porta del Paradiso.

193

Ouro Prêto lies among steep hills in southeastern Brazil. Baroque churches dominate the former mining town.

The Historic Town
of Ouro Prêto, *Brazil*

Among the hibiscus and bougainvillea in the gardens of 18th-century Ouro Prêto, art and rebellion bloomed.

Founded by Portuguese prospectors in the late 1600s, the town thrived as a mining center. Ouro Prêto's name—"black gold"—derived from ore darkened by a high iron content. Isolated in the interior 310 miles northeast of Rio de Janeiro, the town drew musicians and writers, as well as artists and artisans who blended local and European motifs in a unique Brazilian baroque style.

The master of the form was Antônio Francisco Lisbôa, called Aleijadinho—the Little Cripple. Although maimed by disease, this genius continued designing and sculpturing into his 70s. According to legend, when he could no longer tolerate the pain in his fingers, he chopped them off. With

mallet and chisel strapped to the stumps of his fingers by assistants, he continued carving soapstone, granite, and wood into glorious statues and altars.

The intellectual climate of Ouro Prêto helped sow the seeds of Brazil's drive for independence and the abolition of slavery. Joaquim José da Silva Xavier, a soldier and dentist known and loved even today as Tiradentes, or Toothpuller, was the hero of a rebellion against Portuguese rule. Tiradentes and his followers hoped to achieve a republic like the new United States of America. But they were betrayed and captured, and Tiradentes was hanged and quartered.

Ouro Prêto's gold deposits had played out by 1800, and new construction slowed. But along the twisting cobbled streets, the man-made treasures remain, relics of Ouro Prêto's golden age.

Cherubs carved by Aleijadinho, Brazil's Michelangelo, adorn São Francisco Church.

In St. Mary's Church larger-than-life figures of linden wood, carved by the 15th-century master Wit Stwosz, depict scenes in the life of the Virgin Mary.

The Historic Center
of Kraków, *Poland*

Like a lens concentrating light, medieval Kraków concentrated Polish culture in a vibrant urban center. Religion, art, science, scholarship, commerce, and statecraft flourished here for more than five centuries.

From a hill on the bank of the Vistula, a castle dominates the city. It is Wawel, begun in the 11th century and later rebuilt as a Renaissance castle. Medieval chronicles tell of the Wawel dragon that dwelt in a cavern under the hill. A tribal chieftain called Krak slew the dragon and, in legend at least, gave his name to Kraków, Poland's capital until 1596.

In 1241 Tatar armies arrived. The stout castle stood against them, but towns below the hill fell. On their ruins Prince Bolesław the Shy erected a new Kraków. On Wawel Hill rulers built abbeys, schools of art, a renowned library, and churches. Kings hung precious Flemish tapestries on the walls of Wawel Castle and filled its chambers with weapons, paintings, fine furniture, and Oriental rugs. In the Gothic cathedral, burial place of most of Poland's kings, is the Italian Renaissance chapel of the family of Sigismund I.

At Kraków's center, Bolesław designed a market square 600 feet on a side, even today the largest medieval square of any city in Europe. Broad streets led from the four corners of the market to the wall surrounding the city. The covered stalls of the Cloth Hall, where drapers sold textiles from around the world, served the most important manufacturing industry of the Middle Ages.

Overlooking the square are the towers of St. Mary's Church, which still draws faithful Poles every day. From the high tower the legendary trumpeter of Kraków sounded the alarm of Tatar invasion. In the 15th century Kraków's university, the oldest in Eastern Europe after Prague's, had some 18,000 students. In its cherished buildings, Copernicus followed studies that led to the science of modern astronomy. Thus past and present beat together in the pulse of Krakovian life.

Gothic and Renaissance architecture characterize the Cloth Hall in Kraków's Market Square.

The Historic Center
of Warsaw, *Poland*

Adolf Hitler gloated in 1944 that Warsaw was gone. After Nazi looting and demolition—methodical, savage, and thorough—Warsaw was only a name on a map. It stood for death. Early in 1945, after Soviet and Polish troops took the ruined city from the Germans, Varsovians began to come home. They found ashes and rubble where there had been houses, shops, museums, churches, palaces. They found the corpses of their families and neighbors buried beneath the streets. In the honeycombed buildings they found and cleared thousands of mines and unexploded shells and bombs.

In the first days of peace, only a few people existed in Warsaw's cellars and burned-out ruins, compared to a prewar population of 1.3 million. By spring 1945 the original inhabitants had begun to return. A newspaper started publication. A ladies' hairdresser advertised for patrons. One of the first new shops sold flowers.

"Warsaw?" cried one citizen. "Warsaw is life itself!"

The historical city was reborn, in part, through the art of the 18th-century Venetian painter Bernardo Bellotto, called Canaletto. The canvases of Canaletto had depicted Warsaw—its buildings, panoramas, lively street scenes—with such richness and accuracy that the architects and artisans who rebuilt Warsaw used the art as a guide.

Poland's capital since 1611, Warsaw both embodies and symbolizes the spirit of the nation. Historian Lewis Mumford foresaw that Warsaw would again be a "mother-city," nourishing its

Warsaw's Old Town Market Square, in both pictures, is reborn in tribute to a nation's identity.

environment and its people. Varsovians reconstructed the Gothic cathedral, using bricks rescued from the rubble of the original. They rebuilt the Royal Castle and the medieval walls of the old city. With a trove of photographs and documents carefully hidden during the war, they re-created the medieval market squares, 17th-century homes, and the facade of the Grand Theater. Inside, the buildings are modern, to serve the present and the future. The resurrection of old Warsaw defies the evil that tried to destroy it.

Homecoming, January 1945.

Kathmandu Valley, *Nepal*

In 1934 a violent earthquake shook one of earth's oldest surviving kingdoms, destroying priceless icons and threatening a 2,000-year heritage of Hindu and Buddhist art. Almost no one outside the realm noticed. In fact, almost no one remembered that this country even existed. Its lands, suspended among daunting Himalayan mountains and ruled by a xenophobic dynasty, had been closed to the outside world since 1816.

Today the kingdom of Nepal is well known. A new ruler opened its frontiers in 1951, resuming relations with neighboring nations and encouraging trade. Its capital, Kathmandu, founded perhaps in the 10th century and home today to 300,000 people, bustles with bazaars displaying rugs and bronzeware. Tourists trek the surrounding countryside. The many religious shrines, built during Kathmandu's age of prosperity in the 16th, 17th, and 18th centuries, impress believers and nonbelievers alike with their carved facades and gilded metalwork.

Positioned on a profitable trade route between China, Tibet, and India, the Kathmandu Valley for centuries provided an ideal stopover for merchants traveling the arduous mountain terrain. The location proved so strategic that rulers of surrounding kingdoms took turns invading. Successive dynasties invested great wealth in offerings to their respective Hindu and Buddhist deities, building pagoda-roofed palaces, temples, and shrines throughout the valley—and in the process fostering religious tolerance. Hindus and Buddhists, dependent on peaceful relations for survival in this rugged land, learned to worship their separate gods side by side—often even in the same temple.

Fortunately, hundreds of these shrines survived the 1934 earthquake. The valley's 200 square miles encompass one of the densest concentrations of religious monuments on earth. As one British visitor remarked two centuries ago: "The valley consists of as many temples as there are houses and as many idols as there are men."

200

The all-seeing eyes of Buddha survey the Kathmandu Valley from a temple at Swayambhu.

Islamic Cairo, *Egypt*

"Mother of cities . . . boundless in multitudes of buildings, peerless in beauty and splendor." Travelers to medieval Cairo strained to describe the sights before them—a sprawling maze of buildings and alleys teeming with city life. Caravansaries packed with Oriental spices and brocades resounded with the eager bargaining of merchants; theological colleges hummed with discussions of the holy Koran; from slender minarets rang the lyrical call of muezzins to the faithful.

Amid the hubbub stood Cairo's domed mosques, hushed refuges for Cairenes who have followed the Prophet Muḥammad in the worship of Allāh since the seventh century. In 969 an army of the Fāṭimid order of Islam invaded Egypt and built a palace-city on the east bank of the Nile. Two centuries of Fāṭimid rulers raised shrines to Allāh, affirming a legacy that has lasted 1,300 years.

In 1250 a dynasty of warlords—the Mamluks—seized power and exploited Cairo's position on trade routes between Asia and Europe. The city prospered, becoming one of the world's largest urban centers—with a population of half a million—and bursting into world prominence as a cultural and religious center. Islamic art and architecture found elaborate expression: Mosques rippled with fanciful arabesque designs; tiered minarets soared above the city; carved latticework turned window screens into objects of art.

The Ottoman Turks swept across Egypt in 1517. Their capital, İstanbul, soon eclipsed Cairo, but Ottoman devotion to Islam assured the future of Cairo's religious monuments. Islamic Cairo has changed little since then.

Today those distant times continue to reverberate through Cairo. Rather than destroy the old to accommodate the new, Cairenes have initiated conservation programs to preserve for the future the historic buildings of the City of a Thousand Minarets.

Pages 202-203: Swirls of light illuminate the Muḥammad 'Alī Mosque.

The Medina of Fez,
Morocco

"God coineth the parable of a city," exhorts the Koran, with tales of people who denied God's blessings, sought lives of luxury and iniquity, and saw their cities destroyed. Fez heeds those examples; in the city's medina, its old walled quarter, no dweller lives out of sight of a minaret. The arches and arabesques of Fez have witnessed 1,200 years of Muslim devotion.

In the eighth century the Berbers of Morocco bowed to the Islamic faith. A descendant of the Prophet Muḥammad founded a dynasty in a gentle valley of the River Fez where two trade routes crossed. His son channeled into canals and fountains the water precious to a people with a desert heritage and vital to the rituals of Islam. The city spread over both riverbanks. In 859 a pious philanthropist, a lady named Fāṭimah, established a mosque, Al Qarawiyin. It was to develop into a great university—one of the oldest centers of learning in the world. To medieval Fez came poets, scientists, and scholars of Islam and of the Christian and Jewish worlds.

Settlers from Spain and Tunisia brought the craftsmanship that became the hallmark of Fez. In the clamorous bazaars, turbaned merchants bought and sold the fine textiles, jewelry, and leather underlying the city's prosperity.

France took Morocco in 1912 and built a capital at Rabat that drew wealth away from Fez. Independence in 1956 led to more population shifts. Prosperous Fezzis left the medieval medina for modern homes outside its walls. Job seekers from farm and desert crowded into the medina, doubling its population. Fine old houses, once occupied by a single family, now shelter many—too poor to care for the ancient buildings.

But today's parable of Fez includes conservation plans that can save the old city from destruction. Officials hope to house the dense population outside the medina, then to restore the mosques, dwellings, and markets in a Fez newly animated by its medieval example of scholarship and art.

Arts from Moorish Spain embellish the mosaics and engraved brass doors of Fez's royal palace, built in the 13th century by the Marinids, a Berber dynasty.

Side domes and added minarets gather about the great vault of Hagia Sophia, focus of Christianity for nine centuries and of Islam for five more.

The Historic Areas of İstanbul, *Turkey*

"Solomon, I have outdone thee!" exults the Byzantine emperor Justinian. "Outdone thee, outdone thee," echoes the dome soaring far over his head like the vault of heaven. Indeed he has outdone the biblical temple builder, for here in Constantinople, Justinian has reared a church to humble any other before it—the mighty Hagia Sophia, the Church of the Holy Wisdom, at the heart of sixth-century Christendom.

There was little to foretell such grandeur when Byzas the Greek —so the legends say—founded a town here about 660 B.C. and gave it his name: Byzantium. The town sat on a peninsula on the Bosphorus, a vital strait on the sea route linking the Black Sea to the Mediterranean. On one side, Europe; across the strait, Asia. Here, said a traveler, was one key to unlock two worlds, two seas. Small wonder the sprinkle of huts grew to a hub of trade and empire.

In A.D. 330 Rome's Christian emperor Constantine bestowed his throne, and later his name, on Byzantium. But the city gave its old name to the realm: the Byzantine Empire, beacon of art and statecraft for more than a millennium. In 1453 Ottoman Turks took Constantinople; by then it sprawled across both the Bosphorus and the Golden Horn, an inlet at the old city's flank. Now called İstanbul—from the Greek *eis ten Polin,* to the City—it is the only city to straddle two continents.

Today İstanbul is a living museum of Roman walls and aqueducts, Byzantine churches, Islamic bazaars, sultans' palaces and harems, and the minarets that turned churches into mosques as the city turned from Christianity to Islam. Today worshipers crowd the Blue Mosque, fitting rival to Hagia Sophia. Justinian's masterwork is an echoing shell of a museum, its glowing mosaics once whitewashed by Muslims who judged them idolatrous. Still its huge dome floats aloft, rebuilt at least twice, yet serene on shafts of sun as if whispering in triumph, "Time, empires, earthquakes in hundreds, I have outdone you all."

Christ fills the dome of St. Mary Pammakaristos, once a church, now Fethiye Mosque.

The Old City of Jerusalem and Its Walls

From the hubbub of business-as-usual emerge the sounds of a city at prayer. Cries of thanksgiving, murmured pleas, the cadence of bells and chants: The children of Judaism, Christianity, and Islam each go about the business of their Father. Cemeteries clustered side by side on surrounding slopes and valley floors tell the story of the faithful: They came to the House of the Lord in Jerusalem—and stayed.

From a distance Jerusalem's modern skyline contrasts with the exalted image sacred to Jews, Christians, and Muslims everywhere—more than a third of the world's population. Beyond the sprawl of concrete housing blocks and high-rise hotels, beyond museums and theaters, beyond the McDavid's hamburger restaurant with its orange arches, the sacred image sharpens into focus.

Sequestered in the heart of the city, behind 16th-century walls built by Süleyman the Magnificent, stands Old Jerusalem. Here ancient alleys and footpaths wind around stone dwellings and shops that span the centuries. Everywhere the sights, sounds, and smells of many nations mingle.

Beneath medieval arches, vendors hawk wares in Arabic, Yiddish, Hebrew, Armenian, Polish, English. Almost anything can be had: aromatic spices and teas, hand-tooled leather, hard bread, sweet cakes, poultry dead or alive, tourist souvenirs. On hot days, turbaned peddlers dispense cool fruit drinks from ornate brass urns. And on streets too narrow for cars or trucks, porters carry heavy loads the old-fashioned way—on their backs. Residents still use the red metal letterboxes bearing the insignia of George V, a legacy of the British Mandate from 1917 to 1948. Except for the letterboxes, television antennas on rooftops, and the mix-match of Eastern and Western dress, the century might be anyone's guess—a city even King David might recognize.

David, the second ruler of Israel, left his mark on Jerusalem about 1000 B.C. Capturing the fortress town from the Canaanites,

Facing toward Mecca, Muslims celebrate Ramadan with prayer and fasting.

Jewish pilgrims wedge prayers into the Western Wall, believing they ascend directly to God.

He has risen! From the traditional tomb of Christ, the Greek Orthodox Patriarch passes the Holy Fire from candle to candle on Easter Sunday.

209

Islam's Dome of the Rock outshines Jerusalem's old and new buildings. Muslims believe scales will be hung from arches in its courtyard to weigh souls on Judgment Day.

he proclaimed it the capital for his kingdom. The city built on a rock in the Judaean hills has ever since been a focus of division—and survival. The Prophet Isaiah described Jerusalem as "a quiet habitation," but it has endured a host of conquerors: Byzantines, Arabs, Crusaders, Mamluks, Turks, British. Burned, plundered, and razed, Jerusalem has survived to build and rebuild. Roman columns turned 20th-century streetlights reveal the spirit and tenacity of its citizens.

In the old city's half square mile, descendants of the past live in four distinct quarters—Armenian, Jewish, Muslim, Christian—that hold dozens of nationalities, each with its sacred shrines.

Armenians revere the Cathedral of St. James, built by the Crusaders in the 12th century to honor the first bishop of Jerusalem. Jews have fought and died by the millions for the right to worship at the Western Wall, the last remnant of the Lord's Temple. Christians follow Christ's lead along the Via Dolorosa, the Way of the Cross. At its end stands the Church of the Holy Sepulcher, esteemed as the site of the Crucifixion and entombment. From minarets, muezzins call Muslims to the Dome of the Rock, a site that unites the traditions of the three great faiths. This mosque encloses the boulder where the Patriarch Abraham bound his son for sacrifice and from which, centuries later, Muḥammad ascended to the throne of Allāh.

In 1967 history repeated itself. On a June day Israeli paratroopers seized the walled city from Jordanian infantry in bloody combat. Soldiers pulled down the concrete and barbed-wire barriers. For the first time since the reign of Solomon, the son of David, Jerusalem was united under Israel's rule.

Today armed patrols and the occasional burst of gunfire recall the bloodshed of the past. Perhaps peace can only be found in the prophecies. When God returns to the city faith built, then "there shall be no more death, neither sorrow, nor crying, neither shall there be any more pain: for the former things are passed away."

MESSAGES OF MONUMENTS

Everything that happens on earth leaves its mark—somewhere, somehow. Every effort of man leaves a record. Monuments are a special kind of record, with certain remarkable features not often noted. In contrast to other records and relics of man's efforts, monuments uniquely combine two features: They are public, and they are future-oriented. These features, separately and together, give monuments their powerful universal role in creating and perpetuating communities and in dramatizing our shared global community.

Thucydides, in the introduction to his classic *History of the Peloponnesian War*, declared his hope that he was producing a work not for his own age alone but "as a possession for all time." His work has survived with the uncanny power of the immortal word. This is because his were *written* words, and especially because they have been published. By this I mean "made public," first in manuscripts and then in printed books. The printing press and movable type have had the history-making power to make words into monuments, rendering them more public and more future-oriented. Books become monuments, and authors become monument makers.

But the power of the printed word has been limited. Thucydides' message has reached only those who could read his eloquent words in one language or another. Which dramatizes for us by contrast the distinctive universal power of nonverbal, nonliterary monuments. A monument built or sculptured in stone or painted on canvas is legible to everybody—young and old, literate and illiterate. All people can grasp a message from the Pyramids, the Great Wall of China, or the Taj Mahal. They need not read Egyptian, Chinese, Hindi, or any other language.

One of the uniquely constructive roles of monuments comes from their extremely public nature. Monuments built communities in the past—some by inspiring awe, as the Pyramids did for the ruler or as the Parthenon did for the gods, others by providing public services, like the amphitheater at Arles or the Pont du Gard aqueduct, or still others by insuring the public defense, like the Great Wall of China. So, too, monuments like the United States Capitol, the Washington Monument, and the Statue of Liberty build communities in the present for us. Monuments also extend our communities into the future by enlisting future generations in our community. The festivities in 1986 celebrating the 100th anniversary of the building of the Statue of Liberty were a patriotic occasion, reminding us of our shared immigrant heritage.

The Statue of Liberty also illustrates another distinctive feature of monuments—the advantage of great size. In the tradition of the famous colossi, thousands could see it from a distance. This was a legendary virtue of the Colossus of Rhodes, one of the proverbial Seven Wonders of the World. For the Statue of Liberty, it was necessary for the monument to fulfill its welcoming and symbolic function from a small island in a wide harbor. The few who could stand close might miss the colossal message.

Technology—photography, movies, and television—has somewhat neutralized this special advantage of the colossus. Now technology can make anything look colossal and can let us all be there, making all objects potentially public and community reinforcing.

Remember Thucydides' ambition to provide a monument "for all time." He was proclaiming the future-orientation of all monuments, which is perhaps their least appreciated virtue. From our living point of view a monument—Charlemagne's Palace Chapel at Aachen—is an object we can look *back* on. But monument builders, especially the builders of the grandest, most durable monuments like the Pyramids, Hagia Sophia, and Chartres, had *their* eyes on the future. They too were not satisfied to speak only to contemporaries. They too reached out to the generations unborn.

The monument builder, of course, was earnest to make his statue, his mausoleum, or his church as public as possible in his own time. He wanted it to become a byword, bringing people from afar to share his message, and so making his message public through *space*. But he also hoped his monument would become public through *time*. Every great monument builder sought not only conspicuousness but permanence. So he commonly built in stone. He found ways to defy weather, vandals, and rivals. Then we, his intended audience, measure his success by the durability of his work, by its capacity to have a centennial—or a millennial—celebration. "Monument" becomes a synonym for the enduring in literature and all the arts.

We can expect to find as many varieties of monuments as there have been human ambitions and loves and hates. The world's monuments make the whole world a museum. In this museum the accidents of history, the malice of conquerors, and the whims of climate have been the inscrutable curators.

Perhaps the largest class of monuments, and many of those familiar in our history books, are *Intentional*. They were made by somebody in the past on purpose to serve as monuments. All these reassure us and flatter our egos by showing how effective humans can be in reaching out. They encourage us to believe that we too can be effective in our public relations through space and time. Intentional Monuments include the whole range of constructive human efforts—from the humblest gravestone to the Washington Monument, from the Palace Chapel at Aachen to Gaudí's labyrinths, from the Pyramids to the Escorial. We can be cheered that so many past efforts remain visible.

Less cheering to our egos are the countless *By-product Monuments*. These include many of our most appealing tourist sites—the Acropolis in Athens, the Forum in Rome, and Pompeii—relics of the ambitions of earlier ages. They feed our nostalgia. They gratify the Ozymandias syndrome. They stir our delight in the pastness of past glories:

'My name is Ozymandias, king of kings:
Look on my works, ye Mighty, and despair!'
Nothing beside remains. Round the decay
Of that colossal wreck, boundless and bare
The lone and level sands stretch far away.

This evanescence of the grandiose efforts of the past somehow solaces us for our own ineffectiveness, for the triviality of our own achievements. Ancient ruins somehow put us in the same class, subject to the same verdict of mortality, as all past potentates.

An especially interesting feature of By-product Monuments is their ability to frustrate or even contradict the aims of their first creators. The chaste elegance of classic Greek architecture and its Roman sequels becomes the inspiration for their aesthetic antitheses. The intact, unbroken column is classic, but the broken column becomes romantic. It stirs us to fantasies of "the vanity of human wishes," as Dr. Johnson would have put it. We enjoy the aches of nostalgia. Then we delight not in the geometric order of a classic entablature but in the moss-covered random fragments of the crumbling past. Rich Britons in the throes of the classical nostalgia of the late 18th century landscaped their estates with artificial ruins. We add a new dimension to our vision, for we can begin to see the romantic in the classic, Piranesi in Palladio, the broken in the unbroken column.

By-product Monuments—as the World Heritage list reminds us by including the slave-trading center at Gorée Island and the extermination camps at Auschwitz—are sometimes relics not of man's creativity but of his activities most horrendous. Acts of savagery and barbarism, like creative deeds, inevitably leave their own detritus. Tyrants may hire their sycophants and may revise the official accounts and the historians' chronicles to their perverse tastes. But willy-nilly, evil men leave clues to their crimes on, or under, the landscape. Some of these they can never quite revise or erase.

These unintentional monuments remind us of a secondary meaning of "monument." That word, the dictionary tells us, means "a structure, such as a building or sculpture, erected as a memorial." It derives from the Latin *monēre*—"to remind"—which is the plain purpose of a monument. Etymology thus reveals both the public and the future-oriented purposes. But that same Latin *monēre* also means "to warn," from which we have our words "monitor," "monitory," and others. All monuments are in a sense monitory, warning us of the waywardness of history. So they are visible messengers of history as our Cautionary Science.

Monuments preserved by us primarily for their monitory role are symptoms of a sense of history, which is itself a modern phenomenon. Since the Renaissance our energetic, critical scrutiny of the past has made us seek clues in all the shards and flotsam of the past. An effort has been needed to make them into monuments. For past emperors were more intent to destroy the creations of their predecessors, or to imprint their own names on those creations, than to preserve relics of an inhumanity that they themselves were ready to reenact. Unintentional monuments can give archaeology the fascination of a chamber of horrors.

There is still another peculiarly modern kind of monument, another by-product of our sense of history and our technology. I will call these *Artificial Monuments*. They are a product of modern history and archaeology, of modern transportation, advertising, public relations, and organized tourism. Colonial Williamsburg is the apex and the prototype—the serious effort to restore the remains of the past and make them live. But they appear across the United States from Old Sturbridge, Plimoth Plantation, and Mystic Seaport to Shakertown at Pleasant Hill, Dodge City, and Fort Clatsop.

And there are other versions still—the theme parks. These make little pretense at authenticity but offer up gargantuan servings of myth, legend, roller-coaster fun, and cuteness. These fantastically popular modern pseudo-monuments for the whole family include Disneyland, Busch Gardens, and Knott's Berry Farm—and *their* imitations.

Anything takes on a new meaning when we think of it as a monument. It makes us aware of our community and perpetuates that awareness. The awakening object need not be a human creation. Nature out there for all to observe is that most public of public experiences. And the most future-oriented. What Thomas Jefferson and his fellow 18th-century "natural philosophers" called "the economy of nature" displays for us our living links to the past, the present, and the future.

The *Nature Monument* of course differs from all other monuments in not being of our making. But the Nature Monument is not merely a spectacle. We live in it. We call it our environment because it "environs," that is, surrounds us. It inspires awe because we are uncertain what it memorializes. And that very mystery, that uncertainty, ironically inspires the dogmatism, ideology, and arrogance of believers.

Our environment is the Nature Monument wholesale. And there are also Nature Monuments retail: individual creatures. The word "creature," meaning a product of creation, itself suggests a monumental kind of sentiment. So we exclaim admiringly at "all creation!" We imply that there must have been a creator who is there to be remembered and celebrated as we celebrate the king when we admire a pyramid.

We need not be theological to consider every living species as a kind of monument. A Bengal tiger, a redwood tree, a flamingo each offers an opportunity (like that of a man-made statue) for the public sharing of delight. Each such colorful creature reminds us of a whole experience not of our making, a vast community of sights and sounds. These, too, become a remembered community.

Every species, too, is future-oriented. In fact we define a species by its capacity for futurity, for perpetuating its kind into next generations. When we extinguish a species or allow it to be extinguished, when we no longer have the common spectacle of the passenger pigeon, we enjoy one less symbolic agent of community. The extinction of any species is the destruction of a living monument. It dissolves one more unique object that once had the capacity to cement our community of enduring public admiration.

Nature Monuments also have a special kind of uniqueness, which leads us from awe to reverence. Man-made monuments can be re-created, reproduced, restored, and Williamsburgized. Nature Monuments, once destroyed, are gone forever. More dramatically than any other human act, our power to destroy a wilderness or a species reveals mankind's capacity for irreversible destruction. The vivid opposite of the creativity that makes us human.

The Statue of Liberty,
U.S.A.

One hundred tons of copper sheet about as thick as a penny, draped over a stainless steel armature, she looms in New York Harbor and in the hearts of Americans: "Liberty Enlightening the World" or, as most know her, the Statue of Liberty.

Alsatian sculptor Frédéric-Auguste Bartholdi, who designed the 151-foot colossus, has rarely been called a great artist. The statue's stance atop her 154-foot base is less than graceful. Liberty's stern gaze, beetling brow, and downturned mouth recall the face of Bartholdi's overbearing and, ironically, anti-Semitic mother.

But the details of Liberty's appearance are of little importance. She takes her place in the imagination as a positive symbol—an ideal—perhaps *because* she is not distractingly beautiful as art. Bartholdi explained the theory behind the statue: "The immensity of form should be filled with the immensity of thought . . . and the spectator . . . should be impressed, before all things else, with the greatness of the idea."

During her lifetime Liberty has stood for more than one great idea. She came to the United States in 1885—in 214 packing crates—as a gift from France, a memorial to American independence. By the turn of the century she was Mother of Exiles to the immigrant ancestors of nearly half of all Americans. During World War I she became Miss Liberty, a symbol of the Allies' effort to "make the world safe for democracy."

Six million people attended Liberty's 100th birthday party in July 1986. Their exuberance seemed boundless, but it could not match the feelings so many immigrants had as they beheld the statue for the first time. "Looming shadowy through the mist, it brought silence to the decks of the *Florida*," wrote one Italian man. "This symbol of America—this enormous expression of what we had all been taught was the inner meaning of this new country we were coming to—inspired awe."

Liberty, spanking clean with new torch raised high, celebrates her centennial with fireworks.

Independence Hall,
_U.S.A._

Independence Hall has no street address. It stands midway between Fifth and Sixth on Philadelphia's Chestnut Street. But no monument occupies a more distinct place in the history of the United States of America.

Here in the Assembly Room, on July 2, 1776, members of the Second Continental Congress resolved "That these United Colonies are, and of right ought to be, free and independent States." By August, 51 members had signed the Declaration of Independence, and in 1781, nine months before the British were defeated in the Revolutionary War, the Congress met here to ratify the Articles of Confederation that welded the thirteen colonies into a union. Six years later they adopted the Constitution of the United States as the nation's basic law.

The modest brick structure in which history was made took shape on the sketch pad of Andrew Hamilton, Speaker of the Assembly of the colony of Pennsylvania. The Assembly sought a more dignified meeting place than the private homes and taverns it had been frequenting. By 1753 the structure was built, complete with a steeple to hold a 2,080-pound bronze bell.

The Liberty Bell began its career on a sour note. When tested, it cracked under the impact of its clapper. It was recast once to repair the crack and again to improve its unattractive tone, but town residents still complained: "From its uncommon size and unusual sound, it is extremely dangerous and may prove fatal to those afflicted with sickness."

Cracked again during a funeral, the Liberty Bell now hangs silent outside Independence Hall. But the words of the Founding Fathers still ring out. The adoption of the Declaration of Independence, wrote John Adams, "ought to be solemnized with Pomp and Parade, with Shews, Games, Sports, Guns, Bells, Bonfires, and Illuminations from one End of this Continent to the other from This time forward forevermore." So it has been, so it will be—every Fourth of July.

Original items on the Assembly Room dais include a silver inkstand used by signers of the Declaration of Independence and a chair occupied by George Washington.

Haitians say that the Citadel's builders were confined to the fortress lest they betray the plan of its dungeons, passageways, and ammunition depots.

The Citadel and Sans Souci National History Park, *Haiti*

To efface the cruel memory of slavery in Haiti, the monument would need to be massive. The Citadel is. Its stone prow, beetling 3,000 feet above the northern plains, dominates not only the landscape but also the history of Haiti, the only nation ever to rise out of slavery and proclaim itself free.

In 1805, after 14 years of bloody revolution against French colonial rule, Gen. Henri Christophe began building the fortress in case Napoléon's forces should return. Although Christophe knew the enemy would land on the coast, he was determined to build a bastion on their only route inland, where he could wage a fight to the death. He understood the necessity of this symbolic gesture: Haiti would be a nation of freemen as mighty as any. To accomplish this end quickly, he had declared himself king of the northern provinces, while the south remained a republic under a rival general.

Henry I, as he called himself, had spared nothing to strengthen his domain. He had conscripted a thousand former slaves a year to drag the guns and stone blocks up the mountain to the Citadel, which even today can be reached only by foot or horseback. It is said that many lost their lives during the Citadel's construction and that Henry once commanded his elite guard to march over the parapet ledge to prove, in death, their loyalty.

While the Citadel stood for brute defensive force, Christophe's palace at the foot of the mountain represented the highest order of civilization. Named after a plantation once on the site, Sans Souci covered 20 acres with baroque arcades, terraces, and gardens. Built of bricks plastered with yellow stucco, it was filled with European tapestries, sculptures, and paintings. Sans Souci was Christophe's last retreat when his subjects rebelled in 1820 and joined forces with the republic in the south. The king, Haitians still recount with pride, accepted his fate and shot himself through the heart with a specially reserved silver bullet. A modest memorial rests on the Citadel's parade ground.

This Citadel cannon bears the crest of the French man-of-war from which it was salvaged.

Gorée Island, *Senegal*

"It is impossible to speak in these places," wrote an American journalist. Not speak in this graceful house the color of sunset? Where stairways curve upward to airy chambers with windows that welcome sea breezes?

These spiraling stairs embrace a pit of darkness. A black hole with dungeons, chains, manacles, and the nameless souls of millions sold into slavery. In more than a hundred houses like this House of Slaves, African men, women, and children waited to leave for the New World from Gorée Island, an outcrop of black basalt off the westernmost tip of Africa.

Beyond the darkness shines a rectangle of light. They walked through the rectangle onto a 200-foot pier. If the men weighed too little, if the women's breasts were not firm enough, if the children's teeth were not strong enough, they were shoved off the pier to the sharks. If they passed inspection after three or four months in chains, they lay down in ships, humans packed like sardines—some ten million people between the early 16th century and 1848, when the French abolished slavery on Gorée. If they did not die on the Atlantic, they became slaves in the Americas or the West Indies.

The Portuguese, British, Dutch, and French all vied for and controlled Gorée Island during the centuries of the slave trade. Today Gorée is part of independent Senegal and the only boats that leave are ferries, mainly carrying tourists two and a half miles back to Dakar, Senegal's capital.

Visitors spend their days on Gorée in courtyards shaded by acacias. They admire the mansions where slavers lived above slaves—elegant structures blending African and European architectural styles, homes built by slaves who crushed seashells to make lime mortar and chiseled basalt into blocks. Tourists bask on Gorée's sandy beach, snap pictures with their cameras, sip wine and chat in cafés.

But still, in the House of Slaves on Rue Saint-Germain, it is impossible to speak.

The House of Slaves on Gorée Island was the point of no return for thousands of Africans headed for bondage in the New World.

The Great Wall, *China*

For as long as there has been China, there has been the Great Wall, a legendary rampart that seems an integral part of the land it crosses, winding almost 4,000 miles over mountain, desert, and plain. Built as a barrier at the northern edge of civilization, the wall has come to symbolize China's national character—its unity, industry, and xenophobia.

Qin Shi Huangdi, China's first emperor, began to connect the walls of several feudal states in 221 B.C. to protect his newly unified empire from northern barbarians—and to keep his peacetime army occupied. During the 12-year project, perhaps as many as 400,000 laborers died from accidents, disease, and exhaustion; thousands were rumored to be buried within the earthen battlements.

But the Great Wall did not stop invaders from the north. Taking advantage of political weakness within China, Genghis Khan and his Mongols swept through in 1211, and more than four centuries later a traitorous army officer opened a gate for the Manchus.

The wall did, however, keep *in* the Chinese, helping to foster a strong national identity as well as a profound fear of, and contempt for, the outer "demon regions." Often, foreign conquerors were absorbed into the Chinese way of life, adopting the language, dress, and culture of their subjects.

In the 1400s and 1500s the Ming emperors rebuilt the wall on a grand scale, mostly with brick and stone. But centuries of neglect and war took their toll. So did the Cultural Revolution, when farmers pilfered stone from the wall to repair houses and build pigsties. In places the wall simply disappeared. Finally, in 1977, the government proclaimed it illegal to remove any stones. Today the Love Our China and Repair Our Great Wall Social Contribution Activity Committee keeps vigil. Sections of the wall, restored to their Ming grandeur, attract millions of tourists a year—Chinese and barbarian alike.

Five horsemen could ride abreast here on the Great Wall near Beijing. The wall, 25 feet high in places, stretches halfway across China.

The Porta Nigra at Trier, West Germany, is one of the world's best preserved Roman city gates.

Above: A fortress in the Middle Ages, the amphitheater in Arles, France, now holds bullfights.
Opposite: Built into a hillside, the theater of Orange in southern France once seated up to 10,000.

Expressions of Power: Far-flung Monuments of the Roman Empire

Atop a rocky mound in the town of Arles in southern France stands an 1,800-year-old Roman amphitheater where 26,000 spectators once viewed gladiatorial contests. In nearby Orange a Roman theater built around 10 B.C. still provides a stage for plays. And four hundred miles to the north, a hundred-foot-high Roman gate—now called the Porta Nigra because of its soot-blackened sandstone blocks—rises above the traffic of Trier, West Germany.

Few civilizations have been as adept as the Romans at expressing power through architecture. At its height the Roman Empire extended from Britain to Syria. To earn the respect and dedication of their imperial subjects, the Romans built imposing city gates and commemorative arches, huge amphitheaters, bathhouses, aqueducts, forums, temples, and theaters. Many of these still stand—at Baalbek in Lebanon, Leptis Magna in Libya, El Jemm in Tunisia, Nîmes in France, and Bath in England. They have endured, in part, because of the adaptability of the Roman builder.

Though the empire favored building styles based on Roman models, it allowed for variations according to local customs, terrain, climate, and materials. The Romans preferred to build with concrete and brick. But where stone was abundant, as in parts of France, North Africa, and Syria, they altered both architectural plans and ornamental decoration to suit the native material. In France's Provence region, an area colonized by Greeks centuries earlier, the Romans carved the hard stone into ornament so delicate it rivaled embellishments on the buildings of Rome itself. In North Africa, one of the wealthiest Roman provinces and a region rich in soft rock, the stonework was larger, grander, and more daring.

Because of the care taken in their design, many of these Roman monuments survive today—reminders of an empire's great provincial cities that flourished more than 2,000 years ago.

The Pont du Gard Roman Aqueduct,
France

Massive, majestic, and efficient, the Pont du Gard is a fitting metaphor for the Roman Empire. Whereas the Greeks built monuments to celebrate divinity, the Romans triumphed more in feats of civil engineering. The Pont du Gard was part of an aqueduct built about 19 B.C. that carried four million gallons of water a day downhill from a mountain spring to the city of Nemausus, 31 miles away.

Today the imposing Pont du Gard stands in a desolate, scrub-dry area of southern France. But in the days of the emperor Augustus, Nemausus prospered. Now known as Nîmes, the city was located on the main road between Italy and Spain. Augustus favored the city by stationing the veterans of his successful Egyptian campaign there, swelling the population to 40,000. Historians think that when Marcus Agrippa, governor of Gaul and water commissioner for the Roman Empire, visited Nemausus in 19 B.C., he decided an aqueduct was needed to supply the public baths, fountains, and pools the Romans liked to install in their showcase colonies. The overflow from these waterworks flushed the city sewers.

The Romans built the Pont du Gard by using pulleys and winches to hoist the solid limestone blocks, weighing as much as six tons each, into place up to 145 feet above the River Gard. In a carefully measured rhythm, 6 arches vault across the river plain; above them runs a row of 11 arches topped by 35 more, with a sloping channel forming the uppermost tier. The base columns were angled at the edges to prevent damage by frequent floods. Jutting stones supported scaffolding during construction and later repairs. To minimize evaporation and contamination of the fresh water, ten-foot-long slabs covered the open channel on top. When Henry James visited the bridge in 1878, he observed "a kind of manly beauty, that of an object constructed not to please but to serve, and impressive simply from the scale on which it carries out this intention."

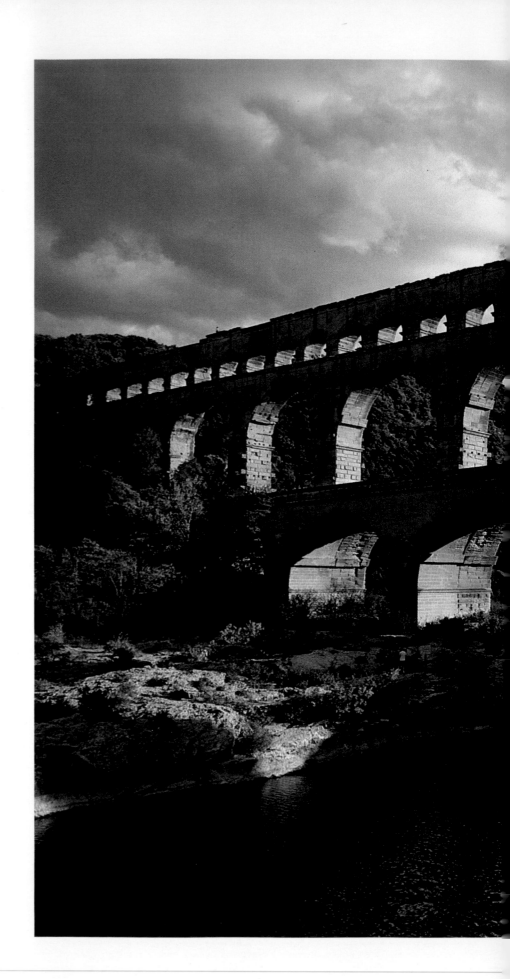

A masterpiece of Roman engineering, the Pont du Gard was part of an aqueduct that could supply each inhabitant of Nemausus with a hundred gallons of water a day.

"Art is long, and Time is fleeting." These words, written by Henry Wadsworth Longfellow in *A Psalm of Life,* explain why monument builders employ art to transcend time. And it is why, in honoring royalty, deities, great people, and great ideas, monuments honor artists as well.

Who can gaze at the exquisite Taj Mahal, built by a grieving husband to entomb a beloved wife, and fail to praise the craftsmen who spent nearly a quarter of a century creating it? Who can visit the Pyramids at Gîza, where Egyptian kings were lionized, and fail to admire the ancient minds that conceived their perfect symmetry?

Fontainebleau, in the midst of a forest 40 miles south of Paris, was built as a residence for French rulers. But beginning in the 1530s, it became a monument to Renaissance art and architecture as François I assembled Italian artists there to decorate the palace. Primaticcio's slender stucco figures set the standard for female beauty used by French sculptors of the late 16th century.

King Stanislas I of Poland, living in exile in Nancy, France, conceived the Place Royale, now Place Stanislas, as a city center to house his court and honor his benefactor, King Louis XV. Today the three-acre square is considered one of the best examples of 18th-century French architecture—a tribute to architect Emmanuel Héré and to artists Jean Lamour, who designed the gilded wrought-iron grilles and gateways, and Barthélémy Guibal, who designed the fountains at the corners of the square.

Throughout Barcelona, Spain, the flamboyant architecture of Antonio Gaudí prevails. Park Güell, Güell Palace, and the Temple of the Holy Family display his inventive use of mortar and tile, organic forms, and elaborate shapes. In 1952, a hundred years after his birth, all of Gaudí's buildings were declared historical monuments. All of Barcelona, many say, is a tribute to this great artist.

Pages 232-33: Ceramic tiles decorate a serpentine bench in Gaudí's Park Güell, Barcelona.

Above: The grillwork of Jean Lamour frames the Fountain of Amphitrite in the Place Stanislas, Nancy.
Opposite: At Fontainebleau, near Paris, Primaticcio's stucco figures grace the King's Staircase.

231

In an underground chapel honoring Queen Kinga of Poland, miners have carved virtually everything—from the massive stairways to the chandelier beads—out of salt.

The Wieliczka Salt Mine,
Poland

Deep beneath the southern Polish town of Wieliczka lies an age-old gallery of poor man's marble—works of art sculptured in salt. Since the 17th century, miners have used the skills of their trade to carve masterpieces in Europe's oldest saltworks, which date back a thousand years. During the Middle Ages the mine provided Poland's kings with a fourth of the state income.

Wieliczka's 2,000 grottoes stretch 180 miles on nine levels. To ward off evil spirits lurking in the mine, self-taught artists transformed salt into altars, biblical bas-reliefs, and statues of saints, heroes, and legendary figures. In 1689 an early miner-artist carved a salt chapel honoring St. Anthony, the patron saint of miners. On the walls of a 177-foot-long chapel dedicated to Queen Kinga, 20th-century miners chiseled bas-reliefs of "The Last Supper" and other biblical scenes. Legend says Kinga tossed her engagement ring into a briny spring in her native Hungary and magically retrieved it in Wieliczka, bringing salt to Poland as a queenly dowry.

During World War II, Nazis paved the floor of one grotto with concrete and set up an aircraft engine factory, safe from Allied bombs. Other chambers have since become a recreation hall, movie theater, café, and sanatorium where asthma sufferers seek cures in the cool, pollutant-free air.

An underground museum preserves salt-encrusted equipment and tools left behind by miners. In the Middle Ages they brewed salt from brine or hacked out rock salt with picks and dislodged it with sticks. The men raised brine or salt blocks to the surface with windlasses and treadmills; later they brought horses underground to do the job with capstans. Steam engines supplanted the horses, and oil lanterns replaced tallow torches before electricity modernized the mine. Braving fires, explosive gases, cave-ins, and the ghosts that lurked in the shadows and saline mists, the miners of Wieliczka have built a monument to art and industry.

Candlelight glows on Queen Kinga, the miners' patroness.

235

Records in
Wood and Stone

A polished monolith, tipped with gold and laced with hieroglyphic script, glorifies a pharaoh and the gods he worshiped. In a totem pole's deep relief, wolf and bear, hawk and beaver crouch together to tell the tale of one great family. Glyphs engraved on a massive slab of limestone pay tribute to a Maya ruler. Obelisks, totem poles, stelae: From the Old World to the New, people have drawn on fundamental materials—wood and stone— to create enduring records of their history, customs, and beliefs.

Tradition and technology have shaped the expression of this common human impulse. To celebrate prosperity or military victory, Egyptian pharaohs of ancient Thebes erected obelisks of hard red granite up to 105 feet high. Dedicated to the sun god, the tapered monoliths were surmounted by a tip that flashed in the sunlight. Artisans used copper blades and emery to inscribe figures and hieroglyphs that spoke of royal power and devotion to the deities.

In a similar marriage of pictures and text, the Maya stelae at Copán immortalized the city's elite. With wood, stone, and bone tools, Maya sculptors carved portraits of their rulers from soft volcanic stone. Animals real and unreal, gods from the underworld, and glyphs in deep relief explained a king's descent from historical or mythical ancestors and, thus, his right to rule.

With no system of writing to record their history, the Haida Indians of Canada's Anthony Island honored their dead and told tales of family lineage and tribal events in a language of symbols, often rooted in the natural world. Using stone and metal tools, this small community of fishermen and hunters shaped the fine, firm wood of the giant western cedar into totem poles up to 78 feet tall. Only the Pacific Northwest Indians carved these wooden columns. But diverse peoples worldwide raised records in stone: Greeks and Tibetans erected stelae; Phoenicians, Romans, and Americans built towering obelisks.

Pharaoh Ramesses II raised this 82-foot-tall obelisk at Egypt's Luxor Temple.

On Canada's Anthony Island a Haida mortuary pole depicts a human figure held by a grizzly.

Maya stelae overlook the Great Plaza at Copán, Honduras. One shows rulers facing east and west.

237

Memphis and the Pyramids from Gîza to Dahshûr, *Egypt*

Monuments for the ages to ponder, the Sphinx and the three Great Pyramids at Gîza have fascinated people for 5,000 years. Even today, scholars debate how these massive structures were built—and why. About 80 pyramids line the Nile's west bank. The most important, dating mainly from the Old Kingdom of the third millennium B.C., rise along the 21-mile stretch from Gîza to Dahshûr. The ancient Greeks considered Gîza's trio the most wondrous of the Seven Wonders.

The pyramid credited to King Khufu—Cheops in Greek—is the biggest, its square base covering 13.1 acres. Its apex originally towered as high as a 50-story skyscraper. Now the top 31 feet are gone—lost to erosion or looted for construction in nearby Cairo. Once encased with smooth white limestone, each of its triangular faces spans five acres; 2.3 million stone blocks, each weighing an average of 2.5 to 3 tons, constitute a total bulk of 6.25 million tons. All this rock was quarried, dressed, and raised into position in less than two decades without the benefit of pulleys or draft animals or even the wheel. To do the job, ancient engineers probably relied on crowbars, sledges, rollers, ramps—and an almost unlimited labor supply.

Gîza's man-made mountains are also remarkable for their accurate construction. Their sides point precisely to the cardinal directions of the compass; other pyramids show accurate alignments with the sun. Most scholars believe these colossal structures were primarily royal tombs.

Between Gîza and Dahshûr lies Memphis, the capital and chief port of the Old Kingdom. Inhabited for 3,000 years, Memphis probably peaked with the golden age of pyramid building. Certainly it declined long before the rise of Greece and Rome. Today Saharan sands and villages blanket its 840-acre ruins. Archaeologists have never completely surveyed Memphis or excavated more than 10 percent of its center. Like the Great Pyramids, this ancient city continues to kindle man's imagination.

239

Giza's inscrutable Sphinx, its face scarred by latter-day conquerors who used it for target practice, still reigns before the Pyramid of King Khafre, the son of Khufu.

The Palace Chapel of Charlemagne at Aachen,
West Germany

An architectural miracle, half human and half divine, proclaimed Charlemagne's contemporaries after the dedication of his Palace Chapel at Aachen in 805. But few could foresee that the chapel would come to symbolize the political, cultural, and spiritual renewal of Europe after 400 years of anarchy.

Charlemagne himself would not have been surprised. Though Aachen was an insignificant town, he chose it for his capital because it lay near the heart of his realm, which reached from the North Sea to the Mediterranean. From this imperial center Charlemagne would revive the laws and culture of ancient Rome, encourage the making of new books, and direct the building of fine churches and monasteries. Ultimately, he would transform Aachen into a second Rome, fitting home for the founder of the Holy Roman Empire.

The centerpiece of his grand scheme for Aachen was the Palace Chapel, the most imposing structure Europe had seen in centuries. Its octagonal shape conjured up Byzantine splendor; Roman architecture inspired its massive piers and rounded arches.

Charlemagne's chapel embodied the union of church and state and reinforced his position as a Western potentate. On a second-floor gallery, between heaven and earth, he placed his throne, facing the high altar. For Charlemagne was very pious; according to his court biographer, he attended services three or four times a day and loved to sing "in low tone, and with others." Hundreds were employed to pray for him constantly in three shifts that required 30 altars.

Gone now is Charlemagne's palace, with its library, 167-foot-long reception hall, and marble pool large enough for a hundred bathers. Though a cathedral later engulfed the chapel, the octagonal masterpiece remains almost unchanged after 1,100 years, miraculously surviving the bombs of World War II. Today it stands as the greatest monument to the man who revived the ideas and ideals of ancient Rome.

240

On a panel from his gold reliquary, Charlemagne offers a model of his octagonal chapel to the Virgin Mary.

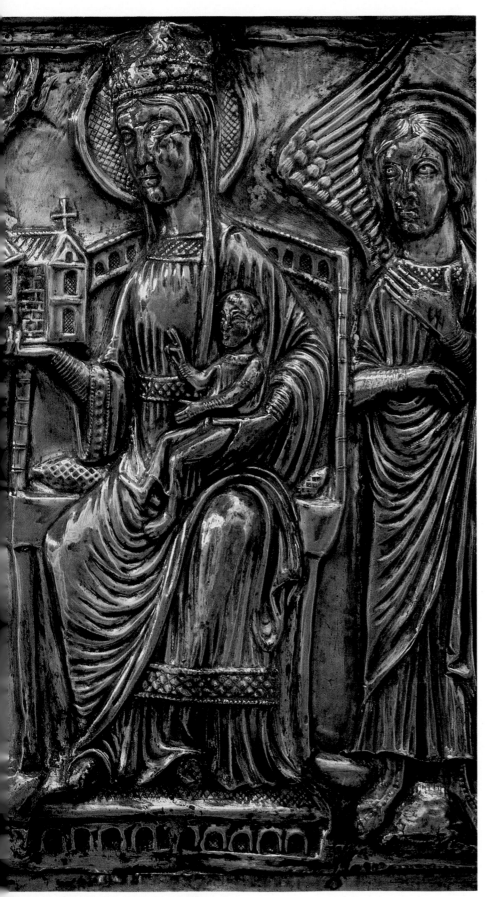

On this throne made of Greek marble, Charlemagne sang, prayed, and heard Mass.

El Escorial. Its name, "the slag heap"—taken from local iron mines—hardly evokes its role as symbol of the Spanish Empire and bastion of the Roman Catholic faith. Here, 30 miles north of Madrid, Philip II retreated occasionally from the secular affairs of his empire, the first upon which the sun truly never set.

Philip's reasons for building his monastery and palace, begun in 1563, were twofold: to honor his father, Charles V, and to commemorate a victory over the French on St. Lawrence's feast day. Eleven Spanish monarchs are interred at the Escorial, and St. Lawrence is remembered in the grid pattern of the ground plan, said to resemble the gridiron on which the martyr was roasted alive.

The Escorial is at once austere and lavish, qualities it shared with Philip himself: stark gray granite walls without; within, paintings by such masters as Titian, El Greco, and Hieronymus Bosch. The staggering cost of the building, financed by gold and silver from Spain's colonies in the New World, caused much grumbling in the kingdom. The project took 20,000 workmen 21 years to complete. Philip supervised the construction through a spyglass from his vantage point on a neighboring hill.

Philip saw the Escorial as his stronghold against the rising tide of Protestant heresy—and also as his own guarantee of salvation through the perpetual prayer of the monks who lived there. He began a collection of religious artifacts. Today the trove's 7,000 relics include St. Jerome's head, Mary Magdalene's arm, and St. Maurice's body. Altogether, 10

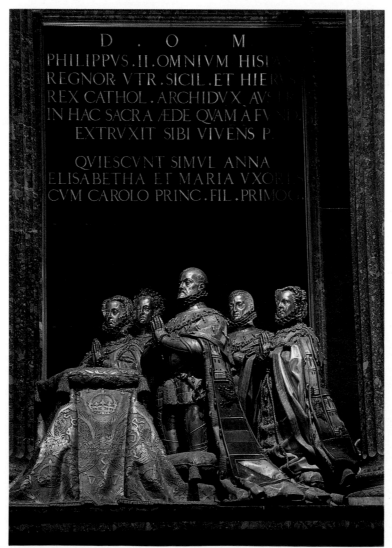

Spain's Philip II and his family kneel, life size, beside the Escorial's high altar.

Restoration in the 1960s saved the Escorial from, among other things, billions of termites.

bodies, 144 heads, and 306 limbs are stored in cupboards near the high altar. A ring of Mary Queen of Scots rests here as well; she sent it to her Catholic ally moments before she was beheaded.

Philip died more slowly, from cancer. He languished almost two months, watching Mass in the church through a wooden partition next to his bed. His successors spent little time at the Escorial. Perhaps the building, so much a reflection of the man who built it, seemed too stern and uncompromising to be comfortable.

Before the remains of kings and queens were brought to this mausoleum, they rotted for years in a vault called the *pudridero,* or fermenting pit.

The Taj Mahal, *India*

In 1631 a woman, faithfully following her husband to a battlefield in India, died there giving birth to her fourteenth child and was buried hastily in a nearby garden. Every Friday, the Muslim holy day, her disconsolate husband visited the grave until military matters called him away. Still overcome by his loss, he planned a final resting place that would bespeak the perfection of their love.

Two decades later Shāh Jahān, the fifth Mogul emperor of India, completed his Taj Mahal. The exquisite mausoleum he raised on the banks of the Yamuna River in Agra enshrines the remains of Arjūmand Bānū Baygam, better known as Mumtāz Mahal, the Chosen One of the Palace.

For 22 years master craftsmen guided 20,000 laborers working the finest materials. Together they created this triumph of Mogul architecture in a tradition stemming from the dynasty's Central Asian roots but mindful of its Indian setting. A Persian dome balanced by four Indian cupolas crowns the white marble tomb, which holds two royal cenotaphs, for Shāh Jahān joined his beloved in death. Surfaces inside and out bear flawlessly executed Persian floral patterns of inlaid diamonds, garnets, turquoise, sapphires, and onyx.

With its slender minarets, the tomb's riverfront aspect most inspired Shāh Jahān, who arrived by barge from his residential fort upriver. But visitors entering from the town of Agra first encounter the Taj through the arched frame of a red sandstone gateway that yields to the clean lines of cypresses and the calm pools of a formal garden. In Mogul times, flowers, fruit trees, and flowering shrubs proliferated in this Islamic Garden of Eden.

An ailing Shāh Jahān was overthrown by his third son in 1658. Thereafter a prisoner in the Agra Fort, the deposed ruler could take comfort in the view from his chamber window: a grieving husband's tribute now regarded as a universal symbol of love.

"A sigh made stone," the Taj Mahal is captured in the reflection of a garden pool.

245

The Auschwitz-Birkenau Concentration Camps, *Poland*

Hell once lived on earth, in a marshy meadow of southern Poland. From 1940 to 1945 the camps of Auschwitz-Birkenau served the ideals of Adolf Hitler's Third Reich. Today they make the world contemplate an evil it might rather forget.

Electrified barbed-wire fences and machine guns in guard towers surrounded Auschwitz: its gallows, crematoriums, pyres, gas chambers, barracks where people slept stacked on shelves, grounds where nameless shadows shuffled from one misery to another, known only by the numbers tattooed on their forearms.

In the autumn of 1941, as chestnuts ripened on the trees about the small railroad station, 12,000 Russian prisoners of war arrived. Nine months later all but 150 were dead: starved, beaten, poisoned, or shot by the Nazis. A million Poles, Jew and gentile alike, lost their lives here. In one night 4,000 Gypsies were killed on the orders of Heinrich Himmler.

Freight cars delivered slave labor for the I. G. Farben chemical works and other German factories. In the spring of 1942 thousands of East European Jews stood terrified under the blossoming chestnuts to be appraised by black-booted SS officers with their death's-head badges, guns, whips, and snarling dogs. Men and women strong enough to work were waved to the left. Most—and usually the children—were waved to the right, to the gas chambers. This ceremony the Nazis designated *Begrüssung*—Welcome!

Hitler's plan for an Aryan super-race brought his Final Solution —the annihilation of European Jews. At Auschwitz and the other death camps, six million Jews died in what Himmler proclaimed to be "a page of glory in our history."

The survivors speak: *The crying of the people at Auschwitz could tear apart the heavens. . . . I saw people . . . crawling on the ground like worms. . . . There was such stench. . . . People knew it was corpses burning. . . . I have not told you of our experiences to harrow you but to strengthen you.*

Like blazing gibbets, the lights of Auschwitz glared upon the agony and murder of almost four million people from 24 nations.

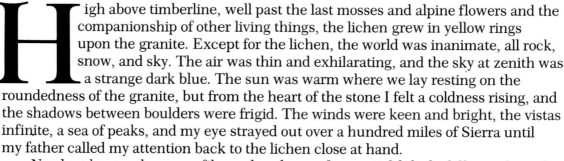

THE COMPANIONSHIP OF LIVING THINGS

High above timberline, well past the last mosses and alpine flowers and the companionship of other living things, the lichen grew in yellow rings upon the granite. Except for the lichen, the world was inanimate, all rock, snow, and sky. The air was thin and exhilarating, and the sky at zenith was a strange dark blue. The sun was warm where we lay resting on the roundedness of the granite, but from the heart of the stone I felt a coldness rising, and the shadows between boulders were frigid. The winds were keen and bright, the vistas infinite, a sea of peaks, and my eye strayed out over a hundred miles of Sierra until my father called my attention back to the lichen close at hand.

No plant keeps a lower profile, and under my fingers it felt little different from the rock. The yellow rings and whorls might have been aboriginal rock paintings. The growth rate of lichen had been measured recently, my father said—not this particular species, but one like it—and in a year it had advanced one-sixteenth of an inch across its rock.

With that I considered lichen, and the wonders of the plant came home. That each of these rings was hundreds of years old. That a plant can survive without soil, on bare rock. That lichen in fact is not *one* plant, but two, a fungus and an alga. That the fungus stores water for the alga, and the alga photosynthesizes food for the fungus.

The lichen was not alone, after all. Here in this high terrain of violent extremes, in the sleet and ice of winter and the ultraviolet light of summer, the lichen prospered and was its own company. It was a rudimentary community unto itself.

The interdependence of lichen is miraculous but commonplace. Interdependence is the rule on this planet. The first organism must have existed alone and isolated, drifting in its warm and empty Archeozoic sea through the eternities of solitude that had to pass before a second variety of life diverged from it, but life has never been alone since. All life today is mutually dependent. "When we try to pick out anything by itself, we find it hitched to everything else in the universe," wrote the naturalist John Muir.

Life, that inextricable commodity, is now everywhere on the planet: on the floor of the abyss, high in the atmosphere, in the hottest deserts and coldest glaciers. Life on earth falls into three broad provinces: the poles, the temperate zone, and the tropics. In the tropics, where the fabric of life is most tightly woven, with the deepest pile, the interactions of living things are Byzantine in complexity. But even in polar regions, where the fabric of life is threadbare, no life stands alone. Polar bears have the seals they depend on, glacier worms have their algae, and Muir's observation on the difficulty of picking things out by themselves holds true.

John Muir's mountains were the Sierra Nevada of California, and those happen to be my mountains too. I first began hiking purposefully in the Sierra when I was six.

The Sierra Nevada is a good place to go for a beginner's course on life on the planet. The range falls entirely within the temperate zone, yet it contains, in its vertical zonation, abbreviated representations of earth's two other broad regimes of life. Gaining altitude in the Sierra, one gains de facto degrees of latitude. Starting up the east side, a walker departs the Sonoran Zone, where he might as well be in the dry tropics, passes through the Transition Zone, which corresponds roughly to the global latitude where he actually is, ascends to the Canadian Zone, where he might as well be in Saskatchewan, to the Hudsonian, where he might be at Hudson's Bay, to the Arctic-Alpine, where he might be in Alaska north of tree line. The Sierra is a desert range where life is sparse and its pattern unconfusing—a good place for a John Muir or a small boy to pick things out and see how they are hitched to everything else in the universe. In the Sierra Nevada all the various ways living things have of relating to one another are on display.

There is predation, the most abrupt and dramatic of those relationships. The evidence is everywhere. It lies about in scat. Breaking up the droppings of Sierra coyotes and owls to learn what they ate is pleasant, serendipitous work, the matrix crumbling away to reveal the bones of the rodents and snakes that have fallen to tooth or claw.

There is the variety of predation called parasitism. A Sierra hiker has more lessons on that relationship than he wants or needs, especially in spring and early summer, when the mosquitoes are most numerous. One humming late-spring evening in the Canadian Zone, my family fought back, preying on our parasites, slapping mosquitoes until we had filled two tin cups with tiny bodies. In the night some unknown, surgically precise scavenger, demonstrating its own style of predation, finished the job, and the next morning there was nothing in the cups but mosquito legs and proboscises.

There is competition. In the great wedges of rocky talus that spill from the sides of Sierra peaks live two species of haymaker. The marmot is a high-altitude woodchuck, the pika a tiny, small-eared relative of the rabbit. Amid the jumbles of angular boulders, the big rodent and the little rodent compete in cutting and drying the alpine grasses that will sustain them through the long months of the Sierra's imitation Alaskan winter.

There is symbiosis, the interdependence of the sort illustrated above timberline by lichen. The word "symbiosis" was made popular, indeed, by the fungus expert Heinrich de Bary, who used it to describe the relationship of the fungus and the alga in lichen.

In the Sierra Nevada, and in ranges immediately east and west, grow the noblest trees on earth: the giant sequoia, the biggest thing that has ever lived; the coast redwood, the tallest; and the bristlecone pine, the oldest tree on earth. Whereas redwoods grow close together in cathedral-dim groves, giant sequoias grow in relative isolation from one another, on rocky soils, in thin air. The giant sequoia lives for the small eternity of 3,000 years. It is wind pollinated, reproducing independently of hummingbirds, bees, and other insects. Giant individuals like the trees called General Sherman and General Grant seem to stand in tall and massive freedom from symbiotic liaisons. In fact, those generals have feet of fungus. Conifers depend on a symbiotic relationship with mycorrhiza, or fungus roots. The threadlike hyphae of the fungi are far better at searching out nutrients than are the root hairs of the trees. A bristlecone, by the time it nears its fifth millennium, has proved itself nearly immortal in its wind-bitten bark and gnarled branches, but underground its mycorrhiza have passed through hundreds of generations.

The Sierra boyhood was formative. I came to like travel in wild places better than almost anything in life. When I was 22, I spent five weeks walking with two friends across the Brooks Range of Alaska. Life in high latitudes is austere. We walked days across the tundra without seeing anything move in it; then we met caribou and the whole landscape seemed to move. Now that bison are gone, caribou make the last great northern herds. When a migration of these big boreal deer is passing, the tundra might be a chill and simplified Serengeti. Whereas African herds are mixed—wildebeest, zebra, impala—the arctic herds, under the reductionism of high latitude, are all one animal, *Rangifer tarandus,* the barren-ground caribou. I glimpsed in the Brooks Range that most earthshaking of zoological spectacles: *the herd,* ten-thousand-hoofed but single-minded, a living river, its chuffs and snorts and ungulate murmurs merging like the babble of a stream. When the migration is at full tide, the very terrain seems to quicken and flow.

On the barren grounds the bread of wolves is caribou. In the choppy, distance-devouring gait of caribou—chins high, antlers tipped back, heels clicking in the odd way of caribou heels—I sensed an urgency, as if each animal believed it was behind schedule, and in their worried double time I could detect the herd's choreographer.

The zonation of my home mountains could not prepare me for the wet tropics. Two-fifths of earth's species live in the rain forest between the Tropics of Capricorn and Cancer. Sun and water are plentiful, tropical environments have been fairly stable over time, and the diversification of habitats and the speciation of plants and animals have run wilder than in any other environment. The vast single-species stands of trees common in the temperate zone are unknown around the Equator. In tropical forest there can be hundreds of species of trees on a given acre.

In the early 1960s we were taught that as many as one million insect species might exist on earth. In the early 1970s Terry Erwin of the Smithsonian Institution developed techniques for fogging the crowns of the tropical forest with insecticide and counting what fell to earth. The blizzards of unknown arthropods that dropped overwhelmed all our notions of insect diversity, of *life's* diversity. From studies in several jungles Erwin has extrapolated that from ten to thirty million insect species live in the tropical canopy.

The tropical forest of our movies and adventure books is a jungle of predation and parasitism. The real jungle, with its humidity, insect hum, and shadows, is more remarkable for its symbionts. There is some redness in tooth and claw, but more than that a mad mutualism, symbionts on all sides striking bargains with one another.

The most ubiquitous and clever of jungle symbionts are probably the ants. Ants are the free radicals of the jungle, combining with almost anything. One ant species, the leaf cutters, are cellar gardeners. Leaf-cutter armies travel the forest floor in jiggly columns, each ant a standard-bearer carrying home the irregular green banner of the leaf fragment it has cut. The leaves are not to eat—not directly. They are compost for farms that the ants will later harvest. Like the algae in lichen, like the giant sequoias, leaf cutters have combined their fates with fungi.

The wettest of wet tropical environments, save for the blue deserts of the open equatorial ocean, is the coral reef. The reef is among the most biologically productive of ecosystems, marine or terrestrial.

My own first corals were in the Palau Islands of the western Pacific. As I drifted over the reef in mask and snorkel, huge clams countersunk in coral heads half-closed defensively before me. Transparent shrimp backed away over the convolutions of brain coral. Blennies peeked out from their tube corals. Damselfish turned tail to flee to their forests of staghorn coral, then faced about to watch me through the branches. It was a world of fluid motions and gaudy and electric colors never seen in the world of air.

Predators are everywhere on the reef. Sharks patrol the reef front. Sea snakes insinuate the coral crevices. Crown-of-thorns starfish flow glacially over living coral rock, devour the polyps, and leave dead rock behind. But on the reef, as in the rain forest, symbiosis is the relationship that catches the eye and the imagination. Clownfish run for protection to sea anemones and *bathe* in the tentacles, immune to the sting. Bug-eyed gobies guard the blind shrimp that maintain the sand holes the two creatures share, odd couples and strange bedfellows.

At the very foundation of the reef is the symbiosis between a coelenterate, the coral polyp, and a small one-celled plant. Within their tissues all reef-building corals have algae. Corals are, in that sense, the lichen of the sea. The algae in coral, fertilized by the metabolic wastes of the polyps, photosynthesize, multiply, and leak organic compounds that the polyps use as food. Neither organism would find sufficient sustenance without the other. For the sake of their resident algae, the corals must always build toward the light, and the result is the coral atoll and the coral reef.

The coral atoll is the planet in microcosm. According to the Gaia theory advanced by James Lovelock and others, the entire earth makes a kind of reef in space. The ecosphere—Gaia—is a multiple entity like the coral community or like lichen; a multiple entity multiplied, a super-superorganism. Like a living thing, the earth modifies its environment in favorable ways. Organisms collaborate to regulate atmospheric chemistry in ways that make the planet more livable. The Gaia theory is good poetry, certainly, if not yet perfect science. It generates a good planetary chauvinism. If Dr. Lovelock is right, or even partly right, the boundaries between ecosystems, and between the larger regimes of life—tropical, temperate, and polar—are not iron curtains. They are more like the slim dotted lines that divide postal zones or school districts, and we are all of us symbionts: wolf, caribou, fungus, alga, polyp, and man.

The spherical blue organism of earth, if it is indeed an organism, is unique. So far as we know, it stands alone in the universe. We need to remember that—to leave room for our fellow symbionts, to keep our predatory and parasitic tendencies in check. This is the one living planet. There seems to be no spare.

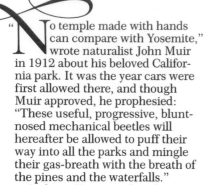

Yosemite National Park, U.S.A.

"No temple made with hands can compare with Yosemite," wrote naturalist John Muir in 1912 about his beloved California park. It was the year cars were first allowed there, and though Muir approved, he prophesied: "These useful, progressive, blunt-nosed mechanical beetles will hereafter be allowed to puff their way into all the parks and mingle their gas-breath with the breath of the pines and the waterfalls."

And into Yosemite they drive—carrying some three million visitors a year who threaten to smother the park with affection.

Their affection is not misplaced. Yosemite's 1,200 square miles embrace a staggering beauty. Three periods of glaciation during the last ice age scoured the park's granite bedrock, leaving bare peaks and rugged terrain where the silt from meltwater lakes turned into alpine meadows that vibrate with color in the spring.

The grandest effect of the glaciation is Yosemite Valley, one mile wide and seven miles long. With spectacular cliffs and waterfalls —among them 1,612-foot Ribbon Falls, the third highest free-leaping cascade in the world—the valley attracts most of Yosemite's visitors. Some come, as Muir advised, to "climb the mountains and get their good tidings," others to hang-glide off 3,200-foot Glacier Point. So many campers lash onto each others' tent poles at night that when someone strikes a tent in the morning, the park staff jokes, the whole camp collapses.

Yosemite has a bank and a beauty parlor, a jail and an annual crime rate. But the park also incorporates five of the seven life zones in the United States—and an amazing variety of plant and animal life. There are three groves of giant sequoias as well as winter walks where you can stoop to watch snow fleas dance. With inspired management and a mindful public, the park will remain forever what it was to John Muir— "about as divine as anything the heart of man can conceive."

The 3,000-foot granite face of El Capitan draws hundreds of climbers a year.

Opposite: Club moss is a friendly tenant for maple trees, which draw nutrients from it with rootlike tendrils.

Unfurling in the ceaseless drip of water on the rain forest floor, hellebore leaves vie for light and space.

Mushrooms, the spore fruit of fungi, poke through the rain forest's dense undergrowth.

Few places in the world offer such ecological variety as 1,400-square-mile Olympic National Park on Washington's Olympic Peninsula. The expanse stretching south from Hurricane Ridge, across flowering alpine meadows to snowcapped Mount Olympus and the Bailey Range, resembles the Swiss Alps. Not far away, the rocky Pacific coast shelters intricate webs of life in tide pools and on massive rock outcrops jutting from the sea.

Just a few miles in from the ocean and downslope from some 60 glaciers lies the park's most remarkable feature—one of the few temperate rain forests in the world. Storms brewing over warm Pacific currents slam into the mountains, dropping 134 inches of rain a year —the highest precipitation in the continental United States.

Walking in the cool rain forest is like being inside a leafy sanctuary with the pungent smell of decaying leaves as incense. Huge conifers, including some of the world's largest specimens of firs, hemlocks, and cedars, reach heights of 230 feet. Branches of big-leaf maple arch outward as far as 40 feet—each limb perhaps a ton of wood, leaf, and hanging moss. Understories of alders and willows filter sunlight into a surrealistic soft green glow. Below, mosses, ferns, lichens, wildflowers, and shrubs compete for limited light amid a seemingly unlimited supply of water. Naturalist Roger Tory Peterson called this luxuriant growth "the greatest weight of living matter, per acre, in the world."

That great bulk hardly changes. Growth balances decay. Tree seedlings can rarely root in the crowded, acidic forest floor, but when an old conifer falls, hundreds of them sprout in colonnades along the decaying trunk. Their roots slowly curl around the nurse log, sometimes leaving the young trees standing on tiptoe after the fallen giant rots. The first saplings to tap the soil's nutrients outdistance their competitors. Centuries later, a soldierly row of survivors reaches full growth, and a tiny part of the forest regains its stature.

255

Iguazú National Park, *Argentina,* and Iguaçu National Park, *Brazil*

The ground shudders and a rumble explodes through the rain forest. A train? An earthquake? A volcanic eruption?

No, the Iguaçu River as it roars out of the jungle and hurls itself over cliffs between Argentina and Brazil—the finale of its twisting journey through Brazil's southern highlands. When the rainy season swells the river, an almost unbroken sheet of silty water pours over a two-mile-wide lava crescent, a cataract nearly as broad as three Niagaras. From August to October, when the river is lower, rock ledges divide the misty waters into almost 300 cascades. "This makes Niagara look like a kitchen faucet," said Eleanor Roosevelt when she first saw the world's widest waterfall.

Above the impact of water on rock hovers a perpetual umbrella of mist a hundred feet high, prompting Guaraní Indians to call this area "the place where clouds are born." They named the falls Iguazú, or "great water." Today the Argentines know them as Iguazú, the Brazilians as Iguaçu. National parks on both sides of the falls protect 925 square miles of subtropical rain forest—one of the world's richest ecosystems.

Sheltered by the falling water, dusky swifts nest on slippery black rocks behind the falls, their eggs resting on ledges barely an inch wide. During the day these daredevils spiral high above the falls, tracing arabesques in the sky as they scoop up insects. At dusk they plummet toward the curtain of water, slice through with wings folded, and, swooping upward, lock onto the rocks with outstretched feet.

Clouds of spray churned up by the thundering water nourish the

Like an inland sea plunging into a chasm, the Iguaçu River tumbles over two-mile-wide cliffs linking Brazil and Argentina to form the world's widest falls.

red soil for miles around. Ferns, mosses, bamboos, and orchids luxuriate on nearly every ledge and cliff not pummeled by water. Each leaf is angled to collect maximum sunlight.

Hundreds of species of trees lean toward the falls, their boughs tangled with pink begonias, flowering vines, and showy bromeliads whose rosettes of spiky leaves form a chalice always filled with water—a useful drinking place and nursery for a miniature world of insects, invertebrates, and amphibians. The branches of host trees become balconies for thick mats of epiphytes, or "air plants," their roots drawing nutrients from dust and mist. Coconut palms stand along the riverbank, silent sentinels as half a million cubic feet of water rumble past each second during the rainy season.

Through the trees dart thousands of jewel-toned butterflies— yellow, orange, iridescent blue, black-and-white with red dots— from the tiniest to the unbelievably gigantic, eight inches from wingtip to wingtip. Pigment colors the wings of all these butterflies except the lustrous blue morphos, whose wings reflect the blue rays of daylight. Male morphos, their eyes sensitive to blue, will sometimes court a blue shirt.

Though the thunderous voice of the falls must have mystified the travel-weary Spanish explorer Álvar Núñez Cabeza de Vaca as he approached them through the rain forest in 1541, this first European visitor was not awed by the spectacle. But to the Guaraní, the emerald jungle surrounding the falls was otherworldly enough to be a burial place for their dead.

Râs Muḥammad, *Egypt*

Just yards away from the rocky desert the Bible calls the "great and terrible wilderness" grows a garden of stupefying color and richness. Iridescent blue "shrubs" and purple "blossoms" sway gently among yellow "fruits" and pink "stones."

This improbable garden blooms beneath the waveless surface of the northern Red Sea, just off the cape of Râs Muḥammad, where the Sinai Peninsula dwindles to a gnarled limestone promontory. But what appears a profusion of plant life is actually a rainbowlike tangle of sea animals, one of the most varied in the world. Sponges, hard and soft corals, urchins, and gorgonians dwell on the side of a reef that plunges as deep as 230 feet.

Millions of coral animals have built the reef over the centuries. This wall grows as each hard coral polyp—a tube topped by a tentacle-ringed mouth—encircles itself with a limestone skeleton atop the skeleton of an ancestor. Hard corals multiply in colonies that produce domes, antlers, pyramids, or bouquets. While most polyps are only millimeters wide, a colony can weigh several hundred pounds.

Delicate as they seem, corals collectively form a voracious hunting machine. At night they extend their polyps and spear tiny floating animals—zooplankton—with minute harpoons that uncoil from cells in their tentacles. Corals also become prey: Crown-of-thorns starfish thrust their stomachs through their mouths to engulf and digest corals; yellow-and-black butterflyfish nibble the polyps. Corals even attack each other, casting lethal spaghetti-like filaments into the polyps of neighboring colonies competing for space on the reef.

But eat-or-be-eaten is not the reef's only rule. Red-and-white shrimp hover near fissures in the coral, waving white antennae to advertise a community service. They climb into the mouths of moray eels and purple-and-yellow angelfish, cleaning out parasites, bits of food, and dead skin. In return, predators refrain from snapping their jaws, keeping the shrimp temporarily secure in this watery jungle.

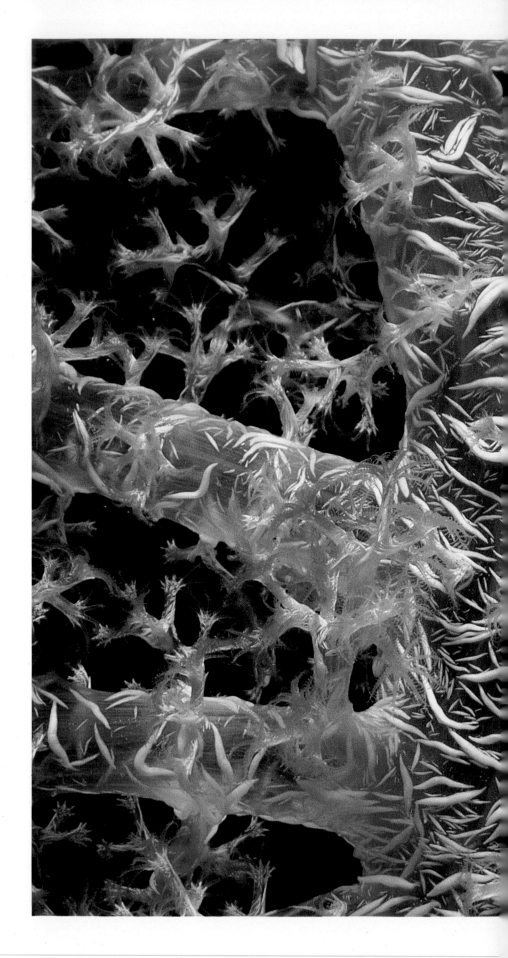

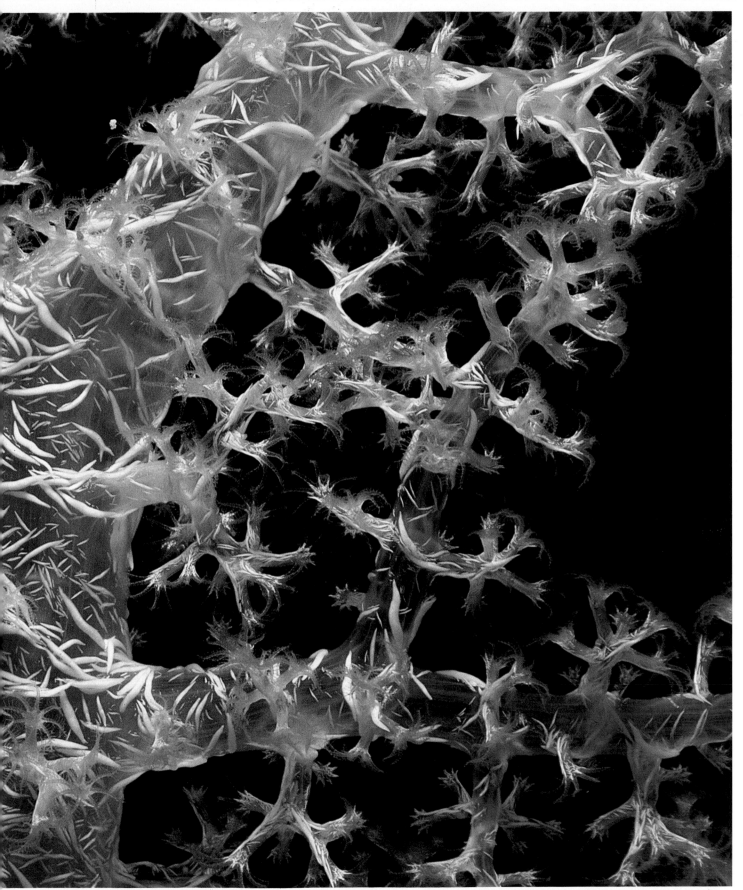

Looking as innocent as cherry blossoms, *Dendronephthya* coral polyps spear plankton with tiny harpoons. These soft corals secrete calcareous spikes to deter predators.

The Great Barrier Reef,
Australia

You can see it from the moon. Parallel to Australia's northeastern coast stretches the world's largest system of coral reefs—largest now or ever, as far as geologists can tell. It is some 1,250 miles long, 80,000 square miles in area (about the size of Great Britain), and hundreds of feet thick—the biggest thing on earth built by living creatures.

Most of the Great Barrier Reef is not a single underwater wall but a thick spatter of individual reefs anchored to a monolithic limestone ridge, itself secreted by those same creatures, tiny coral polyps, over the past 28 million years.

Corals thrive best on the ocean side of a reef, where clear water lets in the sunlight and where the waves of the open sea bring nutrients. Young fringing reefs, which grow just offshore, tend therefore to develop seaward until, ages later, a greatly enlarged reef stands scores of miles from the coast.

This is the mature barrier reef, home to countless interdependent species—hard and soft corals, shellfish, anemones, fish, sponges, and others. They help shape the architecture of the reef, extending it seaward in massive, irregular bulges of coral rock. The angled face of the reef deflects incoming waves, turning some waves back on themselves and sending others sideways into each other. The reef tames the ocean by directing its enormous energy against itself.

As the reef migrates away from shore, many corals on the landward side die off, leaving a lagoon or an enclosed sound. Parrotfish crunch away at the old coral with their beaklike mouths, digesting algae and excreting the rest as sand, as much as a ton a year per fish. Some of the sand washes up on old reefs to make islands— nesting sites for seabirds. More of it ends up on shore, as the brilliant white beaches that attract human sunbathers and land developers.

Corals subdue the sea, build islands, spawn beaches, lay down the very bedrock. Few animals weave themselves so thoroughly into the geological fabric of the planet.

A tube coral snares a careless fish, whose nutrients will be shared with the rest of the colony.

Above: Like many reef animals, this gaping soldierfish feeds by night and shelters in crevices by day.
Opposite: The dark ribbon of Hardy's Channel, a natural passage, winds through the Great Barrier Reef.

Plitvice Lakes
National Park, *Yugoslavia*

A queen prayed for rain and heaven answered. As the sky darkened, villagers saw their monarch's face reflected in the clouds, weeping. As she cried, a downpour quenched the withered earth and created the cascading lakes of Plitvice. So legend says, but nature tells another story.

Forming a watery staircase between the forested mountains and shrub-covered canyons of northwestern Yugoslavia, Plitvice's sixteen lakes spill from one into the next over descending tiers of natural dams. To one visitor, this three-mile-long geological wonder looked as though the "resident giant had walked off leaving his upstairs tap to overflow."

The architects? Tiny organisms in the water that began their work 50,000 years ago. These mosses, algae, and bacteria become encrusted with waterborne minerals and gradually form layers of travertine, a kind of limestone. The travertine deposits grow a third of an inch each year and build up craggy barriers between the lakes. These formations, many of them honeycombed with caves where prehistoric hunters once lived, provide a mossy backdrop for Plitvice's main attraction—falling water.

At every turn along bordering footpaths, the water sings. Tumbling from a variety of heights, streams trickle, spurt, and thunder into azure and emerald pools. At plummet's end the sun paints rainbows in the mist.

Kingfishers skim the pools below the falls to snatch small trout. Wild boars splash in the ponds and wallows, and otters build dens in waterside thickets.

Humans, too, find refuge at Plitvice, once called Satan's playground because it was the scene of lengthy warfare after Ottoman Turks invaded in the 15th century. Today poets, artists, statesmen, and tourists come here to rest, to explore, and to think, following the advice of one enthusiast: "The Plitvice Lakes should only be contemplated, lest one should defile Nature."

Formed by rock that grows, Plitvice's waterfalls flow into the gently moving Korana River.

Los Glaciares
National Park, *Argentina*

The ice ages still cling to the spiny peaks and beech-clad slopes of the southern Andes, where nine glaciers spill into Argentina's Los Glaciares National Park from the southern Patagonian ice field. This mass of ice—largest in the Southern Hemisphere outside Antarctica—rises in some of the coldest, wettest weather on earth. Storms rage for weeks, and howling 125-mile-an-hour winds scour huge trenches in the ice.

Although most of the world's glaciers are retreating, the Moreno Glacier continues to advance, curving 33 miles down a mountainside and poking its snout into Lake Argentino. The glacier's face measures more than two miles wide and 200 feet high. Compressed by its own weight, the glacier has a bluish cast: When light strikes the densely packed ice crystals, they absorb all the colors of the spectrum but blue.

Streams rush over the glacier's snaggled surface and plunge through deep shafts to rivers flowing beneath the ice. Inching forward, the ice creaks, pops, and groans. Fissures honeycomb the glacier and leave giant fingers of ice pointing skyward. Cathedral-size chunks of the face break off and crash into the lake, raising 60-foot-high waves. Every few years the glacier creeps across a narrow arm of the lake, creating a frozen dam. Water builds up and then bursts through in a torrent that floods the valley below.

The advancing glacier sometimes plows down the surrounding beech forest, home to condors, hummingbirds, chinchillas, and deer. Flocks of reddish-green parakeets fly over ice abloom with pink patches of snow algae— the first link in the glacial food chain. Protected from the cold by a natural antifreeze, the algae live on nutrients dissolved in the snow and may serve as food for the dark, inch-long ice worms that wriggle in pools of meltwater or slush on many glaciers. To avoid overheating, the worms burrow into the snow when the midday sun warms the rime-coated remnants of an even colder age.

Made of ice thousands of years old, the 75-square-mile Moreno Glacier noses into Lake Argentino.

Bryce Canyon National Park, *U.S.A.*

he Paiute Indians called it "red rocks standing like men in a bowl-shaped canyon." In their world view Bryce Canyon showed the wrath of a god who had turned its earlier residents— lizards, birds, and humanlike creatures—into stone as punishment for their evil ways.

To geologists the canyon shows a different origin. Sixty million years ago a deep lake covered southern Utah. Sediments carried into the lake by rivers, streams, and runoff eventually turned into limestone layers of varying hardness, 2,000 feet thick. About sixteen million years ago earth's crust stirred, thrusting up the rock and breaking it apart into large plateaus. Water—summer rain and winter snow and ice—transformed these plateaus. At Bryce, water gnawed at the eastern side of the tableland to produce a fantastically carved escarpment. Eroding at different rates, the hard and soft rock make shapes that tickle the urge to name them: Queen Victoria, the Three Wise Men, Wall Street, Tower Bridge, Hindu Temple. . . .

Some of the wayward animals of the Paiute legend must have redeemed themselves: The 56-square-mile national park is home to hundreds of species. At dawn and dusk, mule deer browse among waxy manzanita bushes on the 8,000-foot-high plateau, careful to avoid the park's bobcats, coyotes, and mountain lions. Eagles, hawks, and owls hunt rodents from caves just beneath the plateau's rim. The birds' prey, including marmots, ground squirrels, and prairie dogs, nibble flowers and berries farther down the canyon.

As for the Paiutes, they fought off raiding Utes and Navajos but lost to the press of white settlers who brought livestock to southern Utah in the 1870s. Ebenezer Bryce, a Mormon carpenter from Scotland, tried to graze cattle amid the canyon's towering rocks. Bryce soon moved to Arizona, leaving behind his name and a spirited epithet for the canyon: "A hell of a place to lose a cow!"

Pages 266-67: Minerals in the rock impart color to the spires of Bryce Canyon's Silent City.

Japan's highest peak, Fuji-san rises above the clouds and smoggy haze of the crowded Tōkyō-Kyōto urban corridor in central Japan.

Fuji-san, *Japan*

Its consummate shape is what helps make this volcano so sacred to the pilgrims of the Fujiko sect. On a summer day you can hear them among the hordes of weekend climbers: in white robes and straw sandals, chanting their way up Fuji-san.

Fuji-san. Not Fuji—and only foreigners say Fujiyama (literally "Fujimountain"). San means "mount" and is also the honorific of respect, appropriate for this 12,388-foot-high symbol of Japan.

But like Fuji-san itself, that respect has eroded. Some of the recreational hikers strew the trails with trash. Others try stunts, like bicycling up or playing baseball in the crater. But many climb earnestly: the young, the old, even amputees. Some 500,000 hikers a year, in all. On a summer weekend 30,000 people may be on the trails. No peak so high is climbed so much.

Despite crowds, the pilgrims keep alive the mountain's Shinto traditions. While most hikers ride buses to points about 4,000 feet below the top, the pilgrims begin the trek at the bottom, dressing in white robes and performing rituals at the first of the shrines spaced from base to summit. For the pilgrims, climbing Fuji-san's near-perfect cone celebrates a harmony between nature and humankind so basic that Shinto does not even recognize the Western distinction between the two. In the purity, the ideal form, of the holy mountain's simple lines, the pilgrims seek purity for themselves.

That geometrical beauty typifies composite volcanoes with central vents. Fuji-san is one of earth's finest, its layered cone built by intermittent eruptions, sometimes of ash, sometimes of lava. The last blowup, in 1707, covered Edo, today's Tōkyō, with six inches of ash.

Even before then, centuries of erosion had been at work. Gullies on Fuji-san have now grown so big they endanger the profile that has entranced generations of Japanese poets and artists. Hoping to preserve that which inspires, the Japanese are building a wall across the biggest ravine to impede rockslides —man in symbiosis with mountain.

269

Redwood National Park, U.S.A.

When dinosaurs walked the earth, colossal evergreens forested much of the Northern Hemisphere. Today their descendants, the redwoods and sequoias, grow wild only in temperate corners of China and the American Northwest, survivors of ice ages and chain saws.

To protect earth's tallest living things, Redwood National Park was created along a 50-mile strip of northern California where the Pacific Ocean washes the coastal range. The sea breeze douses the rugged canyons with winter rain and summer fog. Fungi, lichens, ferns, and mosses flourish in the cool, moist shade of coast redwoods that spire to 350 feet, higher than the Statue of Liberty.

Sprouting from pinhead-size seeds, these goliaths mature 400 years later, when their trunks measure as much as 20 feet across. But even the stoutest coast redwood looks slim beside its Sierra Nevada cousin, the giant sequoia, whose 35-foot diameter makes it wider than many city streets.

A sharp, clean aroma rises from the redwood forest floor, where salamanders skitter across a layer of decaying vegetation called duff. Wet weather keeps the trees from drying out, but it soaks the unstable soil and rock below, inviting frequent landslides on the steeper slopes. Winds also topple old trees whose shallow roots can no longer hold their lofty trunks in place.

Yurok Indians used fallen redwoods to build canoes and homes, but commercial logging began during the gold rush. Redwoods yield straight, sap-free timber resistant to decay and insects.

The Yuroks believed the spirit Wah-Pek-oo-May-ow splashed a bitter magic potion on the trees so fire would not eat them, but scientists say it is foot-thick, sapless bark that protects mature redwoods from flames. If severe burning does open wounds, later fires can hollow out the cores, making cavities called goose pens because settlers kept poultry in them. With few natural enemies, redwoods can endure 2,000 years. Their hours, said Emerson, "are peaceful centuries."

Above: Douglas iris and other wildflowers spangle second-growth stands of redwoods.
Opposite: Redwoods reach skyward like the spires of a woodland cathedral.

271

Wildebeests and zebras fan across the Serengeti in hoofed caravans more than six miles long.

Serengeti National Park,
Tanzania

"This is the world as it was in the beginning," said a placard once posted at the entrance to Tanzania's Serengeti National Park, home to the largest herds of plains animals on earth.

The rains shape the rhythm of life here, as they did in the Pleistocene epoch, when immense herds of hoofed animals roamed much of the planet. Wildebeests dominate the Serengeti now. Every November, when the rains begin, nearly one and a half million of these bearded, hunch-shouldered antelope thunder into the park from their wooded refuge to the north. Tracking storm clouds, which they can spot from 60 miles away, they seek the freshly sprouted grass.

Nearly a million gazelles and 200,000 zebras migrate with the wildebeests. In May, as the rains slacken and the grasslands begin to dry, the animals continue their clockwise sweep to the permanent water holes of the western woodlands. The zebras lead the way, chomping down the tall grass and clearing a path for the wildebeests and gazelles. In August the herds return to their northern refuge.

The wildebeests' ceaseless trek defines the Serengeti Plain: 10,000 square miles in Tanzania and Kenya, about half of it protected by the park. Sharing this realm are elephants, some 25 species of hoofed animals, and their predators—lions and leopards, cheetahs, hyenas and wild dogs. Predators reduce the risk of mass starvation by helping to keep hoofed game populations at numbers the land can support.

In the 1890s an epidemic of rinderpest virus decimated the Serengeti's wildlife and domestic cattle. Unimpeded by grazing throngs, the savanna darkened to thick woods. The grasslands began to return in the 1960s, when the trees were toppled by an influx of elephants and burned by safari hunters and Masai herders. As the rinderpest subsided and unusually heavy rains fed the grass, wildebeest numbers jumped a staggering sixfold. But the system remains fragile: A severe drought could kill a million wildebeests in a single season.

273

Etosha National Park,
Namibia

Each year brings the same question: Will the flamingos return to Etosha? In times of drought, sometimes lasting several years, the salt pan in this wildlife reserve in southwestern Africa lies cracked and glistening—"the place of dry water," Africans call it. But in good years, when the monsoon brings 18 inches of rain between January and April, Etosha Pan turns into a shallow lake up to 60 miles long.

Then, out of nowhere it seems, the flamingos arrive by the tens of thousands—more than a million in peak years. Since they migrate at night over sparsely populated areas, it took researchers years to realize that the greater and lesser flamingos of the southwest and those of the Rift Valley lakes in East Africa form one mobile continental flock.

They nest on mud islands secure from major predators, breeding only when the water contains plenty of food. Adults eat algae and tiny crustaceans, strained through hairlike projections in their beaks, and feed their downy gray chicks a red liquid secreted from their throats. Over the years young birds turn pink by eating the same food as adults, which contains red pigments that flamingos reprocess and store in feathers and leg skin. If the rains stop early, parents may abandon their flightless chicks in the evaporating lake. In 1969 park-sponsored Operation Flamingo rescued 20,000 clay-mired orphans. In 1971 25,000 tottered on their spindly legs to water 50 miles away.

Full-time residents of 8,600-square-mile Etosha National Park range from 2,000 elephants to tiny dik-dik antelopes and 378 species of birds. Herds of zebra, springbok, and wildebeest jostle around water holes in the semiarid savanna. Some of Etosha's 200 lions —the zebras' chief predators— flatten their tawny bulks in nearby scrub. Once, when plentiful food in protected surroundings drove the number of lions too high, park biologists put female lions "on the pill," implanting time-release contraceptives in their necks in an effort to restore nature's balance.

In the rainy season, flamingos flock to 1,800-square-mile Etosha Pan, rich in minerals and algae.

Coco-de-mer palms bear 40-pound nuts, the world's largest.

Beneath the rustling palms on a tropical island in the Indian Ocean, a 19th-century British military hero thought he had discovered the Garden of Eden. When Gen. Charles Gordon visited the Seychelles island of Praslin in 1881, he found himself in a lush forest of palms, flowering *bois rouge* trees, thick-leaved *capucins,* and screw pines perched high in the air on stiltlike roots.

In the heart-shaped fruit of *coco-de-mer* palms growing in the Vallée de Mai, Gordon saw proof that Adam and Eve once walked here. Citing the biblical depiction of the heart as the seat of desire, and reasoning that "if curiosity could be excited by any tree, it would be this," he concluded that the coco-de-mer palm was the tree of knowledge that had tempted Eve into sin. The suggestive shape of the twin-cheeked coco-de-mer—the forbidden fruit—stoked Gordon's idea and inspired the local legend that male coco-de-mer trees, with their dangling, yellow-flowered catkins, let go of the earth during storms and stride over to female trees for a frond-smacking night of passion. Fruits of these romances are said to contain a powerful aphrodisiac.

For centuries before French explorers found the palms on Praslin Island in 1768, coco-de-mer nuts had washed up on foreign shores. Nothing like these strange seeds grew in the known world, so they were thought to come from an underwater tree. Hence the name coco-de-mer, or sea coconut.

Today 4,000 coco-de-mer palms stand in primeval splendor in the Vallée de Mai, a 46-acre nature reserve. Sunlight filters through their 20-foot-long fronds to the forest floor, where caecilians—which look like large worms but are distant kin to frogs—burrow deep into the humus. Green geckos sun themselves on pink granite boulders or scamper up the palms, stippling female blossoms with pollen. And rare black parrots whistle in the early morning calm before the trade winds, soft with the scent of vanilla blossoms, rattle the palm fronds of Paradise.

Twenty-foot-long fronds crown the coco-de-mer, known as the prince of palms. Mature trees may reach a hundred feet and live 800 years.

OUR SHARED INHERITANCE

Some days, when my dog is standing next to me outdoors with his shoulder brushing against my knee, I feel as though we're not simply friends and allies but that my legs actually begin inside his body, that my roots stem from him and he is my live ancestor and ancient relation. When we jog together or chase after a rabbit, when he noses me and I rub my hands through the fur on his neck, when he sleeps protectively next to my head on a camping trip, there is a deep comfort in the association which, apart from our friendship, is rather like what I feel when I'm lying at my ease on the ground with thick grass between my fingers and the uneven soft earth under my back and shoulders, gazing into the open sky.

But of course the dog is a creature, even quite *personal,* not like the grass and ground. And just as he's personal, I'm animal. Lolling like a lizard in the sun until I lose track of time, then drinking thirstily—or hunching with my back turned to a cold wind like a horse or a buffalo—I don't have much trouble knowing who I am, at least the part of me that's animal. We don't need to dive repeatedly into big ocean rollers, or hike off-road for 30 miles and sleep in the spruce trees under an alpine glacier, to feel the swell of prehistory in our fluids and bones. We need only make love. Making love—or when you are otherwise at peace, lying alone on your back in the grass facing the sky—you can feel your own mortality stretch out until you know you will die not into a narrow grave, but finally into the folds of the ocean and sky.

Walk in the fields till you ache, till your teeth are chattering, or you're slick with hot sweat. Get so hungry you crouch a bit over your plate as if ready to spear the hand of anybody who tries to touch your food. Sleep fitfully like an animal—or sleep lusciously deeply; plenty of animals do that too. Nature is often with us, a busybody even in the city, intervening guerrilla-fashion against the odds in many of our lace-curtain moments and activities. Though crushed by heavy industry and postindustrial technology, cloverleafed with suburbs, veneered by hothouse transplant species, nature is still chameleon enough to give us rest and pleasure when we need rest and pleasure, if we can manage to accept the gift, until eventually, with a heart attack perhaps, we return to a state of nature anyway, "paying our debt to nature," as the old saw goes.

Feel your heartbeat, touch the hard curve of your skull under your cheek: They are nature too. If I listen to my own breathing, the susurration sounds like small waves gently toppling on a beach, each one stroking the sand while sliding back into the sea. The wind itself hasn't stopped blowing through the arroyos of our cities. Wind and waves, like snow and sunsets, lakes and mountains, will outlast both humanity and wildlife no matter how the world we are transforming ends up. But they're not animate, and most of us, if we have any sort of religious faith or intuition, suspect that God is part of life and life is part of God. God, therefore, isn't "dead" (in the phrase of the 1960s) but possibly is dying, if variety of life counts for very much. Wherever one happens to live, whatever habitat of land or beach or water one may have gotten to know, the spectrum of life and its species is withering, shrinking, and smothering as though in a vise.

I've been staying for a month in Virginia, not far from a pond that is handsomely black in patches, shiny or pewtery in other places, where the sun hits at a slant, or else a muzzy, dreamy amber—if it doesn't mirror a whole brass band of red and yellow autumn trees in the northwest cove. I can see the heads of beavers, perch, and frogs poke up and swim along, then plunge, and various dead snags and curious assemblages of dry-ki sticking out of the water. Enough acres of briary oak woods border one side of the pond that a few animal prints mark the mud and wet leaves at the inlet: scrambly squirrel, fastidious fox, frenetic mink. Although there's a roaring highway on the other side, to go and stroll about makes for a lovely half an hour. An Ophelia mood would be required to imagine threatening factors operating here; and yet a developer could bulldoze the whole woods and parcel up the pond's banks for condominiums in a matter of a dozen days.

As in any temperate dab of woods, I know that breech-clothed Indians once walked this ground, hunting with arrows, cooking in a fire pit. But the idea has no echoes for me, no reality. I don't pause to think about it; it's too far back. To catch a memorable whiff of the subsistence way of living, one must travel to the edge of a true wilderness and maybe see six seals plunked headfirst in the snow outside an Eskimo's hut and watch him skin a polar bear, the outer shell of the animal collapsing upon itself when cut loose from the body like a miscreant beast squashed flat in a TV cartoon—or camp for several nights in a Louisiana bayou on an island ringed around by the coal-red sparks of alligators' eyes floating in the water, with the cries of roosting long-legged birds roused by the earliest streaks of dawn under the starlit sky. We need such self-sustaining communities—lions with their migrating herds of zebras and wildebeests, elephants with their acacia trees, snow leopards and wild sheep in the Himalayas, and moose and pondgrass in Montana, as well as tribal peoples like the Masai, tending cattle near the Ngorongoro Crater, or the Kababish and Hadendowa, herding camels at the fringe of the Sahara with their nomadic culture intact—in order for us in the "developed world" to be able to imagine ourselves some day journeying somewhere else, in the past or present, and seeing or doing wilderness things.

Yet so few obstacles of terrain and mileage matter to us lately, it's hard to reach back. There is no fire of frostbite and snow blindness, no staggeringly unclimbable mountain range heaving up and housing malign spirits, no presiding constancy in the procedures of nature that we notice continually. Besides its hazards and its constancy, nature not long ago was onion-skinned with riddles for everybody who lived in intimacy with it. But we have overridden or sidestepped the hazards, and the riddles have become obscured like starlight above a lighted city. Extreme cold may suddenly feel like being stranded in a wilderness, because we can die from it. So does the ocean still, when we are out on it and it roughens alarmingly. Wild places have no calendar of rules that guarantees our safety at the expense of the rest of nature and promises that it will always be the deer and fish who die to feed us, not us in pursuing them.

Nevertheless, the range of potential encapsuled in us is so far-flung we cannot expect to explore it without immersing ourselves out of our regular depth in nature occasionally. Do we have humor, self-reliance, courage, and sensible judgment when living out of a backpack? Does beauty still buoy our spirits when nobody is around to applaud our exuberance? Can we lie down on a bed of moss miles from home and recoup our strength when it is gone? Although back home we may have noticed nature when the weather dripped or a cat stalked a robin, do we recognize signs in the sky and animals' reactions when it really counts and we're alone?

In an ordinary tract of woods we have to glide far back into ourselves or achieve a kind of preternatural state of exhausted disorientation in order to catch a sense of what the wilderness was. One cannot easily visualize a forest of 150-foot trees from seeing the quarter-grown specimens that our woods comprise nowadays (at what is Dartmouth College in New Hampshire, a 270-foot white pine was felled). Yet on the other hand, simply gazing at the stars—staring at them till you need to clutch the ground so as not to tumble out into them forever and ever—is to look into a final wilderness. More than ancient rock or desiccated desert, they seem to leave us out of consideration. Biblically, the wilderness meant not the exhilarating swarm of handsome, fascinating wildlife on the Serengeti Plain, but where God wasn't and man wasn't. Animals were rocks that squalled and clawed (as some of the enthusiastic folk who tour African game parks inside Land-Rovers would find themselves agreeing if the vehicles broke down and the animals they follow admiringly were suddenly to take note of them as part of the natural scene), not animals as romantic museum pieces, the way we often see them.

Yet I still sometimes meet people who are throwbacks to the old-time frontiersmen—who will cache away a grubstake of supplies somewhere in the Alaska Range to come back to if they have to leave the mountains for a spell. A great many others like to gaze off someplace that they couldn't easily hike to or climb to. Where the Alaska Highway skirts the massifs of the St. Elias Mountains, such people park their cars and stand and stare, suspending the hectic schedule of their trip, ambiguously drawn to, as well as awed by, the bulk and silence of the peaks. Only being able to *come at* such a spot, indulging in a quick, ambitious pleasure jaunt, or, back home, the very possession of space has become the medallion of wealth and luxury—owning property enough for the sky to show, the wind to blow, the birds to nest and trees to grow, with room for vegetation to remain unkempt on a spare tract as well as the obligatory stretch that's tightly trimmed in front of the house. Especially, wealth has grown to mean the freedom to buzz off to exotic locales where tribespeople "still hunt with a blowgun" or eat narwhal, to Moroccan oases where women go voluminously veiled, volcanic islets where puffins nest, Buddhist villages hung with prayer flags, to watch a stout cruise ship poking its stubby snout into Antarctica's bays, to buy a waterskin from a Samburu, visit Doubtful Sound in New Zealand and Ibb and Kawkabān in Yemen. "It's almost too late, it's all going fast," they like to say.

A life even just lived by natural light has become a rare experience. It can be dumbfounding to stop and think of the masterworks of art and literature that were created without electricity—by daylight or by beeswax—from Shakespeare's dramas to the cathedral at Chartres. To imagine oneself at Chartres seven or eight hundred years ago is almost as hard as winging into prehistory. To work a quarter of a century (which seemed miraculously swift at the time) not for either money or fame but in exaltation of God: This may be as far removed from our concept of artistic or other endeavor as it would be to still hunt wildlife for our meals. Brand-new temples of commerce in places like Stamford, Connecticut, might dwarf the cathedral at Chartres, the Duomo in Florence, the Tower of London in absolute scale, and the people pouring into them every morning outnumber the Samburu of the Kenyan veld, the Beni Amer of the Sudanese desert, the Inupiat Eskimos, and other discrete though endangered peoples; but the world is highly organized now to protect only Stamford.

Many of us have a collection of stunningly memorable sites that we have managed to visit—the Capitoline Hill in Rome, the Acropolis in Athens, Granada's Alhambra, Cairo's Sphinx, the Greek temples in Sicily at Agrigento, the old caves on the marvelously wild island of Sámos, Les Invalides in Paris—which because of the resplendent weather, the company of somebody who was with us, the passionate, clairvoyant interval of life at which we saw them, can bring a smile at any time, like a library of astonishments in the mind's eye. And we like to think that nature, like culture and commerce, is still in us, that we contain what we need of it, a love of sunrises and greenery, good food, fresh air and running water, comely topography and outdoor exercise. Though we also contain more than we prefer to acknowledge—nature as rain and ice, swamp and ruthlessness— most of us no longer believe that we are *in* nature, that we swim like fish in the midst of it and will die if the water sours.

Life is a matter of life *and* death, and if we forget that, we shorten our sense of timeliness and purpose. Nature doesn't do face-lifts or even switch on the streetlights. It drags out every minute of the bitter winter and makes no significant exceptions except through a long span of millennia. That is its glory, whereas we have existed like scintillations on the water, living fabulously, dying quickly. We still die quickly but lately have become like laser beams, with a blinding, sunlike power to destroy. In practically a flash we can burn to a crisp whole chunks of nature, constellations of species—tens of thousands each year in tropical rain forests alone, according to the latest estimate—and having lost our sense of rootedness, we feel no fear.

I don't say that if we all go out and buy a dog to walk with, we will restore our sense of linkage to the rest of creation and a proper reverence or respect for it. Nor will the maintenance of parks and preserves do that. But without preserves and parks, and without a homely, intimate acquaintance with animals and plants at home, it seems to me there would be no hope.

Sagarmatha National Park,
Nepal

Sagarmatha. The name means "whose head touches the sky" in Nepali and honors the mighty Himalayan peak that, to generations of Westerners, has symbolized the ultimate challenge to strength, endurance, and determination—Mount Everest.

Named for a British surveyor who saw it in 1852, the mountain rises to 29,028 feet—the world's highest peak—and stands as the centerpiece of Sagarmatha National Park. Unsuccessful attempts to scale the mountain in the 1920s and '30s gave rise to the notion that it was unclimbable—and spread the tale that the mysterious Abominable Snowman prowled its icy flanks.

Why climb Everest? In the immortal words of British climber George Leigh Mallory: "Because it is there." And while struggling toward the summit on the morning of June 7, 1924, Mallory and his companion, Andrew Irvine, disappeared into swirling mist, never to be seen again. Not until May 1953 did Edmund Hillary of New Zealand and his Sherpa guide, Tenzing Norgay, stand together in triumph on top of the mountain.

But success brought trouble, too. Climbers and tourists swarmed into northeastern Nepal, leaving mounds of trash and burning firewood at an alarming rate—some seven tons per climbing expedition. Soon many hillsides were denuded; floods and erosion threatened Sherpa villages and pastures.

To help restore the balance between human needs and a fragile environment and to preserve Sherpa culture, Sagarmatha National Park was established in 1976. Its 450 square miles include three of the world's highest mountains: Everest, Lhotse, and Cho Oyo. Climbers must now provide their own fuel; solar panels and small hydroelectric generators help relieve the demand for firewood; and reforestation programs aim at restoring trees to barren slopes. Such efforts are needed, one observer noted, to regain "harmony between people and land."

Phortse, one of twenty Sherpa villages within Sagarmatha National Park, lies in shadow beneath the brow of Tawoche Peak.

The 13th-century Church of St. John Kaneo crowns a Lake Ohrid promontory.

The Ohrid Region,
Yugoslavia

Ohrid is a beautiful lake, its crystal waters a haven for living fossils, its hilly shores and bluffs a home to humanity since the dawn of history.

Covering 140 square miles, the oval lake lies mostly in southern Yugoslavia's Macedonia region and extends into neighboring Albania. Ohrid's waters are deep—up to 938 feet in places—and so extraordinarily clear that you can peer 70 feet into its depths.

Ohrid is also one of the world's oldest lakes, formed some five million years ago when a huge slab of the earth's crust slipped downward between parallel faults. Its great age, the fact that it escaped ice age glaciation, and a reasonably pollution-free modern environment have made Ohrid a unique habitat for dozens of snail, worm, crab, and sponge species that have lived on earth 50 million years—and were once thought extinct. Scientists have written hundreds of papers about the lake and its aquatic life, including trout and eel species found nowhere else and prized by gourmets.

Humans have inhabited Ohrid's shores since the Stone Age. The old town of Ohrid, on the lake's northeastern side, once bloomed as a center of Byzantine art and learning. Founded in the sixth century B.C. by Illyrian tribes who called it Lychnidus, the town prospered under Roman rule because of its location on the Via Egnatia, the main overland route between the Aegean and Adriatic Seas.

The arrival of Saints Clement and Naum in the ninth century touched off an explosion of intellectual growth that saw the development of Slavic literature and the construction of schools, libraries, and churches. Elements of this cultural activity persist to this day in dozens of well-preserved churches, some of them sited on rocky promontories above the lake.

The town of Ohrid rises like an amphitheater amid hills dotted with vineyards and gardens. Every house along its steep, winding streets commands a view of the lake—a heritage guarded jealously since the town's beginnings.

A setting sun punctuates Ohrid's placid expanse.

285

Göreme Valley and the Rock Sites of Cappadocia, *Turkey*

In a landscape as bizarre as a surrealistic dream live the cave dwellers of Göreme Valley, known in ancient times as Cappadocia. Today the arid, 43-square-mile valley is a district of Anatolia in central Turkey. Its inhabitants, mostly farmers and herdsmen, till their fields and watch their flocks in much the same way their forefathers did.

Volcanoes set the stage for this labyrinthine land five million years ago, when they spewed thick blankets of ash across the area, then covered them with sheets of lava. Over the millennia, wind and water whittled the lava and ash into thousands of free-standing cones, pinnacles, needles, and spires that local residents call *peri bacalari*—fairy chimneys.

The hand of man is also visible amid the valley's cone-strewn scenery. For at least 16 centuries people have lived in Göreme, burrowing chambers and passageways into the soft rock. From the 4th century until the collapse of the Byzantine Empire in the 15th century, the valley prospered as a center of Christian asceticism and worship. At its most populated, around the 10th century, some 40,000 priests, nuns, hermits, and monks lived at Göreme, honeycombing the cliffs and pinnacles with countless dwellings and more than 500 churches—many of them embellished with rock-cut pillars, altars, friezes, and vividly colored frescoes.

Even today local farmers tend vineyards, apple orchards, and wheat fields in the valley—and occasionally occupy time-honored living quarters in this land shaped by nature and adorned by man.

286

Above: Christ's Nativity brightens the domed ceiling of the Karanlik Kilise—Dark Church.
Opposite: Cappadocia's cone dwellings have provided shelter for monks, mystics, and farmers since the fourth century A.D.

Mont-Saint-Michel and Its Bay, *France*

Linking sea and sky, earth and heaven, Mont-Saint-Michel's otherworldly silhouette has drawn the pious, the scholarly, and the curious for many ages.

Until the eighth century, it is said, the mount was part of the French mainland. Celts, Romans, and Christian hermits had all built shrines on the 256-foot rocky pinnacle rising above the Normandy coast. Then, legend tells, in 708 the archangel Michael commanded a bishop to raise a chapel on the summit. Soon thereafter a great wave engulfed the surrounding forest, leaving Mont-Saint-Michel and its chapel towering over a bay at high tide, over swirls of mud and sand at low.

The cult of St. Michael—the warrior angel and conqueror of Satan—swept across war-torn medieval Europe. Seeking the archangel's blessing, pilgrims streamed to the island. Some lost their lives to quicksand or tides that raced faster than a galloping horse.

Over the centuries the faithful piled ever grander churches and cloisters atop the rock, turning earlier structures into a labyrinth of foundations and crypts. The three-story Gothic abbey known as La Merveille is a paragon of 13th-century monastic architecture.

Mont-Saint-Michel's medieval fortifications withstood sieges by both English and French troops. Yet the monks were driven out by decree during the French Revolution; for the next 70 years the abbey lodged prisoners instead.

Today a magnet for tourists, a restored Mont-Saint-Michel is resisting another incursion. The causeway built from the mainland to the island—plus dikes and dams designed to reclaim land from the sea for farming—has hastened the silting of the bay. By 1980 only one tide in nine washed the mount clear of the mainland. France has demolished some of the earthworks, hoping to restore Mont-Saint-Michel's ethereal setting amid the ebb and flow of the waters. If the project fails, nature threatens to fulfill Victor Hugo's prophecy—that Mont-Saint-Michel may one day rise from cabbage and potato fields.

Sacred for more than a millennium, Mont-Saint-Michel shimmers between water and sky.

From the rubble of Tassili-n-Ajjer come intimations of an Eden past.

Tassili-n-Ajjer, *Algeria*

It would be hard to imagine a worse place for people to live—and thrive—than the middle of the Sahara wasteland. But this is precisely where ancient hunters and herdsmen settled, perhaps as long as 8,000 years ago, while most of Europe shivered through the last ice age.

The place is Tassili-n-Ajjer, a barren, sun-scorched plateau and mountain massif in southeastern Algeria that covers 30,000 square miles. Today the region barely supports snakes, spiders, lizards, and a few Tuareg nomads.

But it was not always so. While Europe lay gripped by glaciers, Tassili-n-Ajjer bloomed with lime and olive trees, oaks, oleanders, and myrtles. Elephants, rhinos, hippos, gazelles, giraffes—and people—basked in a warm, moist Mediterranean climate, refreshing themselves in the limpid pools and lakes fed by myriad streams. Then, gradually, Europe's ice retreated. Africa's climate changed. Hot winds began to blow. The lush countryside grew desiccated. Slowly the animals drifted away. So did the people.

But they left abundant evidence of their presence: graves, broken pots, stone animal pens, arrow points and spearheads. And art—thousands upon thousands of paintings and engravings, some atop one another, emblazon the rocky walls of the canyons and ravines that had been the homeland of these unknown Africans.

Scholars have studied the region since the early 1930s, but only recently have they begun to appreciate the full nature and extent of its archaeological and pictorial treasures. Much remains to be explored. The earliest paintings, perhaps 7,000 to 8,000 years old, show round-headed hunters stalking now extinct antelope. Later drawings depict herdsmen and bowmen in realistic detail, the arrival of the horse about 3,000 years ago, and the earliest camel caravans, around A.D. 200. The dry climate has preserved much of the art, making Tassili-n-Ajjer, as one scholar suggests, "the largest open-air museum in the world."

Human and animal figures enliven a rock-shelter near Tanzoumaitak.

The Ngorongoro Conservation Area,
Tanzania

Our ancestors may have watched millions of years ago as 15,000-foot-high Ngorongoro Volcano spewed rock and ash in thunderous explosions, then collapsed. The resulting crater is today a wildlife-filled basin 10 to 12 miles across, ringed by a forested wall 2,000 feet high.

In the Ngorongoro Conservation Area—3,100 square miles of northern Tanzania—extinct volcanoes fringe the Great Rift Valley. Ash from ancient eruptions has preserved traces of some of the oldest hominids, including footprints that prove early humans walked upright 3.6 million years ago.

At Olduvai Gorge, 30 miles from Ngorongoro Crater, Mary and Louis Leakey found fossils of *Australopithecus boisei*, nicknamed "nutcracker man" because of his massive molars, and of the larger brained *Homo habilis*, or "handy man," a tool user thought to be an ancestor of modern humans. Almost two million years ago these early humans camped along a lake at Olduvai, now a sun-parched canyon. They probably tracked herds migrating across the adjoining Serengeti Plain.

Ngorongoro Crater itself contains prehistoric *bau* boards—rocks carved for playing what may be the world's oldest board game, a diversion still enjoyed by local Masai herders. About 15,000 Masai live within the conservation area; their cattle, sheep, and goats share grazing land with an ever growing population of wildlife.

Ngorongoro's grassy floor teems with more than 30,000 animals, from bat-eared foxes to elephants and rhinos. Each spring, hundreds of thousands of migratory flamingos tinge pink the lake in the center of the long-dead volcano.

Pages 292-93: Called "the world's largest zoo," Ngorongoro is also one of the world's largest craters.

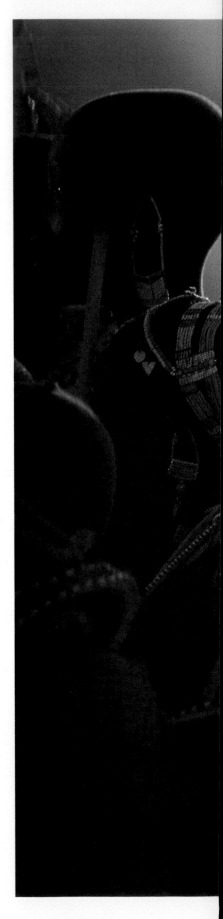

Ngorongoro's lions prey on the region's abundant wildlife, rarely on Masai livestock.

Despite government pressure to modernize, the proud, pastoral Masai cling to traditional dress and customs.

Magpie geese congregate on a lagoon at sundown in Kakadu National Park.

Kakadu National Park,
Australia

There are no alligators in the Alligator River that runs through Kakadu National Park in northern Australia. Only crocodiles. Big ones. Some reach lengths of 20 feet or more where the river mixes with the salty waters of Van Diemen Gulf. Sharks gather here too, near a nub of land aptly named Point Farewell. Smaller crocodiles, a freshwater variety reputedly shy and harmless to humans, live upstream, beyond reach of the tides. Little wonder that European explorers confused their reptiles and misnamed the river.

People live in the park too—as they have for perhaps 40,000 years, ever since they wandered across a land bridge that once linked Australia and New Guinea. They are the Aboriginals. Those who settled this part of Arnhem Land called themselves Gagudju, a name that lives on in 4,800-square-mile Kakadu National Park. The discovery of rich uranium deposits in the area helped spur establishment of the park in 1979 as a way to preserve Aboriginal culture and a delicately balanced ecology.

Kakadu's topography, isolated location, and steaming tropical climate have made it a cauldron of plant and animal life. More than 250 bird species have been counted here—as well as 50 mammal species ranging from anteaters to kangaroos, nearly 100 types of reptiles and amphibians, and 5,000 kinds of insects, including termites that build mud nests up to 20 feet high.

At dusk tens of thousands of magpie geese, spoonbills, herons, egrets, and ibis congregate on a single tidal lagoon. In the rain forest the jungle fowl gather twigs and leaves to construct mounded nests up to 15 feet high and 150 feet around at the base. The bowerbird builds an elaborately decorated archway to lure a mate during the courting season. The long-legged jacana crosses streams and ponds by running across lily pads.

Kakadu's terrain varies from low-lying tidal flats and mangrove swamps to undulating grasslands and woodlands of palm and eucalyptus trees. Then, rising abruptly

297

Traditional Aboriginal X-ray art reveals a subject's skeleton.

from the lowlands, loom the sheer walls of a 700-foot-high escarpment that traces the park's southern and eastern boundaries. During the December-to-April rainy season, a time northern Australians call the Wet, typhoons and torrential downpours feed hundreds of waterfalls. Many of these vanish during the dry season, but a few flow year-round most years, including 650-foot-high Jim Jim Falls, the park's most spectacular cascade.

The escarpment's sandstone walls also preserve a record of Aboriginal history, from realistic portrayals of European settlers in the 1800s to stick-figure paintings dating back at least 25,000 years. The paintings, rendered in blacks, whites, and ocherous reds and yellows, depict humans and animals as well as weapons and tools such as the boomerang and the woven, pouchlike dilly bag.

Some of the oldest paintings show the Tasmanian tiger, believed long extinct in Australia. A later art style, called X-ray art, portrays its human and animal subjects as though they had see-through skin—with skeletons and internal organs in plain view. On the cliffs at Nourlangie, dozens of surrealistic X-ray drawings detail ancestral Aboriginal spirits and ceremonies of a long-ago Dreamtime before the earth and its inhabitants assumed their present forms.

Today some 300 Aboriginals live in the park, hunting and fishing as their ancestors did. Others are being trained as park rangers and managers. As one Aboriginal leader, Big Bill Neidji, put it soon after the park was established: "Our story is in the land . . . It is written in those sacred places. My children will look after those places. That's the law."

The Arnhem Land escarpment rises near Baroalba Springs in northern Australia.

Bali, *Indonesia*

Indonesians refer to the island of Bali as Pulau Dewata—Island of the Gods. Roughly 2,150 square miles, it belongs to the mighty deities said to dwell atop volcanic Mount Agung, "the navel of the world." Bali's human caretakers, duty bound to make their sacred realm beautiful, have created a tropical paradise where rice fields interlock like the facets of an emerald. Carefully tended terrace walls retard erosion and help to retain the rich soils that have made these gardens among the world's most fertile.

Unlike those Indonesian islanders who look to the sea for sustenance, the Balinese turn toward the land and the deities on Mount Agung. Though normally benevolent, wrathful gods received official blame when the 10,000-foot volcano erupted in 1963, destroying villages and taking 1,600 lives.

Of Indonesia's 3,000 inhabited islands, only Bali blends Hindu beliefs with Buddhism and animism. Some 20,000 temples dot the island, attesting to the importance of the spirit world in Balinese life. For centuries this unique religion has withstood the impact of Islam, now the predominant faith in the rest of Indonesia.

Seeking harmony between the lofty gods and the mischievous spirits of sea and earth, the Balinese court cosmic forces through agricultural and other rites that include trance dances, masked dramas, and a steady outpouring of art—music, painting, sculpture, and poetry. Offerings of flowers, fruit, or palm-frond origami are all gifts of beauty designed to keep the gods smiling on the trustees of their holy island.

Above: Irrigated terraces please the rice goddess and feed Bali's 2.5 million people.
Opposite: Carved by a Balinese artist, a mythical bird called Garuda spreads wooden plumage.

The Historic Sanctuary of Machu Picchu, *Peru*

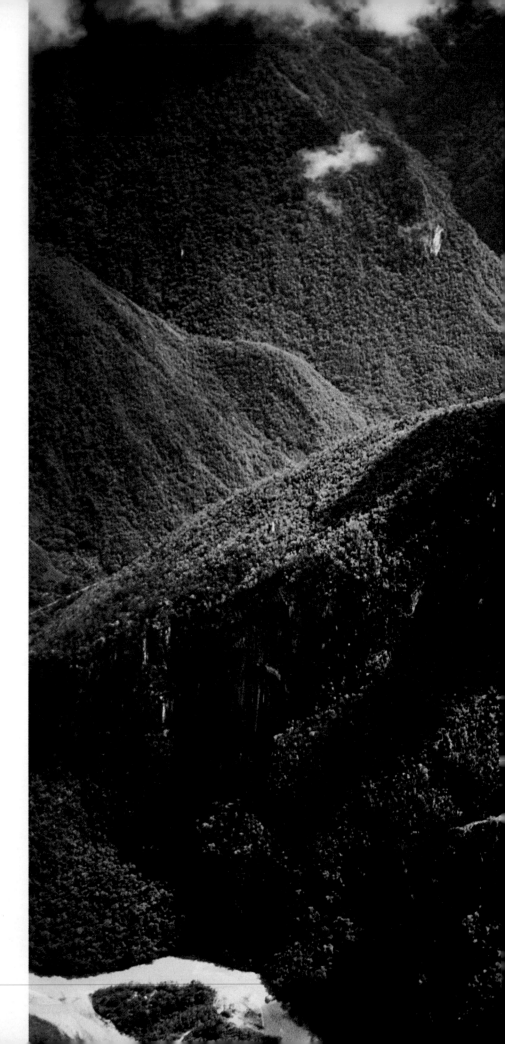

Where the Peruvian Andes stoop down to the jungle 50 miles northwest of Cuzco, the Incas built a sublime city on an almost inaccessible ridge 2,000 feet above the Urubamba River. Once thought to be the last refuge of Incas fleeing the Spanish conquistadores and the hideaway of chosen women known as Virgins of the Sun, Machu Picchu may actually have been a spiritual capital, a trade center, or, as recent studies suggest, a royal estate belonging to the ninth Inca emperor, Pachacuti, founder of the Inca Empire. Built in the 1400s and abandoned in 1534 after the empire fell, the city lay hidden under dense vegetation until 1911, when Indians led American explorer Hiram Bingham to the site.

Inca laborers sculptured the saddle between Machu Picchu (Old Peak) and Huayna Picchu (Great Peak), leveling two square miles of rocky terrain and hewing stairways and terraces from the hillside. Artisans built temples and some 200 dwellings, fitting large rectangular blocks of white granite together so tightly that a knife blade could not slip between them. Trapezoidal shapes—a hallmark of Inca architecture—helped the buildings withstand earthquakes.

Mortarless mosaics of irregular boulders served as retaining walls for terraces. Filled with rich soil from the valley, these level planting areas prevented erosion. In them, farmers grew potatoes and maize, using the sun to calculate planting and harvesting times. Masters of irrigation, the Incas channeled water from a nearby spring into stone aqueducts that nourished the city's gardens and fountains.

The ethereal setting conjures up visions of a gentle people living in harmony with nature. But the role of Machu Picchu in the world of the Incas remains an enigma to this day; only the beauty of their handiwork remains. "And the air came in with lemon blossom fingers," wrote the Chilean poet Pablo Neruda, "cleansing the lonely precinct of the stone."

Terraces and stone walls in the Inca citadel of Machu Picchu cling to a jungle ridge.

A List of World Heritage Sites

As of December 1986, the World Heritage Convention had approved 247 cultural and natural sites for inscription on the World Heritage List of Recorded Sites. They are listed alphabetically here by nominating country in the order in which each site was nominated.

Algeria
Al Qal'a of Beni Hammad
Tassili-n-Ajjer
M'Zab Valley
Djemila
Tipasa
Timgad

Argentina
Los Glaciares National Park
Iguazú National Park

Argentina and Brazil
Jesuit Missions of the Guaranís

Australia
Kakadu National Park
Great Barrier Reef
Willandra Lakes Region
Western Tasmania Wilderness
    National Parks
Lord Howe Island Group
Australian East Coast Temperate
    and Subtropical Rain Forest Parks

Bangladesh
Historic Mosque City of Bagherhat
Ruins of the Buddhist Vihara
    at Paharpur

Benin
Royal Palaces of Abomey

Brazil
Historic Town of Ouro Prêto
Historic Center of Olinda
Historic Center of Salvador (Bahia)
Sanctuary of Bom Jesus in Congonhas
Iguaçu National Park

Bulgaria
Boyana Church
Madara Rider
Thracian Tomb of Kazanlŭk
Rock-hewn Churches of Ivanovo
Ancient City of Nessebar
Rila Monastery
Srebarna Nature Reserve
Pirin National Park
Thracian Tomb of Sveshtari

Canada
L'Anse aux Meadows National
    Historic Park
Nahanni National Park
Dinosaur Provincial Park
Anthony Island
Head-Smashed-In Bison Jump
    Complex
Wood Buffalo National Park
Canadian Rocky Mountain Parks
    including the Burgess Shale
Historic Area of Québec

**Canada and the United States
of America**
Kluane and Wrangell-St. Elias
    National Parks

Colombia
Port, Fortresses, and Group of
    Monuments at Cartagena

Costa Rica
Talamanca Range-La Amistad
    Reserves

Cuba
Old Havana and Its Fortifications

Cyprus
Paphos
Painted Churches in the Troodos
    Region

Ecuador
Galápagos Islands
Historic Center of Quito
Sangay National Park

Egypt
Memphis and Its Necropolis and the
    Pyramid Fields from Gîza to Dahshûr
Ancient Thebes with Its Necropolis
Nubian Monuments from Abu Simbel
    to Philae
Islamic Cairo
Abu Mena

Ethiopia
Simen National Park
Rock-hewn Churches of Lalībela
Fasil Ghebbi in the Gonder Region
Lower Valley of the Āwash
Tiya
Aksum
Lower Valley of the Omo

France
Mont-Saint-Michel and Its Bay
Chartres Cathedral
Palace and Park of Versailles
Basilica and Hill at Vézelay
Decorated Grottoes of the Vézère
    Valley including Lascaux Cave
Palace and Park of Fontainebleau
Château and Estate of Chambord
Amiens Cathedral
The Roman Theater and Its
    Surroundings and the Triumphal
    Arch of Orange
Roman and Romanesque Monuments
    of Arles
Cistercian Abbey of Fontenay
Royal Saltworks of Arc et Senans
Place Stanislas, Place de la Carrière,
    and Place d'Alliance in Nancy
Church of Saint-Savin-sur-Gartempe
Cape Girolata, Cape Porto,
    and Scandola Nature Reserve in Corsica
Pont du Gard Roman Aqueduct

Germany, West
Aachen Cathedral
Speyer Cathedral
Würzburg Residence with the Court
    Gardens and Residence Square
Pilgrimage Church of Wies
Castles of Augustusburg and
    Falkenlust at Brühl
St. Mary's Cathedral and St. Michael's
    Church at Hildesheim
Monuments of Trier

Ghana
Forts and Castles of Ghana
Ashanti Traditional Buildings

Greece
Temple of Apollo Epicurius at Bassae

Guatemala
Tikal National Park
Antigua Guatemala
Archaeological Park and Ruins of
    Quiriguá

Guinea and Ivory Coast
Mount Nimba Strict Nature Reserve

Haiti
The Citadel, Sans Souci, Les Ramiers
    National History Park

Holy See
Vatican City

Honduras
Maya Site of Copán
Río Plátano Biosphere Reserve

India
Ajanta Caves
Ellora Caves
Agra Fort
Taj Mahal
Sun Temple at Konarak
Group of Monuments at
    Mahabalipuram
Kaziranga National Park
Manas Wildlife Sanctuary
Keoladeo National Park
Churches and Convents of Goa
Group of Monuments at Khajuraho
Group of Monuments at Hampi
Fatehpur Sikri

Iran
Tchogha Zanbil
Persepolis
Meidān-e-Shāh of Eşfahān

Iraq
Hatra

Italy
Rock Drawings in Val Camonica
Historic Center of Rome
Church and Dominican Convent of
    Santa Maria delle Grazie in Milan
    with "The Last Supper" by Leonardo
    da Vinci
Historic Center of Florence

Ivory Coast
Taï National Park
Komoé National Park

Jordan
Old City of Jerusalem and Its Walls
Petra
Qaṣr 'Amrah

Lebanon
Anjar
Baalbek
Byblos
Tyre

Libya
Archaeological Site of Leptis Magna
Archaeological Site of Sabratha
Archaeological Site of Cyrene
Rock Art Sites of Tadrart Acacus
Old Town of Ghadames

Malawi
Lake Malawi National Park

Malta
Hal Saflieni Hypogeum
City of Valletta
Ggantija Temples

Morocco
Medina of Fez
Medina of Marrakech

Nepal
Sagarmatha National Park
Kathmandu Valley
Royal Chitwan National Park

New Zealand
Westland and Mount Cook National
Parks
Fiordland National Park

Norway
Urnes Stave Church
Bryggen Area in Bergen
Røros
Rock Drawings of Alta

Pakistan
Archaeological Ruins at Mohenjo
Daro
Taxila
Buddhist Ruins of Takht-i-Bahi
and Neighboring City Remains
at Sahr-i-Bahlol
Historical Monuments of Thatta
Fort and Shalimar Gardens in
Lahore

Panama
Fortifications on the Caribbean Side
of Portobelo-San Lorenzo
Darién National Park

Peru
City of Cuzco
Historic Sanctuary of Machu Picchu
Archaeological Site of Chavín
Huascarán National Park
Archaeological Zone of Chan Chan

Poland
Historic Center of Kraków
Wieliczka Salt Mine
Auschwitz-Birkenau Concentration
Camps
Białowieża National Park
Historic Center of Warsaw

Portugal
Central Zone of the Town of Angra do
Heroísmo in the Azores
Monastery of the Hieronymites and
Tower of Belém in Lisbon
Monastery of Batalha
Convent of Christ in Tomar
Historic Center of Évora

Senegal
Gorée Island
Niokolo Koba National Park
Djoudj National Park

Seychelles
Aldabra Atoll
Vallée de Mai Nature Reserve

Spain
Mosque of Córdoba
The Alhambra and the Generalife
in Granada
Burgos Cathedral
Monastery and Site of the Escorial
in Madrid
Gaudí's Park Güell, Güell Palace,
and Casa Milá in Barcelona
Altamira Cave
Old Town of Segovia and Its
Aqueduct
Churches of the Kingdom of the
Asturias
Old Town of Santiago de Compostela
Old Town of Ávila with Its Extra-
muros Churches
Mudéjar Architecture of Teruel
Historic City of Toledo
Garajonay National Park
Old Town of Cáceres

Sri Lanka
Sacred City of Anuradhapura
Ancient City of Polonnaruwa
Ancient City of Sigiriya

Switzerland
Convent of St. Gall
Benedictine Convent of St. John
at Müstair
Old City of Bern

Syria
Ancient City of Damascus
Ancient City of Bosra
Site of Palmyra
Ancient City of Aleppo

Tanzania
Ngorongoro Conservation Area
Ruins of Kilwa Kisiwani and Ruins of
Songo Mnara
Serengeti National Park
Selous Game Reserve

Tunisia
Medina of Tunis
Archaeological Site of Carthage
Amphitheater of El Jemm
Ichkeul National Park
Punic Town of Kerkouane and
Its Necropolis

Turkey
Historic Areas of İstanbul
Göreme National Park and the
Rock Sites of Cappadocia
Great Mosque and Hospital of Divriği
Hattusha

United Kingdom
Giant's Causeway and Causeway
Coast
Durham Castle and Cathedral
Ironbridge Gorge
Studley Royal Park including the
Ruins of Fountains Abbey
Stonehenge, Avebury, and Associated
Sites
Castles and Town Walls of King
Edward in Gwynedd
St. Kilda

United States of America
Redwood National Park
Mesa Verde National Park
Yellowstone National Park
Grand Canyon National Park
Everglades National Park
Independence Hall National
Historical Park
Mammoth Cave National Park
Olympic National Park
Cahokia Mounds State Historic Site
Great Smoky Mountains National Park
La Fortaleza and San Juan National
Historic Site in Puerto Rico
Statue of Liberty National Monument
Yosemite National Park

Yemen
Old City of Şan'ā'

Yemen, Democratic
Old Walled City of Shibām

Yugoslavia
Old City of Dubrovnik
Stari Ras and Sopočani
Historical Complex of Split with the
Palace of Diocletian
Plitvice Lakes National Park
Ohrid Region
Kotor Region
Durmitor National Park
Studenica Monastery
Škocjan Caves

Zaire
Virunga National Park
Garamba National Park
Kahuzi-Biega National Park
Salonga National Park

Zimbabwe
Mana Pools National Park, Sapi and
Chewore Safari Areas
Great Zimbabwe National Monument
Khami Ruins National Monument

About the Authors
and Photographers

For more than three decades, British broadcaster and best-selling author DAVID ATTENBOROUGH has delighted audiences with his enthusiasm for natural history. Educated as a zoologist at Cambridge University, Attenborough circled the globe in the 1970s and early '80s to create two widely acclaimed television series on evolution, "Life on Earth" and "The Living Planet," both later published in book form. In 1987 he completed a book and a BBC series about the Mediterranean.

American-born DAVID ROBERT AUSTEN has worked as a photographer in Australia since 1975. His photographs have appeared in NATIONAL GEOGRAPHIC stories on Papua New Guinea and Australia's Murray River and Queensland.

A former television photojournalist, JAMES P. BLAIR has been on the National Geographic staff since 1962, traveling worldwide for NATIONAL GEOGRAPHIC and many of the Society's books. In 1977 he received the Overseas Press Club award for best photographic reporting from abroad.

DANIEL J. BOORSTIN, the Librarian of Congress for 12 years, also served as director of the National Museum of American History. An honorary fellow of the American Geographical Society, he is a distinguished historian and the author of 18 books on American and world history, including *Hidden History, The Discoverers,* and a trilogy, *The Americans*—the last volume of which, *The Democratic Experience,* won the 1974 Pulitzer Prize for History.

KENNETH BROWER's interest in ecology has taken him to Alaska, the Galápagos Islands, Borneo, and Micronesia. Best known as author of *The Starship and the Canoe,* Brower has published pieces in NATIONAL GEOGRAPHIC, *The Atlantic, Audubon,* and *Smithsonian.* His books include *With Their Islands Around Them, Wake of the Whale, Micronesia: The Land, the People and the Sea,* and *A Song for Satawal.*

One of Britain's leading architectural historians, MARK GIROUARD has written many books, including *Life in the English Country House, The Victorian Country House,* and *Cities and People.* He is well known in Britain for his radio and television broadcasts and has lectured widely in the United States, Australia, and Britain. Girouard's story on English country houses was published in the November 1985 issue of NATIONAL GEOGRAPHIC.

JACQUETTA HAWKES was educated at Cambridge University and conducted archaeological research in Britain, Ireland, France, and Palestine. During World War II she became the first United Kingdom secretary to UNESCO and later served as vice president of the Council for British Archaeology. Her many works include *A Land, The First Great Civilizations, The Atlas of Early Man,* and *Mortimer Wheeler: Adventurer in Archaeology.*

Essayist and novelist EDWARD HOAGLAND has been called the "Thoreau of our time." In four novels, two travel books, and more than 80 essays, he has described the remote wilderness of British Columbia and the tumult of New York City crowds, the elusive red wolf and big-city boxing. His works include *African Calliope: A Journey to the Sudan, Red Wolves and Black Bears, The Tugman's Passage,* and *Seven Rivers West.*

Award-winning photojournalist FRANS LANTING has journeyed to places such as Madagascar, Suriname, and the Falkland Islands to photograph wildlife and other subjects. His pictures illustrate three books: *Islands of the West: From Baja to Vancouver, Feathers,* and a book about his native Holland.

"Cities are mankind's supreme creation," writes Welsh author JAN MORRIS. During three decades of almost constant travel, Morris has described virtually all of the world's great cities, from Rio de Janeiro to Shanghai, from Sydney to New York. Her books include *Venice,* the *Pax Britannica* trilogy, *The Matter of Wales, Among the Cities,* and *Manhattan '45.*

Since 1982 Peruvian lawyer and diplomat JAVIER PÉREZ DE CUÉLLAR has been Secretary-General of the United Nations. Before assuming that post, Pérez de Cuéllar served as Peru's ambassador to Poland, Switzerland, and Venezuela. In 1969 he became the first Peruvian ambassador to the Soviet Union. He is the author of two books on international law.

Research zoologist GEORGE B. SCHALLER has spent much of the last 30 years studying endangered animals in their habitat: tigers in India, snow leopards in the Himalayas, jaguars in Brazil. Director of Wildlife Conservation International at the New York Zoological Society, Schaller is the author of numerous widely acclaimed books, including *The Year of the Gorilla, Stones of Silence, The Giant Pandas of Wolong,* and *The Serengeti Lion,* which won the 1973 National Book Award. He has also written several articles for NATIONAL GEOGRAPHIC.

Photographer TOMASZ TOMASZEWSKI is vice president of the Polish Art Photographers Union. A regular contributor to the publication *Solidarity Weekly* before it was closed under martial law, he now reports on Poland for Western journals. Tomaszewski and his wife, Małgorzata Niezabitowska, traveled 50,000 miles back and forth across Poland interviewing more than a thousand people for a September 1986 NATIONAL GEOGRAPHIC story on Poland's Jews.

ADAM WOOLFITT is an award-winning, free-lance travel photographer and a regular contributor to magazines that cover the world. Woolfitt's photographs have appeared often in NATIONAL GEOGRAPHIC, depicting places as diverse as Westminster, Bordeaux, Edinburgh, and Washington, D. C.

Acknowledgments

We wish to thank the many individuals, groups, and institutions who helped in the preparation of *Our World's Heritage.*

We are grateful for the assistance of François-Bernard Huyghe, Anne Raidl, and Margaret van Vliet of the UNESCO Division of Cultural Heritage and to N. Ishwaran, Jane Robertson, and Bernd von Droste of the UNESCO Division of Ecological Sciences.

Our thanks go to Jeremy Harrison and James Thorsell of IUCN; to Chantal Fouquet, Delphine Lapeyre, and Florence Portelette of the ICOMOS International Secretariat; and to Ellen Delage, Russell V. Keune, and Terry B. Morton of US/ICOMOS. We are also indebted to James H. Charleton, Ernest Allen Connally, Richard Cook, Robert C. Milne, William Penn Mott, Jr., and John Poppeliers, all with the National Park Service.

In addition, the following deserve our special thanks: Stu Coleman, Great Smoky Mountains National Park; Alan Crivelli; Mercer Cross and George Stuart, National Geographic Society; Lewis D. Cutliff, Mammoth Cave National Park; Hiroshi Daifuku; Victoria Dawson; Paul A. Dunn, Johns Hopkins University; Susan Evans, Pennsylvania State University; Zahi Hawass, Egyptian Antiquities Organization; Robert C. Heyder, Mesa Verde National Park; Susan L. Huntington, Ohio State University; Roderick Hutchinson, Yellowstone National Park; Gisele Hyvert, UNDP, Haiti; Rosen Iliev, Srebarna Nature Reserve; International Crane Foundation; Vassos Karageorghis, Department of Antiquities, Cyprus; Conrad Kent, Ohio Wesleyan University; Carleton Knight III; Elżbieta Kotarska; Charles Love, Western Wyoming College; Eleanor Mannikka, University of Michigan; John J. McCusker, University of Maryland; Barbara Mertz; Tanyo Michev, Bulgarian Academy of Sciences; Mingma Norbu Sherpa, King Mahendra Trust; John G. Morris, National Geographic Paris Office; Jennifer Moseley, National Geographic United Kingdom Office; Michael E. Moseley, University of Florida; National Geographic Administrative Services, Illustrations Library, Library, Photographic Laboratory, Translations Division, and Travel Office; Dotcho Nikolov, Rila Monastery National Museum; J. D. Ovington, Australian National Parks and Wildlife; M. S. Nagaraja Rao, Archaeological Survey of India; Susan E. Recce, U. S. Fish and Wildlife Service; Richard B. Renshaw-Beauchamp, British Columbia Provincial Museum; Candace Roper; Patricia J. Scharlin; M. K. Seely, Desert Ecological Research Unit, Namibia; Walter M. Spink, University of Michigan; Matthew W. Stolper, Oriental Institute, University of Chicago; J. Gary Taylor; David L. Thompson, Howard University; D. Tweddle, Lake Malawi National Park; Denyse Vaillancourt; Robert J. Whelan; World Wildlife Fund—U. S. and abroad; Zhang Changshou, Chinese Academy of Social Sciences.

Illustrations Credits

Abbreviations for terms appearing below: (t)-top; (b)-bottom; (l)-left; (r)-right; NGP-National Geographic Photographer; NGS-National Geographic Staff.

Cover stamping, Carl R. Mukri. Logo, Gerard Huerta. Deluxe edition end-papers: photograph of marble by Joseph H. Bailey, NGP. Pages 2-3, James P. Blair, NGP.

Legacy for a Small Planet

8, Georg Gerster. 9, Robert Caputo. 10-11, Map: base painting by Rob Wood, SRW; cartography by Tibor G. Toth. 12, The Bettmann Archive. 15, James P. Blair, NGP. 16-17, Wolfgang Steche, Visum. 18-19, Frans Lanting. 20-23, James P. Blair, NGP.

Windows on the Past

28-29, Tom Bean, DRK Photo. 30, Christopher Brown. 31, W. E. Garrett, NGS. 32-33, Katia Krafft, Explorer. 34, Pat O'Hara. 34-35, Paul Chesley, Photographers/Aspen. 36-37, Pat O'Hara. 38, Cary Wolinsky, Trillium Stock. 39, David Robert Austen. 40-41, Sam Abell. 42-43, Jim Brandenburg. 44-45, Chip Clark, Australasian Nature Transparencies: Grant Dixon. 46-47, James H. Robinson. 48(t), Australasian Nature Transparencies: Otto Rogge. 48(b), Wayne Lynch. 48-49, David L. Brill. 50-51, David Robert Austen. 52, Frans Lanting. 52-53, Tui De Roy.

Testaments of Vanished Cultures

58-59, Mario Ruspoli and Caisse Nationale des Sites et Monuments Historiques, Paris. 60-61, Adam Woolfitt, Susan Griggs. 62-63, Farrell Grehan. 64-65, Georg Gerster. 66, Jodi Cobb, NGP. 67, Nathan Benn. 68-69, James P. Blair, NGP. 70-71, O. Louis Mazzatenta, NGS. 72-73, Michael S. Yamashita, Woodfin Camp. 74-75, Philippe Roy, Explorer. 76, James P. Blair, NGP. 76-77, Richard A. Cooke III. 78-79, Kate Bader. 80-81, Bruno Barbey, Magnum. 82-83, James P. Blair, NGP. 84-85, James Balog, Black Star. 86-87, David Muench. 88, David Hiser, Photographers/Aspen. 89, Sven O. Lindblad, Photo Researchers. 90-91, W. E. Garrett, NGS.

Realms Royal & Sacred

96-105, Adam Woolfitt. 106-107, Marc Riboud. 107(t), Adam Woolfitt. 107(b), Robert Caputo. 108-111, Adam Woolfitt. 112, Georg Gerster. 113, John Elk III. 114-115, Adam Woolfitt. 116-117, Nathan Benn. 118-119, Ric Ergenbright. 119, Burt Glinn, Magnum. 120(t), Adam Woolfitt. 120(b), Robert Caputo. 121, Cary Wolinsky, Trillium Stock. 122-123, Bill Curtsinger. 124-131, Adam Woolfitt. 132-135, James L. Stanfield, NGP.

The Silent Cataclysm

140-141, Antonio Camoyán, INCAFO. 142, Gerard Sioen, Agence C.E.D.R.I. 142-143, Nathan Benn. 144-145, Stephen J. Krasemann, DRK Photo. 146(t), Connie Toops. 146(b), George J. Sanker, DRK Photo. 146-147, Michael Freeman. 148-149, Brian Milne, First Light. 149(t), Winston Fraser. 150-151, William L. Franklin. 152-153, George B. Schaller. 154, Wolfgang Salb, F.R.E.E., Ltd. 155(l), Rod Brindamour. 155(r), Kjell B. Sandved. 156-157, David Robert Austen. 158-159, William E. Thompson. 160-161, James P. Blair, NGP. 162-163, Belinda Wright. 164-165, Pat Lanza Field. 166-167, Alan Root, Okapia, Photo Researchers. 167, Bill Curtsinger. 168-169, Craig R. Sholley.

The Urban Landscape

174-175, Cotton Coulson. 176-177, Adam Woolfitt. 178-179, Steve Raymer, NGP. 180, Jonathan Blair, Woodfin Camp. 181, Gerd Ludwig, Visum. 182-183, James L. Stanfield, NGP. 183(t), Daniel Wiener. 183(b), William Albert Allard. 184-185, Stephanie Maze. 186-187, Lynn Abercrombie. 188-189, Michel Guillard, Scope. 190-191, James L. Amos, NGP. 192, Bruno Barbey, Magnum. 193, SCALA/Art Resource, New York. 194-195, Stephanie Maze. 196-199, Tomasz Tomaszewski. 199(t), Leonard Sempolinski. 200-201, Bruno Barbey, Magnum. 202-203, Tim Thompson. 204-205, Bruno Barbey, Magnum. 206-207, James L. Stanfield, NGP. 207, Otis Imboden. 208(t), James L. Stanfield, NGP. 208(b), Gordon W. Gahan. 209, Jodi Cobb, NGP. 210-211, Gordon W. Gahan, Photo Researchers.

Messages of Monuments

216-217, Robb Kendrick. 218-219, Ted Spiegel. 220-221, James P. Blair, NGP. 222-223, Gordon W. Gahan. 224-225, Georg Gerster. 226-233, Adam Woolfitt. 234-235, Tomasz Tomaszewski. 236, Farrell Grehan, Photo Researchers. 237(t), Art Wolfe. 237(b), David Alan Harvey. 238-239, Bill Ellzey. 240-241, Ann Münchow. 241, Adam Woolfitt. 242, Fred Mayer, Woodfin Camp. 242-243, Adam Woolfitt, Courtesy of Patrimonio Nacional, Spain. 244-245, Pete Turner, Image Bank. 246-247, Raymond Depardon, Magnum.

The Companionship of Living Things

252-255, Pat O'Hara. 256-257, James P. Blair, NGP. 258-259, Jeffrey L. Rotman Photography. 260(t), Australasian Nature Transparencies: Ron and Valerie Taylor. 260(b), Paul A. Zahl. 261, Brian Brake, Photo Researchers. 262-263, Byron Crader, Ric Ergenbright Photography. 264-265, Galen Rowell, Mountain Light. 266-267, David Allen Harvey. 268-269, George F. Mobley,

NGP. 270-271, Chuck Place. 272-273, Mitsuaki Iwago. 274-275, Des and Jen Bartlett. 276-277, Bill Curtsinger.

Our Shared Inheritance

282-283, Ric Ergenbright. 284-285, James L. Stanfield, NGP. 286, Nicolas Thibaut, Explorer. 287, James L. Stanfield, NGP. 288-289, David Barnes, Aperture. 290-291, Thomas J. Abercrombie, NGS. 292-295, Frans Lanting. 296-299, David Robert Austen. 300, Melinda Berge, Photographers/Aspen. 301, David Robert Austen. 302-303, Loren McIntyre.

For information on the World Heritage Convention, write to

The Secretariat
World Heritage Committee
UNESCO
7, place de Fontenoy
75700 Paris, France

To preserve the cultural and natural properties designated as World Heritage sites, the World Heritage Fund provides support for research, training, conservation projects, and emergency measures to save sites threatened by deterioration or destruction. Contributions to the World Heritage Fund may be sent to the Secretariat at the above address or

in United States dollars to

Chase Manhattan Bank
International Banking Office
410 Park Avenue
New York, New York 10022

Make check payable to the order of UNESCO Account No. 949-1-191558.

in any currency to

Compte UNESCO
Société Générale
Agence AG, Bureau FB
45, avenue Kléber
75784 Paris Cedex 16, France

Make check payable to the order of Compte UNESCO 03301/5-770.002-4.

Please clearly indicate that your donation is intended for the World Heritage Fund.

Type composition by the Typographic section of National Geographic Production Services, Pre-Press Division. Color separations by Chanticleer Co., Inc., New York, N.Y.; The Lanman Companies, Washington, D. C.; Lincoln Graphics Inc., Cherry Hill, N. J. Printed and bound by R. R. Donnelley and Sons Co., Chicago, Ill. Paper by Mead Paper Co., New York, N.Y.

Library of Congress CIP Data

Our world's heritage.

   Includes index.
   1. Historic sites.   2. Natural areas.
I. National Geographic Society (U. S.)
CC135.O87 1987   909   87-17174
ISBN 0-87044-696-7 (alk. paper)
ISBN 0-87044-698-3 (deluxe: alk. paper)
ISBN 0-87044-697-5 (lib. bdg.: alk. paper)